# Norm Dilemmas in Humanitarian Intervention

NATO, an organisation brought together to function as an anti-Communist alliance, faced existential questions after the unexpected collapse of the USSR at the beginning of the 1990s. Intervention in the conflict in Bosnia between 1992 and 1995 gave it a renewed sense of purpose and a redefining of its core mission. Abe argues that an impetus for this change was the norm dilemma that the conflict in Bosnia represented. On the one hand a state which oversaw the massacre of its civilians was in breach of international norms, but on the other hand intervention by outside states would have breached the norms of sovereign integrity and non-use of force. NATO, as an international governance organisation, thus became a vehicle for avoiding this kind of dilemma.

A detailed case study of NATO during the Bosnian War, this book explores how the differing views and preferences among the Western states on the intervention in Bosnia were reconciled as they agreed on the outline of NATO's reform. It examines detailed decision-making processes in Britain, France, Germany and the United States. In particular Abe analyses why conflicting norms led to an emphasis on conflict prevention capacity rather than simply on armed intervention capacity.

**Yuki Abe** is Associate Professor in Faculty of Law at Kumamoto University, Japan. He is the author of 'Norm Dilemmas and International Organizational Development: Humanitarian Intervention in the Crisis of Bosnia and the Reorganization of North Atlantic Treaty Organization', *Contemporary Security Policy* 37 (1) 2016: 62–88.

# Routledge Advances in International Relations and Global Politics

135 **Resistance, Power, and Conceptions of Political Order in Islamist Organizations**
Comparing Hezbollah and Hamas
*Maren Koss*

136 **Christianity and American State Violence in Iraq**
Priestly or Prophetic?
*Christopher A. Morrissey*

137 **Small States and Hegemonic Competition in Southeast Asia**
Pursuing Autonomy, Security and Development amid Great Power Politics
*Chih-Mao Tang*

138 **Empires of Knowledge in International Relations**
Education and Science as Sources of Power for the State
*Anna Wojciuk*

139 **Joining the Non-Proliferation Treaty**
Deterrence, Non-Proliferation and the American Alliance
*Edited by John Baylis and Yoko Iwama*

140 **New Geographies of Global Policy-Making**
South-South Networks and Rural Development Strategies
*Carolina Milhorance*

141 **Norm Dilemmas in Humanitarian Intervention**
How Bosnia Changed NATO
*Yuki Abe*

For information about the series: https://www.routledge.com/Routledge-Advances-in-International-Relations-and-Global-Politics/book-series/IRGP

# Norm Dilemmas in Humanitarian Intervention
How Bosnia Changed NATO

Yuki Abe

LONDON AND NEW YORK

First published 2019
by Routledge
2 Park Square, Milton Park, Abingdon, Oxon OX14 4RN

and by Routledge
52 Vanderbilt Avenue, New York, NY 10017

First issued in paperback 2020

*Routledge is an imprint of the Taylor & Francis Group, an informa business*

© 2019 Yuki Abe

The right of Yuki Abe to be identified as author of this work has been asserted by him in accordance with sections 77 and 78 of the Copyright, Designs and Patents Act 1988.

All rights reserved. No part of this book may be reprinted or reproduced or utilised in any form or by any electronic, mechanical, or other means, now known or hereafter invented, including photocopying and recording, or in any information storage or retrieval system, without permission in writing from the publishers.

*Trademark notice*: Product or corporate names may be trademarks or registered trademarks, and are used only for identification and explanation without intent to infringe.

*British Library Cataloguing-in-Publication Data*
A catalogue record for this book is available from the British Library

*Library of Congress Cataloging-in-Publication Data*
A catalog record for this book has been requested

ISBN 13: 978-0-367-66304-9 (pbk)
ISBN 13: 978-1-138-36756-2 (hbk)

Typeset in Galliard
by codeMantra

For my parents

# Contents

*List of figures* ix
*List of tables* xi
*Abbreviations* xiii
*Acknowledgements* xv

1 Introduction: post-Cold War NATO and international security governance 1

2 Norms, dilemmas and governance: theoretical investigation of NATO in the post-Cold War era 15

3 Reforming NATO through Bosnia: addressing normative expectations beyond borders 35

4 Beyond intervention or non-intervention: Britain's view on the reform of NATO through Bosnia 62

5 Rapprochement with NATO: France's attempt to construct a new European security order 87

6 From intervention to prevention: Germany's debate on humanitarianism, pacifism and international responsibility 109

7 The dilemmas of intervention and the reform of NATO: American response to the war in Bosnia 134

8 Conclusion: norm dilemmas and international security governance 155

*Bibliography* 167
*Index* 181

# List of figures

2.1 How normative action in response to humanitarian tragedy was linked with the reorganisation of NATO 30
3.1 The number of articles using the word 'ethnic cleansing' or 'genocide' 42
6.1 Evaluation on NATO membership in Germany (in percentage) 128

# List of tables

| | | |
|---|---|---|
| 3.1 | The war in the former Yugoslavia and international mediations (1991–1993) | 44 |
| 3.2 | European attitudes towards intervention in Bosnia, 1994 (in percentage) | 48 |
| 3.3 | NATO's main reforms | 54 |
| 4.1 | Support for the British government's policy towards Bosnia (in percentage) | 73 |
| 4.2 | Public opinion on policies towards Bosnia (in percentage) | 74 |
| 5.1 | France's public opinion towards intervention in Bosnia in 1994 (in percentage) | 98 |
| 5.2 | French rapprochement with NATO | 99 |
| 6.1 | Germany's foreign military engagements from 1992 to 1995 (in percentage) | 122 |
| 6.2 | Preference on German foreign activities in 1992 and 1996 | 124 |
| 8.1 | Debates in each case study | 161 |

# Abbreviations

| | |
|---|---|
| ACCHAN | Allied Command Channel |
| ACLANT | Allied Command Atlantic |
| AFMED | Allied Forces Mediterranean |
| AFSOUTH | Allied Forces Southern Europe |
| ARRC | Allied Rapid Reaction Corps |
| AWACS | Airborne Warning and Control System |
| CDU | Christlich Demokratische Union Deutschlands (Christian Democratic Union of Germany) |
| CFSP | Common Foreign and Security Policy |
| CJTF | Combined Joint Task Force |
| CSCE | Conference on Security and Cooperation in Europe |
| CSU | Christlich-Soziale Union in Bayern (Christian Social Union in Bavaria) |
| DPC | Defence Planning Committee |
| EC | European Community |
| ESDI | European Security Defence Identity |
| EU | European Union |
| FDP | Freie Demokratische Partei (Free Democratic Party) |
| ICFY | International Conference on the Former Yugoslavia |
| ICISS | International Commission on Intervention and State Sovereignty |
| IFOR | Implementation Force |
| IMS | International Military Staff |
| IR | International Relations |
| IWG | Inter-agency Working Group |
| MP(s) | Member(s) of Parliament |
| NATO | North Atlantic Treaty Organization |
| NPG | Nuclear Planning Group |
| OSCE | Organization for Security and Co-operation in Europe |
| PCG | Policy Coordination Group |
| PDS | Partei des Demokratischen Sozialismus (Party of Democratic Socialism) |
| PKO | Peacekeeping Operation |

| | |
|---|---|
| PPCG | Provisional Policy Coordination Group |
| R2P | Responsibility to Protect |
| RAF | Royal Air Force |
| RPR | Rassemblement pour la Républiqu (Rally for the Republic) |
| RRF | Rapid Reaction Force |
| SACEUR | Supreme Allied Commander Europe |
| SHAPE | Supreme Headquarters Allied Powers Europe |
| SPD | Sozialdemokratische Partei Deutschlands (Social Democratic Party of Germany) |
| UDF | Union pour la Démocratie Française (Union for French Democracy) |
| UN | United Nations |
| UNPROFOR | United Nations Protection Force |
| VOPP | Vance-Owen Peace Plan |
| WEU | Western European Union |

# Acknowledgements

The content of this book is based on my PhD thesis, submitted to the Department of Politics, University of Sheffield. I would like to express my sincere gratitude to all those who have given me tremendous support over the years in converting it into a book. Above all I thank Professor John Hobson for all of his support and advice, including reading countless drafts from its murky stage. He has always shown me which direction I should take at every single juncture over the course of my research. Without his leadership and encouragement, as well as many insights from his works, I could not have completed this book.

I truly appreciate invaluable comments from the examiners of my PhD thesis, Professor Mark Webber and Professor Brian White. Their insights have broadened my view and will definitely push my research forward. I would like to take this opportunity to show my gratitude to them.

I am also indebted to many mentors, particularly Professor Daishiro Nomiya, who has always given me encouragement and help to carry on with my research. His rigid attitude towards social science has set an example to which I aspire. Professor Kozo Kato's strong support has pushed me forward to break through the deadlocks I have come across in my research process. I am grateful to Professor Glenn Hook and Professor Koichi Nakano for giving me the chance to study in Sheffield. I would also like to thank Professor Takeshi Kawasaki and Professor Takeshi Kishikawa for their support since my undergraduate days. Their kindness and support will always remain in my mind.

Conversations with Bhubhindar Singh have always been a source of joy and a stimulus for my research. I cannot count how many times his vast knowledge on constructivism has helped me out of a puzzle. I have also incurred many debts of thanks to many people. Shih-Yu Cho, Alejandro Garnica Fernandez, Yaman Koçak, Olalla Liñares Segade, Bona Muzaka, Oybek Madiyev and Roberto Zepeda's friendship and help have played an indispensable part. Taisuke Fujita, who has been my role model, has always provided me with support and advice whenever problems struck me. My thanks also go to Yasuhiro Nishiwaki for our numerous exchanges of opinions. I also appreciate Sarah Cooke's help in my postgraduate days and Rachel Grantham's skilful editing work. Nevertheless, all the remaining mistakes and shortcomings of this book are of course mine.

During my stint at the German Institute for Japanese Studies (DIJ), Professor Florian Coulmas, the then Director, proffered me a chance to work there. In addition, it was a wonderful experience to work with Professor Axel Klein. I would also like to express my gratitude to all the DIJ members.

I am grateful to my colleagues at the Faculty of Law, Kumamoto University, Japan. Their professionalism and interdisciplinary conversation have been a constant source of inspiration. I thank them for creating such a stimulating atmosphere. Likewise, the financial support from Kumamoto University is always much appreciated.

Without the funding from the programme for overseas study by the Ministry of Education, Japan, it would have been impossible to come and study in the United Kingdom. I appreciate this programme for giving me this opportunity to fully devote myself to my own research.

The abridged version of this book was published in 'Norm Dilemmas and International Organizational Development: Humanitarian Intervention in the Crisis of Bosnia and the Reorganization of North Atlantic Treaty Organization', *Contemporary Security Policy* 37 (1) 2016: 62–88. I thank Taylor & Francis for giving its permission to publish.

Simon Bates and ShengBin Tan of Routledge have always been very supportive in helping to bring the book into print. I also express my gratitude to the anonymous reviewer for giving me very useful suggestions and constructive comments. I sincerely thank all of them.

I owe my deepest debt to my family. My parents, Shunji and Michiko, who have been supporting my long journey as a student, know more than anyone else that it has not been easy to come to this stage. Many thanks go to my brother Koji, who has been a personal guide in my life for me to follow. Finally, I would also like to convey my biggest thanks to my wife, Sachiyo. Conversation with her always gives me new insights as well as laughs. I appreciate her support, patience and encouragement to complete this book.

# 1 Introduction
## Post-Cold War NATO and international security governance

**The transformation of NATO and the research question**

On 28 February 1994, the North Atlantic Treaty Organization (NATO) shot down four Serb fighter planes violating the no-fly zone over Bosnia-Herzegovina under a series of United Nations missions. The British newspaper, *The Independent*, reported this news as follows:

> IT HAS taken 45 years, but it has finally happened. Nato, the strongest military alliance in history, the defender of Western civilisation, the guardian of individual liberty, has fired its first shots in anger. ... When the foreign ministers of 12 Western countries signed the treaty establishing the North Atlantic Treaty Organisation on 4 April 1949, it is a fair bet that none of them expected the alliance to fire its first shots in the middle of the Balkans.[1]

Why and how did this unexpected action of the Alliance actually happen? Paradoxically, it was after the disappearance of its enemy that this military organisation, created to confront the Communist bloc, resorted to armed force for the first time in its history – this operation was targeted at the military clashes within Bosnia.

In light of International Relations (IR) theories, post-Cold War NATO is both anomalous and inexplicable. Its conventional wisdom, particularly understood in neorealist (as well as classical realist) terms, contends that the incentive for states to ally with others emanates from the need to oppose their common adversary, and it follows that the rationale for binding them together disappears simultaneously with the demise of this adversary (cf. Snyder 1997; Walt 1987; Waltz 1979). In other words, Alliances should not outlive the enemy that they are created to address and, based on this view, it was predicted that disbandment of NATO would ensue from the disintegration of the Soviet Union. For example, Kenneth Waltz (1993: 74) remarked, 'we must wonder how long NATO will last as an effective organization. ... war-winning coalitions collapse on the morrow of victory', while John Mearsheimer (1990: 52) also anticipated that

> it is the Soviet threat that provides the glue that holds NATO together. Take away that offensive threat and the United States is likely to abandon the Continent, whereupon the defensive alliance it has headed for forty years may disintegrate.

## 2  Introduction

In the actual political world too, former French President Charles De Gaulle once mentioned that 'NATO is a transitional organism, born of the Soviet threat and destined to disappear when, one day, that threat disappears'.[2]

Yet NATO still exists; furthermore, it has initiated undertakings which were never expected of its original role: the first instance was the intervention in Bosnia, broadly speaking, the former Yugoslav War.[3] Through its involvement in the so-called 'out-of-area' of the Alliance, a comprehensive overhaul was carried out in order to more effectively respond to this sort of foreign contingency.

This experience is now said to have become the turning point in efforts by Alliance members to establish a new rationale for NATO as Javier Solana (1996b: 4), then NATO Secretary General, stated that 'the experience in Bosnia will have a profound effect on the future course of European security and particularly the role of NATO within it'. Since its first operation, it has engaged in air strikes in Kosovo (1999); peacekeeping in Macedonia (2001); and other activities, including Operation Active Endeavour in the Mediterranean (September 2001–October 2016); Operation Eagle Assist (October 2001–May 2002); the International Security Assistance Force (ISAF) in Afghanistan (December 2001–December 2014), which was followed by a new mission called Resolute Support Mission (January 2015–); the NATO Training Mission-Iraq (NTM-I) (January 2004–December 2011); NATO Assistance to the African Union Mission in Sudan (AMIS) (June 2005–December 2007); Pakistan Earthquake Relief Operation (October 2005); Operation Allied Provider off the coast of Somalia (October–December 2008); and Operation Unified Protector in the case of Libya (March to October 2011).[4]

Obviously, it is impossible to deploy a general argument that encompasses all of the characteristics developed until today because NATO activities now cover various fields and undertakings. However, it is worthwhile to investigate the case in which NATO started foreign operations for the first time: namely, the war in Bosnia. This will give implications on how the foundations of today's posture of NATO were laid. This book examines that question.

## Social norms and international security governance: explaining NATO's reorganisation

### *Brief theoretical comparison*

NATO's intervention in Bosnia and its subsequent reform pose some theoretical questions. Although an intensive examination is reserved for Chapter 2, here a short overview is proffered to make clear what argument this book aims to present.

From the neorealist angle, showing the aforementioned view of NATO's disintegration, not only its continued survival but also its intervention in the Balkans, is anomalous. Neorealism contends that states intervene in other countries' conflicts when their tangible material interests are involved.[5] However, NATO states intervened in this war, although they outspokenly articulated that none of their tangible interests were at stake – rather they were more anxious about being dragged into what they perceived as 'ethnically complex' rivalries.[6] As will be shown in the case study chapters, similar views are easily found in the statements made by political leaders at that time.

Considering these points, non-intervention should have been chosen as an optimal policy, and thus there would have been no need for NATO to be reorganised in order to deal with such regional contingencies that posed no threat to member states' security. However, military intervention was carried out and, subsequently, NATO reform was conducted to address similar sorts of regional contingencies.

Meanwhile, from the neoliberal institutionalist strand, it can be assumed that NATO was called upon because it had more institutional advantages than others in terms of reducing transaction costs in adaptation to the new security circumstances (Wallander 2000; Wallander and Keohane 1999). Put another way, NATO, the most viable military organisation in Europe, was seen as capable of coping with the crisis in the Balkans swiftly. In reality, nevertheless, there was public doubt whether NATO's institutional assets, geared up for high-intensity warfare, were really suited to this sort of low-intensity conflict. Furthermore, there was no consensus among its members on whether this former anti-Communist Alliance should have been employed for this foreign war beyond its territory. In fact, its members' uncoordinated views became a cause of head-on confrontation over what action NATO should take on Bosnia. Before considering whether its assets were usable or not, it should be explained how a new consensus was created for NATO to begin a traditionally unassigned undertaking to address a foreign humanitarian crisis.

Comparing these alternative hypotheses, this book deploys an argument founded around constructivism. But it is different from orthodox constructivist understandings. How it differs and how it aims to advance constructivist studies are explicated in the next section.

*Constructivism, humanitarian intervention and Bosnia*

This book analyses the question raised earlier on the reform of NATO through Bosnia by focussing on normative elements in the 'state-society' relations of its members.[7] It presents an 'internal' logic of institution-building in response to social normative expectations from domestic society. In this ontological sense of centring on the role of normative influences in policymaking processes, this argument rests on constructivist insights.[8]

Constructivists in IR have argued that conforming to normative expectations constitutes state domestic legitimacy. States are embedded within a tight relationship with their society. Being embedded within society means that social expectations that spring from the bottom up, founded around the 'logic of appropriateness' of certain social norms, must receive proper responses (March and Olsen 1998; also see Adler 1997; Hopf 1998; Kratochwil 1989; Wendt 1999). As Mlada Bukovansky (2002: 2) remarks that 'Political legitimacy is conceptualized

## 4  Introduction

and contested through the medium of political culture', what is regarded as legitimate is knitted together with people's collective cognitive understandings and constituted through the contest and evaluation for matching them. In this light, it has been analysed how foreign policies are formed to meet domestic norms (cf. Berger 1998; Duffield 1999; Hopf 2002; Katzenstein 1996a).

The conduct of what we call 'humanitarian intervention' is also hugely dependent on social normative contexts.[9] Martha Finnemore (2003) shows that decisions over the use of armed forces are influenced by collective normative understandings of legitimate military action. She argues (2003: 2) that 'Patterns of military intervention have changed over the history of the state system', just as what was once accepted as reasonable grounds for intervention, such as protection of White Christians and ruthless collection of debts from other sovereignties, is now likely to be the target of criticisms claiming that this is inappropriate and immoral conducts of state policy. These changed patterns are 'not the result of new weapons technologies or altered power capabilities in the system' but 'state understandings about the purpose to which [states] can and should use force' (Finnemore 2003: 2–3). With the expansion of universal human rights and related norms, it might be conceivable, in today's context, for public pressure for action to be generated from exposure to shocking images of appalling humanitarian tragedies on television.

In fact, the crisis in Bosnia, entailing ethnic cleansing and massacres of civilians considered by many to amount to genocide, attracted public attention and propelled the Western states to respond to this humanitarian disaster. Put differently, inaction in the face of excessively deteriorating conditions would be otherwise regarded and reprimanded as inappropriate. Traditionally, intervention in a foreign war such as this has not been regarded as one of the state's ordinary activities; nevertheless, normative contexts anticipate that grave humanitarian atrocities must be stopped, regardless of whether they are inside or outside national borders, therefore triggering pressure on governments. In illustrating why the Western states intervened in Bosnia, the argument of this book starts with its core claim that state policy is constructed under social normative influence.

### *Norms and dilemmas*

This book takes a further theoretical step by questioning whether or not such social anticipation can be seamlessly reflected in actual politics. It contemplates the difficulty with humanitarian intervention, which is that social normative expectations do not clearly tell us how to form concrete policies to achieve goals. It may well be claimed that whilst cessation of violence occurring in a foreign country is desirable, adoption of countermeasures would breach principles of 'sovereign integrity' and 'non-use of force', both of which are stipulated in the Charter of the United Nations. Moreover, if armed intervention brings about casualties among local civilians and soldiers of intervening states, even those who supported the action on normative grounds may wonder how legitimate it is to engage in combat activity in other states and, at the same time, voices calling for troops to be withdrawn from the field of battle will become louder. Thus, meeting what is socially recognised as appropriate can provoke conflicts with other existing norms and interests. This book calls this situation 'norm dilemmas'.[10]

The war in Bosnia confronted state leaders with this problem in all its actuality. Whereas 'something must be done' was largely claimed, opinions over 'how to deal with it' were divided. Many people were wary about being deeply involved in this foreign war, while casualties of the Western states' soldiers and personnel raised criticisms against their government's mishandlings. Additionally, as a natural result of the fact that dealing with other countries' internal military conflicts had not originally been considered a proper state undertaking, there were no shared understandings nor common institutional frameworks among states on how to take action. Hence, international action was not only too indecisive to put an immediate end to the war but also brought about confusion and even serious friction among the intervening states. After all, their crisis response failed to resolve it swiftly and resulted in NATO member states' being reprimanded by their populations for falling short of the normative requirements.

As Chapter 2 explicates, this book proposes that normative influence be differently analysed at the *general* and *practical* discussion levels. Grave human rights violations may be 'generally' seen as too inhumane to ignore, but putting action into 'practice' collides with other norms of sovereignty and non-use of armed forces and other interests. This is because normative concerns transcend territorial limits and bring foreign human tragedy to the domestic political table, but the policy to be deployed is founded around the sovereign state system. More concretely, norms rooted in cosmopolitan values define social appropriateness from a geographically unconstrained angle, whereas other norms work to stabilise politics among states, such as with the rule of non-intervention and abstention from the use of armed forces. This gap generates 'norm dilemmas' for state decision makers.

How are they to respond to such circumstances? Given that a state's domestic legitimacy is constituted by the match between social norms and its policy, however, meeting social expectations triggers another conflict. This book presents an analytical perspective that norm dilemmas prompt states to develop international organisations. That is to say, if *international* mechanisms exist which can help them to effectively cope with regional contingencies, the problems that accompany intervention are more likely to be pre-empted, and they may enhance their *domestic* legitimacy by addressing normative expectations appropriately. For this reason, states move towards the development of institutions for effective security management on the international stage.

After the war in Bosnia, it can be supposed that this experience led NATO governments to recalibrate the role of the Alliance in the post-Cold War era – in order to avoid any repetition of such confusion and public reprimands, they coordinated their mutual understandings and common rules as to how they should address security contingencies in a more efficient manner and, for this reason, how NATO should be reformed. This book examines this claim by tracing how

6  *Introduction*

it started its first activity in its out-of-area (Chapter 3) and how its individual member states saw the war in Bosnia and the role of the Alliance through their engagements (Chapters 4–7).

*Why not 'norms all the way down'?*

Normative influence is not always reflected in international institutions in a straightforward manner, but the dilemmas it triggers propel states to reform them to meet normative expectations. Through this process, addressing foreign humanitarian tragedy was injected into this military organisation, NATO.

Certainly, it can be conceivable that the rise of humanitarian normative pressure against the crisis in Bosnia not only pushed for international action but also urged its reform for the same purpose (cf. Kitchen 2009, 2010). Concurring on the significance of normative influence, however, this book asks some more questions. If the humanitarian concerns for the Bosnian situations had been the sole driving force, the Western states' military intervention should have been made instantly, with no difficulty, and all necessary means would have been promptly used to achieve the desired goal. As it will be explicated, the support for action on the tragedy in Bosnia soon became fragmented because it was also demanded that armed forces not be used unconditionally and that soldiers and personnel not be endangered in operations. The dilemmas in realising normative claims blocked concrete action.

Additionally, if attention had been paid to humanitarianism, a more aggressive principle could have been adopted in NATO to willingly and forcefully intervene in foreign human rights abuses while caring little about sovereign integrity, the use of force, concomitant human casualties, and other related costs. Instead, the book finds, more stress was laid in NATO on conflict 'prevention' because it would help its members to avoid the occurrence of norm dilemmas before armed intervention became inevitable. This perspective can provide a more nuanced explanation of why a particular form of the post-Cold War NATO was prioritised over others.

Since the end of the Cold War, NATO has expanded its range and engaged in various activities on a global scale. Nevertheless, criticism has always accompanied these operations as long as they entailed the exercise of military force in foreign terrains. Hence, conflict prevention has been preferred to intervention. By investigating NATO's first foreign military operation in Bosnia, the book considers what implications can be drawn regarding the basis of its subsequent development.

## Purpose and implications

There are three objectives to this book. They aim to develop new insights on (1) constructivism, in particular its norm contestation debates; (2) European security and NATO; and (3) humanitarian interventions. These points are explicated as follows.

First, this book aims to proffer another constructivist perspective on institution development, 'another' meaning to add a different view to the existing literature. There are numerous constructivist examinations on norms' effects in international politics, and they are certainly valid in each studied context. Instead, the book purports to account for what has been insufficiently explored and thereby to provide some implications in this field. It investigates how state policymakers respond when they are confronted by conflicting normative demands.

Of course, constructivists have held that norms are always in competition with other norms and interests, and therefore state leaders are struck by dilemmas in making decisions. In recent years in particular, scholars, among others Antje Wiener (2008, 2014), have contended that because there exist many kinds of norms in the world, working differently, contestations among norms are triggered. As she explains, some norms constitute desirable goals for states to pursue at the macro level, while others manage interstate relations as organising principles and provide standard procedures as a guide for state behaviours at the micro level. Because of their different influence, contestations are provoked over appropriate state policy.

Observing norms clashing with each other, Wiener and other scholars have moved towards analyses on how a new intermediary norm was created (Wiener 2008, 2014), how norms change and are modified through contestations (Sandholtz 2007), how countermovement is triggered to block challenges posed by new norms (Bloomfield 2016) and under what conditions new norms can override existing ones (Panke and Petersohn 2012, 2016). Meanwhile, the book takes a different direction. As it is often stated that norms are surely malleable but also resilient to change once they are consolidated (cf. Adler 1997; Hopf 1998), state leaders are sometimes required to conform to all of them, even though they are incompatible. The book investigates whether state policymakers can accommodate contradictory norms and interests at the same time, instead of choosing one of them. Indeed, the term 'dilemmas' that the book treats is not new. Yet it aims to present an analytical perspective on how norm dilemmas lead states to facilitate the development of international organisations. In the world, where intervention and non-intervention have ample justifiable grounds, states look for a third way to prevent globally spreading humanitarian concerns from causing frictions with conventionally existing norms and interests.

Second, the book sheds light on how NATO embarked on its new missions beyond its borders. With the growing salience of its activities since the end of the Cold War, a substantial bulk of literature has been produced. There are expositions, such as analysis on the 'political bargaining' of its member states to launch new undertakings by John Deni (2007); adaptation to the new security environment through the efforts of NATO bureaucrats by Seth Johnston (2017); the association between power and identity to understand NATO's persistence and transformation by Michael Williams (2007); inter-Alliance conflicts within NATO members and their reparation by Lawrence Kaplan (2004), Philip Gordon and Jeremy Shapiro (2004), Janice Bially Mattern (2005), Wallace Thies (2009) and Lucile Eznack (2012; also see Thomas Risse-Kappen 1995); its identity change

8  *Introduction*

from a defensive organisation to a global Alliance based on democratic values by Veronica Kitchen (2009, 2010); its role as a 'club' among states sharing information, ideas, resources and different geographic benefits by Ivan Dinev Ivanov (2011); and NATO's historical development and adaptation to the post-Cold War environment by Julian Lindley-French (2006) and Rebecca Moore (2007), and especially after the end of the Cold War period by Catherine McArdle Kelleher (1995); Rob De Wijk (1997); David Yost (1998); Sten Rynning (2005); Martin Smith (2006); James Sperling and Victor Papacosma (2012); and, from an IR theoretical viewpoint, Mark Webber, James Sperling and Martin Smith (2012).

Given the variety of these expositions and issues, it is impossible for a single study to systematically cover all the characteristics of NATO – furthermore, it has now expanded its engagements to a broader range of activities through various conflicts. Hence, this book limits its range to the period of the first security crisis in post-Cold War Europe, i.e. Bosnia, and examines how this affected NATO's overhaul reflecting its members' experiences. Considering the increasing emphasis on the reaction to low-intensity conflicts since the end of the Cold War (North Atlantic Treaty Organization 2010), analysing the Bosnian case proffers an insight into the subsequent development of the Alliance.

Third, this book contemplates humanitarian interventions in general from a broader angle. The Responsibility to Protect (R2P) (ICISS 2001: 2001) notably suggests that collective experiences of interventions have deepened examinations on conditions under which the use of force can be legitimised. As it also admits, however, any intervention has difficulty in escaping criticism, even if it has sufficiently justifiable legal and moral grounds, because it is a military action conducted to meddle in other countries' affairs.[11] As NATO states' involvement in the Balkans will illustrate, norm dilemmas led them to prioritise conflict prevention to make compatible the claims of intervention and non-intervention. In this respect, it is interesting that the R2P also discusses a concept of 'the Responsibility to Prevent' (ICISS 2001: Chapter 3) as one of its key concepts. Beyond the binary choice of either intervention or non-intervention, there is a discussion leading states to a preventive approach.

Undoubtedly, conflict prevention is more desirable than intervention – for instance in terms of the legality of the use of force and the infringement of sovereignty, the cost of military action and collateral human casualties. Its paradox is, however, that a small and minor military clash is least likely to attract global attention until it deteriorates too desperately to handle. The findings of the book will proffer a view on the logic of how conflict prevention is adopted in international politics. The details of this point will be considered in the concluding chapter.

## Methodology

This book treats norms as collective ideational notions on standards of appropriate behaviour for actors (cf. Hurd 2003; Katzenstein 1996b). It identifies their effects in pronounced justifications. People justify their acts by appealing to values and ideals, which their audience also share (see Chapter 2 and Finnemore 2003: 15). For example, military intervention is justified by stressing moral purposes to save human lives, while non-intervention is contended on legal and social principles to refrain from military conduct and to prohibit stronger states' unilateral imposition. These values are employed because they are believed to be collectively shared as legitimate among the public – otherwise, people would not refer to them. Thus, analysing what values are stressed to justify intervention and non-intervention helps us to ascertain what are accepted as norms within a society.

It should be considered how to assess the causal logic of the book's argument about normative influence. For this purpose, it makes clear what evidence either confirms or disproves its claims. In weighing the importance of defining 'What evidence would convince us that we are wrong' (King et al. 1994: 19), criteria for specifying what outcomes contradict the book's expectations are set forth.

The most significant rationale for this book to rest on constructivism is that state preference is guided by collective notions of social appropriateness. More concretely speaking, if the war in Bosnia had been regarded by popular opinion as a mere domestic affair in the Balkans even in the face of ongoing genocide, no response would have been demanded and, therefore, there would have been no need to discuss NATO's reconstitution to address such crises. Additionally, if non-normative considerations pushed international intervention, such as geostrategic elements and material interests, it cannot be said that intervention in Bosnia and NATO reforms were socially expected. If a strong case can be made for such materialist logics, then clearly this undermines this book's argument.

To attest that a response to the war in the Balkans was normatively demanded, the book explores, based around a 'process tracing' approach (Bennett and Checkel 2015), how the response to Bosnia led member states to reorganise NATO. Each chapter qualitatively reads through all relevant archives of major newspapers and political journals in Britain, France and Germany during the crisis in the Balkans (1991–1995). This book thoroughly examined all the relevant articles of the following newspapers and journals – Britain: *The Daily Telegraph*, *The Guardian*, *The Financial Times*, *The Independent* and *The Times*; France: *Le Monde* and *Le Monde Diplomatique*; Germany: *Frankfurter Allgemeine Zeitung*, *Süddeutsche Zeitung*, *Der Spiegel* and *Die Zeit*; and America: *The New York Times* and *The Washington Post*.

It primarily focusses on broadsheet newspapers, not the broadcast media and the tabloids, both of which intuitively seem to exert influence on public opinion. The reasons for excluding them are methodological. The broadcast media are excluded because they are not traceable as they leave no written records as to what they said at that time; meanwhile, the print media are always traceable. On the other hand, it is true that the tabloids are widely read and discuss incidents like Bosnia in a more sensational manner – it is perfectly possible to pick up such expressions which could have been used to exaggerate domestic discussion at that time. Then, there would be a considerable danger of appearing to support the book's argument with exaggerated language, leading the reader to question the validity of its findings and argument. To develop a balanced discussion within the limited space of the book, it was decided to focus principally on broadsheet newspapers.

Additionally, in order to avert the pitfall of 'cherry-picking' or 'selection bias' of information – namely, deliberately choosing convenient, and ignoring inconvenient, evidence – Chapter 3 provides quantitative data about social pressure at the collective level. This method is based on the findings of media studies that the terms 'genocide' and 'ethnic cleansing' caught public attention and 'framed' the tragedy of Bosnia, or the former Yugoslavia, which, as a consequence, contributed to the emergence of social pressure to urge action (Gow et al. 1996; Kent 2006). How frequently these terms were used in major newspapers is counted. Through this method, it can be expected that the higher the number, the higher the pressure generated on the governments of the NATO states. Counterfactually, if only a few articles were found throughout this period, this would suggest that the Balkan conflict was not so often discussed in the public sphere in the Western states, implying insensitivity to genocide or ethnic cleansing. Alternatively, if the war was merely considered 'another country's domestic affair', there was no need for NATO to be socially reformed, disproving this book's argument. The details are explicated in Chapter 3. Proceeding this way, it aims to measure invisible factors in a systematic manner.

Next, it should be explained whether or not the political leaders of the intervening states were influenced by bottom-up pressure. The causal linkage cannot be established if they were insulated from the pressure. This point is examined through their statements in parliamentary archives, speeches, memoirs and autobiographies. The following governmental archives were comprehensively analysed – Britain: *Hansard*; France: *La Politique Étrangère de la France*; Germany: *Drucksache* and *Plenarprotokoll*; and America: *The Congressional Record* and all speeches and transcripts of American presidents provided by the American Presidency Project, by the University of California, Santa Barbara.[12]

As observable implications, the following claims should be examined if this argument is deemed to be valid – whether political leaders were placed under social pressure not to ignore the war in Bosnia and how its influence directed the course of their discussion and behaviour. By scrutinising their pronounced statements and decisions, the causal linkage between normative expectations and policymaking is traced. If relevant evidence cannot be discovered, this book's claims will turn out to be invalidated.

Finally, the process of how experiences in Bosnia were converted into interstate 'collective' understandings on NATO's new roles needs to be examined. First, the book points out the fact that each state had different views on the role of NATO in the post-Soviet threat period as well as on the way to approach Bosnia. These differences are identified by analysing the proclaimed opinions of decision makers and the actual policies of each state. Second, the book explores why political leaders of each state found it necessary to coordinate interstate common understandings through their engagement in the Balkans. The logic of this process is that even if state leaders try to respond to domestic pressures to take action on foreign contingencies, this cannot be realised without adequate construction of an international mechanism because uncoordinated joint perspectives prevent states from organising coherent policy at the international level.

To evince this logic, the book investigates decision makers' views on conducting reforms in NATO by analysing primary sources and how they were actually reflected in collective discussion in the Alliance by reading through its official statements, communiqués and other press release documents. Besides the aforementioned newspapers and governmental archives, all relevant archives of NATO's official documents (such as summit and ministerial decisions, communiqués, speeches and press releases) were comprehensively examined,[13] while all relevant back numbers of *NATO Review* (NATO-run journal) were also examined (from 1991 to 1996). By contemplating these materials, why each individual NATO member unanimously agreed on the reform of NATO for conflict prevention will be elucidated.

## Chapter outline

The structure of the next chapters is as follows: Chapter 2 clarifies the theoretical position of this book. First, it examines how the persistence of the post-Cold War NATO has been explained by intensively comparing IR theories, (neo)realism, neoliberal institutionalism and constructivism. Second, the question is investigated as to why the Western states intervened in the war in Bosnia by comparing geostrategic reasons based on (neo)realism and normative ones based on constructivism. Third, it is discussed how what this book calls 'norm dilemmas' are caused and why this facilitated NATO's reform through its members' engagement in Bosnia.

Chapter 3 takes apart how NATO's new activity in Bosnia was initiated through an investigation of the international-level debate. First, it reveals that at the initial stage of international response, no consensus existed among the Western states on how to cope with such a crisis in the Balkans – accordingly, NATO, a former anti-Soviet Alliance, was not expected to be utilised in this war. The European states (especially France) saw it as an opportunity to establish an independent capability of the European Union under the phrase 'the hour of Europe', while Britain and the United States were very reluctant to be involved in this foreign crisis. Second, it examines how the aforementioned differing views resulted in a stalemate of international mediation efforts and even in a severe inter-Alliance confrontation. Third, in the face of this stalemate, it analyses how the Western states' handling was assessed on the domestic front. Fourth, it shows that the experiences in the Balkans facilitated the decision makers of the Western states to coordinate their common understandings on conflict management and to redesign NATO's role for security governance beyond its borders. Such an orientation can be found in the post-Bosnia NATO summits in 1995 and 1996, in particular.

Chapters 4–7 explore the cases of Britain, France, Germany and the United States, respectively. Among all the NATO members, these countries are selected because their involvement in Bosnia lasted from start to finish, including military engagements and the ceasefire monitoring after the war. Especially, military involvement is an important condition for selection because it changes the contents of debates significantly. It is true that including each member state of the Alliance should enhance the argument of the book but would not change it significantly as long as NATO's decision was made by its members' unanimous consensus.

The routes of each state to reach the agreement on NATO's reform were different, depending on their own intrinsic conditions. The rest of the chapters elucidate through what processes they formulated the idea of conflict prevention as one of NATO's new undertakings.

Chapter 4 takes up the British case. Britain's initial reaction can be characterised as quite unwilling and cautious of getting bogged down in what was regarded as an 'ethnic quagmire' in the Balkans. Nevertheless, after facing rising domestic pressures along the lines that 'something must be done', the British government increased its commitment. This half-hearted involvement, however, became a target of criticisms from the interventionist and non-interventionist camps. The opposition parties, Labour and the Liberal Democrats, denounced the government's insufficient response to this humanitarian tragedy, while the Conservatives reprimanded Prime Minister John Major for the government's excessive involvement, where no British interests were implicated. Furthermore, on the international stage, the British government was confronted by a serious dispute with its Allies. London's objection to aerial bombardments due to the risk to its own troops deployed in Bosnia severely clashed with the view of Washington, which had no soldiers on the ground and promoted a tough-line policy. Consequently, the government leaders found themselves circumscribed by the attacks from the inside of parliament and from outside too. This experience made them realise the necessity of establishing a new security system, one which would enable them to react to regional contingencies at an early phase so that they could pre-empt these criticisms and avoid inter-Alliance confrontation, through which Britain agreed to give NATO a new rationale for conflict management.

Chapter 5 investigates France's new partnership with NATO. After a near 30-year interval, the French government decided to go back to the main bodies of the Alliance through the involvement in the Balkans. This case study argues that this historic turn was made possible by the quest of French political leaders for a new international security framework to meet normative anticipation. France took initiatives in addressing the war with a view to create Europe's own security cooperation; nevertheless, its policy was denounced as its personnel incurred casualties in this operation. As a result, the government was placed in a dilemma: if it chose to stay, it would be criticised for risking its soldiers' lives; meanwhile, if it decided on withdrawal, it would be condemned for leaving the catastrophe behind while acknowledging its policy failure. At this juncture, the French leaders made a turn to the Alliance for the purpose of establishing international capabilities for effective security governance so that they could deal with regional contingencies with no human casualties. The chapter elucidates how France's rapprochement with NATO was initiated.

Chapter 6 explores how Germany, a country that has strong revulsion against military action, reacted to Bosnia. This crisis created a normative 'trilemma' for the German government – i.e. 'never again Auschwitz' (i.e. action to stop humanitarian catastrophe), 'never again war' (i.e. no war engagement) and 'never again alone' (i.e. working together with its Allies cooperatively). In Germany, whereas response to the crisis was hugely voiced, it was also publicly contended that no military measures should be utilised, especially in light of the German historical and constitutional contexts. At the same time, the government faced more pressure from its NATO partners to join their military operation as a responsible member. This experience prompted the German decision makers to move towards the reorganisation of NATO viz. to build international mechanisms for conflict prevention so that it could solve these contingencies before military intervention became inevitable. This explanation clarifies how Germany tried to maintain cooperative relationships with its Allies while holding on to its 'culture of reticence' on the use of force.

Chapter 7 discusses how the United States sought international cooperation with its Allies to address contingencies. Initially, its decision makers outspokenly made clear their reluctant views – they saw no compelling reason to take measures. Despite this attitude, the Washington government became increasingly involved as public recrimination against inaction mounted. However, this, in turn, provoked another criticism: for bringing America to 'another Vietnam'. Moreover, the government was confronted by a grave diplomatic row when its tough-line approach of launching aerial bombardment clashed with the Europeans. Thus, the Washington leaders were struck by domestic reprimands and the international confrontation with its Allies – as a consequence, the Bill Clinton administration was blamed for failing to show clear leadership in the post-Cold War world. Through this experience, the United States also pushed for NATO reform for the purpose of effective conflict management. This chapter makes clear why and how this hegemonic leader in the Alliance also needed to coordinate common understandings and set out international frameworks for security governance.

Finally, the concluding chapter reiterates what has been argued and considers the entire argument in the wider context of the IR literature. In addition, it examines implications drawn from this exposition, such as for contemporary NATO and humanitarian intervention.

## Notes

1 Tony Barber, 'Western governments owe public an explanation on Bosnia: Nato has fired its first shots in anger', *The Independent*, 1 March 1994.
2 Quoted in Goulden (1996: 29).
3 Wars broke out in Slovenia and Croatia in 1991, followed by Bosnia in 1992, when they declared their independence. Therefore, these wars are collectively called 'the war in the former Yugoslavia'. This book primarily uses the expression 'the war in

Bosnia' not simply because it was the longest and biggest one but also because it helps to make clear where the focus is placed, i.e. the war which resulted in NATO's military intervention in 1995. However, when primary and secondary literature is quoted, the war in 'the former Yugoslavia' is sometimes employed. In any case, they both mean the same war in the early 1990s.

4 Cf. www.nato.int/cps/en/natohq/topics_52060.htm (Accessed on 1 July 2018).
5 Concerning such a neorealist view grounded in cost-benefit calculations, see Waltz (1979).
6 Although this view based on the ethnic rivalries in Bosnia is now denied by many pieces of literature (see Chapter 7), this expression is just used to describe the discussions at that time.
7 On state-society relations, see Hobson (1997, 2000).
8 This book refers to constructivism as the 'conventional' variant, which treats norms as empirically explaining social phenomena, not the 'critical' form, which adopts different methodological and epistemological grounds. On this categorisation, see Hopf (1998). There are many reviews and accounts on constructivism today; among others, see, e.g. Wendt (1999), Kratochwil (1989), Hurd (2010), Adler (1997), Finnemore and Sikkink (2001).
9 As Finnemore (2003: 10) says that what 'humanitarian' means has been historically changing over time, it is difficult to find a solid definition. Nevertheless, this book defines it as a military intervention in a third country to halt armed conflicts there and to improve excessively critical conditions of the lives of local civilians caused by the conflicts. On humanitarian interventions in general, see Holzgrefe and Keohane (2003), Ramsbotham and Woodhouse (1996), Roberts (1996), Seybolt (2008).
10 For example, the term is used by Holzgrefe and Keohane (2003), Finnemore (2008). This notion will be carefully developed in Chapter 2.
11 It should be added that not only concerning the use of force, intervention would cause another controversy, such as whether intervention from the outside helps the intervened to develop the will of freedom, because freedom is contradictorily imposed by others in this case (cf. Walzer 1977: Chapter 6).
12 www.presidency.ucsb.edu/index.php
13 www.nato.int/docu/comm.htm

## 2 Norms, dilemmas and governance
Theoretical investigation of NATO in the post-Cold War era

### Introduction

This chapter considers the theoretical background of this book. The first section contemplates how International Relations (IR) theories have explained NATO after 1989. It reviews how its persistence after the demise of the Soviet Union has been discussed by neorealism (as well as classical realism), neoliberal institutionalism and constructivism.

After this investigation, the second part considers the first-step question about why the Western states intervened in the war in Bosnia. In comparison with alternative explanations, such as strategic interests and refugee influx, this section holds that normative pressure from their societies not to ignore humanitarian disasters pushed NATO governments to respond to this crisis. This argument, grounded in constructivism, claims that a new moral purpose was given to the Alliance by their reflecting this social normative influence.

The third part tackles the second-step puzzle: how to explain NATO's reorganisation. It examines why its member states decided to recreate this defensive alliance by establishing a new capability for crisis management. Here, it presents the idea of 'norm dilemmas'. The outcry for action on the devastating situations in Bosnia urged international action; nevertheless, to do so caused intense controversies over the interference in other states' domestic affairs with the use of force, the dispatch of troops to a battlefield and the fear of entanglement. Additionally, this section also makes clear that the lack of interstate frameworks for joint operations resulted in a severe diplomatic row among the Western states.

This chapter proposes that normative influence be separately examined at the *general* and *practical* discussion levels, because state policy is made within a web of different demands. Based on this discussion, even if action against humanitarian tragedy is 'generally' viewed as morally desirable, it does not follow that the approach will also be agreed upon as putting action into 'practice' will spark conflicts as well as bring other norms into play. Accordingly, this leaves state decision makers with a dilemma over their course of action.

The fourth part proffers an analytical perspective: to prevent the experience of norm dilemmas from repeating itself, states were motivated to coordinate their understandings on how to conduct effective security management and, based upon these, re-established NATO. It is certainly possible to assume that normative demands to stop the killings in foreign countries pushed for international intervention and, in due course, became a driving force to reorganise NATO. However, this scenario makes it difficult to account for why its member states stalled as soon as they initiated intervention, despite the fact that action to Bosnia was endorsed by public support. In addition, supposing that this is correct, NATO should have been recreated to forcefully intervene in similar foreign crises while caring little about violations of sovereign integrity, the non-use of force and potential human casualties in operations. Instead, shedding light on norm dilemmas elucidates more nuanced aspects of its reforms with an emphasis on 'crisis prevention' to address contingencies before military intervention becomes inevitable.

Humanitarian norms recognise no territorial borders and define what states should aspire to from a cosmopolitan perspective. However, this collides with other norms and interests established in the sovereignty-based world. Indeed, the principle of non-intervention and the prohibition of the use of armed force have also been long established as desirable standards of state behaviour. In the world where these different and conflicting claims are cohabiting, international governance mechanisms are needed to avoid their clash. This chapter considers the theoretical foundations concerning why norm dilemmas during the war in Bosnia prompted the organisational development in NATO of effective crisis prevention and management.

## NATO and its persistence

The first task is to get a bird's-eye view on how NATO in the post-Cold War era has been discussed, and to clarify what problems have been left unexplored or insufficiently investigated in the existing literature. This section analyses the arguments proposed by classical realism/neorealism, neoliberalism and constructivism.

### Review of the existing literature[1]

#### Classical realism and neorealism

The conventional wisdom of International Relations, particularly understood in classical realist and neorealist terms, tells us that alliances lose their *raison d'être* with the disappearance of the common adversary that they were formed to oppose. This means, states should aggregate their capabilities by forming alliances to counter threats posed by common enemies – with their demise, the rationale for cooperation with allies also disappears (Snyder 1997; Walt 1987; Waltz 1979. Also see Kissinger 1964, 1965, 1994; Liska 1962). Alliances have been thought of as a form of statecraft to balance power so that states can counter common adversaries for their own survival.

Following this understanding, NATO should have dissolved with the disappearance of the Communist regime as had actually been predicted. In addition to some quotations at the beginning of Chapter 1, Kenneth Waltz said that 'NATO is a disappointing thing. It is a question of how long it is going to remain as a significant institution even though its name may linger on',[2] while Owen Harries (1993: 41) remarks that 'The political "West" is not a natural construct but a highly artificial one. ... It is extremely doubtful whether it can now survive the disappearance of that enemy' (also see Mearsheimer 1990; Waltz 1993).

Yet NATO still exists; moreover, it has engaged in activities that were never expected when it was created. Of course, alternative explanations have also been provided by the realist camp. They have argued, for instance, that NATO would continue so long as Russia's trajectory remained uncertain (in the early 1990s in particular) (Glaser 1993). Likewise, it would still be demanded because the presence of American troops in NATO avoids the fear of 'renationalisation', i.e. the resurgence of security dilemmas caused by each country's 'nationalistic, competitive, autonomous noncooperative approach' (Art 1996: 5). Put another way, a singular dominant power, the United States, can deter latent rivalries in alliances and hence prevent their breakup.

Given that these discussions are valid in today's contexts, nevertheless, they can only give an account of NATO's survival for the purpose of collective defence and prevention of intra-alliance tension. They do not elucidate NATO's new activities, such as the so-called 'non-Article 5 missions' viz. operations other than collective defence, e.g. crisis management and ceasefire monitoring. Since the war in Bosnia, the first security crisis in Europe after the decline of East-West confrontation, NATO states have launched such new undertakings. In addition to NATO's continuance, therefore, it is necessary to answer the questions of why new roles were given to this military alliance. To be sure, its persistence should be reasonably illustrated if Bosnia is perceived as a war that would impair its members' tangible interests directly; however, it is hard to find supporting evidence for this as elucidated in the subsequent chapters. For the present, it can at least be said that more detailed accounts are needed to consider how NATO developed through the war in Bosnia.

*Neoliberal institutionalism*

Neoliberal institutionalists have offered alternative accounts for NATO's continuance. Celeste A. Wallander (2000) presents an institutionalist explanation by utilising the transaction costs approach. This says that NATO's institutional assets, developed during the Cold War, helped the members to adapt to the changed environment more easily and to cope with unexpected problems more economically than would have been possible through the creation of 'new' institutions for 'new' issues. Likewise, she and Keohane (1999) also argue that 'inclusive security institutions' – considering NATO – designed not only to deal with threats from the outer enemies but various other risks are also likely to be able to adapt to a new environment.

In a similar vein, and paying attention to institutional traits, Robert McCalla (1996) holds that an organisation manned by over 3,750 employees in Brussels alone (in 1995) is unlikely to dissolve easily. Ivan Dinev Ivanov (2011) also explains its persistence by focussing attention on this institutional advantage, analysing NATO as a diverse and heterogeneous 'club' in which its members can exclusively share information, ideas, resources, facilities and access to the geographical benefits of other members. John Deni (2007) and Seth Johnston (2017) shed light on its member states' and NATO bureaucrats' endeavour to adapt to the new security environment.

Undoubtedly, it seems plausible that the robustness of a highly established institution may enable it to survive in new surroundings (cf. Keohane 1984; Keohane and Martin 1995: 42). Indeed, these views proffer the reasons for NATO's persistence after the disappearance of the Soviet Union and why NATO, the most advanced military organisation in Europe, was chosen when confronted by the war in Bosnia, rather than other organisations, such as the European Union (EU), the Organization for Security and Co-operation in Europe (OSCE), the United Nations or the Western European Union (WEU). In short, NATO's institutional advantages reduce transaction costs in adapting to new security circumstances, which therefore enabled its members to cope with this crisis effectively.[3]

Such neoliberal institutional explanations, nevertheless, do not clarify the motives as to why the member states evolved new security mechanisms in NATO, particularly for the purpose of addressing foreign contingencies. In reality, its adaptation to the new security environment was more complicated than assumed by these perspectives. For example, while neoliberals emphasise its institutionalised aspects, it was actually said that General John Shalikashvili, then NATO Supreme Allied Commander Europe (SACEUR), was 'wary about the fact that no structures existed within the Alliance for out-of-area operations such as Bosnia' (Kaufman 2002: 33). This aspect was also pointed out by a newspaper at that time:

> Bosnia was never going to be Nato's kind of war. The alliance was designated to deter an invasion by 200 divisions from the Warsaw Pact, and the concept of conflict management outside the Nato area was added only after the Soviet threat evaporated.
> 
> All the equipment, training and strategy is still largely geared towards 'high intensity' warfare, based on the use of main battle tanks, heavy artillery and supporting arms. A 'low intensity' conflict, or a policing operation such as Bosnia, requires a totally different force and skills.[4]

In fact, it was also argued, with regard to Bosnia, that 'the internal transformation of NATO lagged behind the external transformation' (Deni 2007: 65). Even though NATO was an institution developed as a 'collective defence' alliance, its infrastructure was not necessarily applicable to other activities, such as 'conflict management'.

Additionally, it should first be explained why NATO states gave it such new tasks beyond their national borders, tasks that had never been thought of at the time of its founding. Without answering this question, it is not possible to discuss how (and whether) its institutional assets helped its members to carry out new missions. After all, the rationale of NATO's reorganisation remains unexplored.

## Constructivism

From the viewpoint of constructivism, collective identity, common democratic values and social norms by allies are emphasised because the role of alliances is not limited to shaping a balance of power in international politics. The study of a 'security community', originated by Karl Deutsch and his associates (1957) and reinvigorated by Emanuel Adler and Michael Barnett (1998), sees alliances as an international entity in which states no longer regard each other as enemies because they have generated a sense of we-feelings. While the earlier group focussed on the emergence of a non-war community through the change in technology and demography, the increase in economic transaction and the formation of mutual trust, Adler and Barnett develop the original thoughts by putting forward an argument founded upon collective identity.

From this perspective, the duration of alliances can be explained irrespective of the existence of common military threats. Thomas Risse-Kappen (1995, 1996) discusses how coalitions of states founded on common liberal democratic values and norms outlive the disappearance of common threats and continue as a security community. Adler (2008: 206–208) also illustrates continuance and change in a 'cooperative security community' by casting light on the 'recognition of the indivisibility, comprehensiveness, and inclusiveness of security', particularly born out of the 1975 Helsinki process, which paved the way for the Alliance's adopt of it in the post-Communist threat period. Even though this 'military' organisation cannot be characterised as a purely pacific and democratic community, Helene Sjursen (2004) states that a sense of common history and a sense of sharing a common destiny glue NATO members together even after the collapse of the Soviet Union. Likewise, a common identity can serve as the basis for the creation of new policy to espouse while dealing with defined problems to be addressed using democratic values (Kitchen 2009, 2010, also see Duffield 2001 and Williams 2007).

An alliance whose members share a specific identity is more likely to live longer than one simply formed to counter a common adversary. However, that alone does not identify by which processes NATO reorganisation was carried out. As will be discussed in the next section, it may well be said that Bosnia was perceived as a challenge to its members' democratic values and became a trigger to embark on new undertakings. Indeed, this book agrees that normative attention directed people's eyes to this conflict. Nevertheless, such expectations did not immediately come to fruition as a policy – they stalled for fear of involvement while their relationship deteriorated considerably over how to approach it. Bosnia was surely related to its reorganisation, but the process of reaching that reorganisation was more troublesome.

It is true that such confusion and conflicts within NATO should not be over-emphasised because they have never been unusual. The strength of this unique alliance is that its shared democratic principles and values have worked as a 'self-healing' mechanism to help it find ways for reconciliation, which is why it has endured longer than any other alliance in history (Thies 2009: 23, also Bially Mattern 2001, 2005; Eznack 2012). This book concurs with this understanding.

Nevertheless, it is still necessary to answer concretely how NATO sorted out the discord caused by the war in Bosnia and what concrete reforms it envisioned by reflecting on its experiences.

## Research question

The question left in the existing literature on the post-Cold War NATO can be summarised as its transformation 'process' and 'logic', i.e. how the former anti-Soviet alliance evolved into a security organisation, which manages regional crises outside of its territory. As will be revealed, at the beginning of the 1990s, the views of each member state about the future of NATO were not identical and lacked clarity; but they gradually converged over the course of their involvement in the Balkans, reaching a common idea of NATO's new roles in crisis management. To investigate this question is to elucidate how NATO states constructed their 'collective understandings' on its appropriate posture and new purpose in the post-Cold War period.

This question is explored with a special focus on NATO states' activity in the war in Bosnia (1992–1995) or, broadly speaking, the former Yugoslavia, and its subsequent reforms after the war. NATO's engagement in this war brought an indispensable impact on its reorganisation, as it is now widely argued that 'NATO's involvement in the crisis in the former Yugoslavia had a very significant influence on the transformation of NATO. It is no exaggeration to say that without this involvement the transformation would have taken a quite different course' (De Wijk 1997: 109). Similarly, 'NATO's role in crisis management and peace operations has emerged under the press of necessity, and the agenda has been driven by events, mainly in the former Yugoslavia' (Yost 1998: 190). Thus, it is pertinent enough to discuss its reform through its engagements in this conflict. By analysing this case, this book aims to induce some implications on how the current posture of NATO was constructed after the disappearance of its military threat.

For a procedural reason, this question is investigated by dividing it into two steps: (1) why intervention? – why did the members of the Alliance decide to take action towards this out-of-area strife in the Balkans? – and (2) why reorganisation? – why did the experience in this conflict prompt them to redesign an anti-Communist alliance by creating a new *raison d'être* as a security organisation for crisis management? The following sections tackle these questions, respectively.

## The first step: why intervention? State-society relations

### Strategic reasons?

In investigating the international response to the war in Bosnia, presumably it is first conceived that strategic calculation pushed the Western states towards an intervention to secure their material interests relating to the area, as can be

*Norms, dilemmas and governance* 21

anticipated along the realist thinking tradition.[5] Their initial reaction, however, shows a stark contrast to this expectation. Decision makers in some countries (Britain and the United States) were very reluctant and even cautious about getting involved in this conflict. Although the following chapters examine this in detail, it will suffice to mention here that London decision makers almost unanimously tried to keep away from this 'quagmire without exit' (Chapter 4), while American decision makers also feared commitment to this war by drawing on the lessons they learned in Vietnam (Chapter 7). For example, Lawrence Eagleburger, then Secretary of State (and also former U.S. ambassador to Yugoslavia), stated that 'Until the Bosnians, Serbs, and Croats decide to stop killing each other, there is nothing the outside world can do about it'.[6] Rather, the U.S. government was more concerned about a possible deterioration in the relationship with the Soviet Union by intervening in the former Eastern bloc, as it was said that it 'had no stomach for making Gorbachev's life more difficult' (Simms 2002: 53). From the angle of interest-based calculations, non-intervention was considered a more strategic policy.

It is true that some European states, such as the European Community (EC) Troika (constituted by those three countries that had/have/will hold the EC Presidency) and pro-EC countries, particularly France, were planning to take more action against this crisis; however, their intention is difficult to interpret as a strategic one. As investigated in Chapter 3, this initial response came chiefly from the Europeans' ambition to deepen political integration in Europe by addressing their initiatives. Hence, it is problematic to connect this attitude with geostrategic calculations because it was not formed by concerns over their security and interests being impaired by the war.

Alternatively, it can be assumed that states might have been pushed to take action over worries about the refugee influx from the Balkans. According to the report by the United Nations High Commissioner for Refugees (2000: 229), Britain received 13,000 refugees, France received 15,000 and Germany received 345,000 during the war. These high figures, especially for Germany, appear to have motivated the West European countries to intervene to stop them.

The problem is, nevertheless, to what extent this concern alone can account for the entire policymaking of the Western states. To prevent the refugee influx alone, it should have been theoretically possible that the closure of national borders, as well as the deportation of refugees, could have first been adopted; moreover, such a policy should have been welcomed by many of the public in the NATO states. Yet the reality does not seem to fit with this supposition. In addition to the refugee inflow in Europe, what also mattered was the magnitude of internally displaced persons within Bosnia. Around 1.1 million were driven from their homes (United Nations High Commissioner for Refugees 2000: 229), and their image was distributed by the media; this added normative pressure for action against the governments of the European states (cf. De Wijk 1997: 54). Therefore, refugee concerns appear as one of the elements that have urged international action, instead of generating a call to refrain from involvement in the crisis. As Chapter 6 reveals in the case of Germany, where the highest number of refugees were accepted, most German foreign policy specialists deny that the refugee issue played a decisive role in Bonn's policymaking but unanimously agree that domestic normative pressure to impel action against this humanitarian tragedy was more important in directing the government's eyes to the Balkans.

Again, the refugee influx can never be dismissed as irrelevant. The task of the following chapters is to examine to what extent it can illustrate the Western states' decision-making and to contemplate how people reacted when confronted by the crisis in Bosnia. In any case, a more solid account is needed to understand what prompted international action to this crisis.

### Normative pressure?

The vast secondary literature supports the idea that not strategic factors but social pressure not to ignore the humanitarian crisis in the Balkans urged the Western governments to take action (e.g. Gow 1997: 197; Kaufman 2002: 81; Lucarelli 2000: 135–139 and 208; Simms 2002: 57–58). In addition to this consensus, this study plans to explore the rise of domestic normative pressure. It is certainly hard to document the effect of such an invisible non-material element as normative pressure. Taking this difficulty into account, it uses two methods to demonstrate it.

First, this book comprehensively examines the qualitative contents of major newspapers and the governmental archives in Britain, France, Germany and the United States. By doing so in a process tracing manner, Chapters 4–7 make clear how the war in Bosnia was discussed in each country and what political leaders thought about public arguments and bottom-up pressure. Each case study reveals that they felt pressed by public debate not simply because inaction would be regarded as inappropriate and illegitimate but also because failing to properly put out the fire would generate a surge of criticism condemning their capability in manoeuvring within foreign affairs.

The second way is to uncover qualitative data on social pressure. Although the first method thoroughly analyses all available materials, it is difficult to cast off the impression of selection bias by picking up information to suit the argument made here. To avert this potential pitfall, the frequency of the media utilisation of the terms 'genocide' and 'ethnic cleansing' was counted as these were words which, according to the findings of media studies, attracted public attention and helped to generate the public outcry that 'something must be done'. The result of this investigation is shown in Figure 3.1 in Chapter 3.

To document how society responded to the Balkan crisis is the task of this book outlined in the following chapters. Nevertheless, here, a tentative expectation is posed that public outcry played an important role in leading state policy towards the Balkans.

### Constructivist explanations for intervention

Why did a foreign war in the Balkans occurring away from their homelands attract public attention in the Western states? First of all, as an external condition to making this happen, the development of the media network was indispensable.

The so-called 'CNN effect' is part of this context.[7] Without information about humanitarian disasters to be disseminated, people would not show any reaction even if such an incident was actually taking place. In this sense, such a technological development is an important condition. From a wider perspective, Anthony Giddens (1990: 63–64) relates globalisation to the information evolution in the current era, where time and space have been compressed with a historically unprecedented speed. The development and expansion of the media network nowadays has enabled humanitarian tragedy of a foreign country to be circulated instantly and extensively and, it is assumed, the war in Bosnia was also subject to this influence (e.g. Kent 2006).[8]

Nevertheless, the media is, after all, a means to make a humanitarian tragedy widely known at a rapid speed – what is more important is how people respond when they see it. If a grave abuse of human rights is viewed as an internal affair of a foreign country, no further discussion is deployed. Conversely, if it is regarded as a global concern, international action is demanded. The kind of reaction that will be provoked is dependent on the normative contexts into which information flows.[9]

In this respect, constructivists have explored how the use of military force has been guided by social collective understandings on legitimate social purposes. State behaviour is not determined by the 'logic of consequence' based on individual/rational cost-benefit calculations but by the 'logic of appropriateness' to meet collective social normative contexts (March and Olsen 1998). Martha Finnemore (1996b, 2003) holds that humanitarian intervention is not a recent phenomenon but has happened even in the nineteenth century – however, the reasons why it should be performed have never been the same. Before the twentieth century, intervention was carried out only to save white Christians, whereas the massacre of Armenians by the Ottoman Turks did not provoke such discussion, although both were common knowledge even at that time (Finnemore 2003: 63–64). Today, if this style of intervention was repeated or declared, it would be regarded as 'racist and barbaric' and be a target of criticism for political incorrectness (2003: 4). According to Finnemore, these changes are explained not by strategic calculations but rather by changes in normative structure on an appropriate use of force. As states justify their intervention – i.e. the breach of sovereign integrity with military forces – by drawing on and articulating 'shared values and expectations that other decision makers and other publics in other states hold' (2003: 15), legitimate military action depends to a large extent on social normative contexts that engulf states and societies.

In the contemporary context, 'shared values and expectations' for legitimate military intervention are principally based on humanitarian purposes – as state leaders justify their use of force for halting grave human right abuses, and particularly genocide. Neta Crawford, along with Finnemore, argues that, from a historical viewpoint, the rise of human rights consciousness, which is deeply imbued in the present normative structure, is attributed to the abolition of slavery and the slave trade, decolonisation and, of course, the expansion of universal human rights as such (Crawford 2002: Chapter 9; Finnemore 2003: 66–73).[10] Taking these points into account, when people are exposed to images of excessive humanitarian tragedy, it is likely that normative pressure will be generated for necessary actions to be taken, even if it happens within other states.

Concerning NATO's intervention, Veronica Kitchen (2009: 106) contends that 'The killing in Yugoslavia had to be stopped not because it posed a direct threat to European or transatlantic security (though it did pose an indirect one), but rather because it posed a threat to Atlantic sensibilities and the narrative of the values-based identity', while Karin Fierke (1996: 489) writes that 'public demands that "something be done" in response to successive onslaughts against the civilian populations in Bosnia' urged the Western states to take measures to deal with this crisis. Lene Hansen (2006: 111–114 in particular) also remarks that what she calls 'genocide discourse' based upon moral and legal responsibility to prevent it formed the Western states' measures to respond to this crisis.

As the following chapters demonstrate, the war in Bosnia caught public attention, which pushed the Western governments to take action against it. This perspective elucidates why NATO took on these new tasks 'out-of-area', even though its members' material interests were unlikely to be impaired. Although careful examination is required in each case, it may well be said, for the present, that NATO states' intervention in Bosnia cannot be fully understood unless the social normative environments circumscribing state decision makers and societies are considered.

*Summary*

To answer the first question of why Western states intervened in the Balkans, normative pressure arising from domestic society played an indispensable role in the formation of states' intervention policy. Without incorporating social normative aspects into the analysis, NATO's activities in the Balkans cannot be sufficiently explained.

As an extension of this argument, the purpose of NATO's reorganisation seems also to be directed by these elements. Why an alliance created in 1949 was reconstituted to address external humanitarian contingencies requires understanding what role a military organisation is intersubjectively expected to play; the role is determined by collective notions of whether excessively deteriorating humanitarian situations abroad are seen as tragedies to be addressed or as domestic issues within a foreign country. Obviously, a military organisation is created to solve security problems, but the question of whether states should tackle a particular situation is 'embedded in larger complexes of constitutive metavalues' (Reus-Smit 1997: 556, also cf. Wendt 1992, 1994, 1999; Hall 1999); the new moral purpose of NATO was revitalised by constitutive collective understandings among/within states. For this reason, the constructivist perspective proffers a theoretical background as the first step of the discussion.

# The second step: why was NATO reorganised?

This section analyses how NATO was reorganised after its member states' involvement in the Balkans. So far, the relationship between the normative influence and NATO's intervention has been discussed. Here, how this experience was reflected in more concrete reforms of the Alliance and what logic worked to account for this transformation are investigated.

## Problems in addressing what is socially regarded as appropriate

### Dilemmas caused by normative influence

As the previous sections discussed the effect of normative force as an important factor in explaining the 'purpose of intervention' (Finnemore 2003), this book uncovers problems that arise in the 'process of intervention'. Given that public outcry over human rights violations makes it inappropriate for state leaders to stand idly by and watch atrocities going on, they will, nevertheless, soon face a problem in meeting demands to intervene because to do so inevitably entails confrontation with other norms and interests. Supposing that intervention is undertaken genuinely on humanitarian grounds, it is a breach of 'The necessary condition for sovereignty among states' as well as 'obviously not peaceable activity' (Finnemore 2003: 7–8), which could result in the deaths of local civilians and also soldiers from intervening states.[11] In other words, what is collectively assumed as appropriate can, when put into practice, cause clashes with other norms and interests such as:

- Respect for sovereign integrity;
- Non-use of force;
- Zero casualties (no killing of local civilians and intervening soldiers).

From the military angle, the standard of 'zero casualties' is regarded as a norm to be abided by in war operations (Gentry 2006; cf. Kahl 2007). However, it can also be interpreted as an aversion to the nation's soldiers coming home in body bags, which is founded around cost-benefit calculations. Thus, application of normative expectations provokes conflicts not only with other norms but also with interests and other related concerns, including the following:

- Interest-based claims (e.g. the fear of being bogged down in foreign crises and possible deterioration in the relationship with regional powers, such as Russia);[12]
- Other concerns over details of military engagements (e.g. aerial bombardment alone or also deployment of ground troops? How long will they stay there?).[13]

Of course, raising a voice for action to avert humanitarian disasters does not mean that people are happy to see armed forces used unconditionally and their soldiers and personnel killed in operation – rather, mishandling by their government of such a situation would be harshly criticised. As Roland Paris (2014: 575) contends, 'No matter how carefully coercive operations may be planned and conducted, they almost always cause collateral damage and accidental deaths – they break things and kill innocent people'. Here, 'norm dilemmas' are caused 'among' norms and 'between' norms and interests – this study defines this concept as meaning that implementing what is considered normatively appropriate generates friction with other social demands. However contradictory they are, all demands are expected to be kept simultaneously. British Foreign Secretary Malcolm Rifkind, during the crisis in Bosnia, touched on this difficulty by remarking that

> 'something must be done' may not be sustained if involvement in a bitter conflict in a country in which no vital national interests are at stake results in casualties. The clamour for action can turn, almost overnight, into an equally vigorous clamour to 'bring our boys home'.
> (Rifkind 1995: 8–9)

This statement precisely depicts the dilemmas lying in humanitarian intervention processes.

Thus, normative expectations are not always realised in policy because different discussions are going on between what goals are regarded as appropriate and how to achieve this social appropriateness. Finnemore (2008: 198) also states in her examination of humanitarian intervention that 'Any policy decision of consequence is taken within a dense web of normative claims that often conflict with one another and create serious ethical dilemmas for decision makers', while suggesting this as a constructivist research agenda. As Thomas Risse-Kappen (1994: 187) claims, 'Decision makers are always exposed to several and often contradictory policy concepts'. In other words, what is questioned in this context is how states make decisions under the circumstances of norm dilemmas.

This research proposes that the effects of norms be examined by separating the *general* and *practical* discussion levels. Normative attention, particularly that emanating from cosmopolitan sources, transcends territorial limits and sets up new political agendas that have not been conceived as proper concerns of the state, such as halting violence on the 'inside' of a third country. Put differently, even if they are anticipated as a desirable goal at the general discussion level, such new agendas are not readily accepted in terms of traditional politics because other norms are also presented as appropriate standards for state behaviours. Hence, intervention, even for humanitarian purposes, generates conflicts with other criteria at the level of practical discussion.

## *No international frameworks for security management*

At the practical discussion level, there is another question as to whether what is socially viewed as desirable beyond the territorial limits can smoothly be met because policies are literally made on a state-by-state basis. In actual intervention, if a number of specific states do not share some sort of mutual understandings on how to perform their activity, it can be expected that 'confusion' as well as 'confrontation' will ensue. On the one hand, the confusion that is referred to concerns the problem of whether efficient international conflict management can be produced. International joint action is unlikely to be deployed with no difficulty unless there is a clear formulation of how to mobilise it. On the other hand, the confrontation that is referred to here is that if some states, for example prefer a military approach, while others continue to push for a peaceful one through their activity, the difference between these policies is likely to result in conflicts 'within' the intervening states.

In NATO states' intervention in the Balkans, with respect to the aspect of confusion, the unpreparedness of the various Western states is said to have hindered them from taking appropriate measures. With hindsight, international mediation efforts at the initial stage were not backed by military support, which meant that the local parties in Bosnia could not be pushed to comply with agreements struck around the negotiating table. Nevertheless, NATO was not prepared and even assumed at that time that armed forces would be needed over the course of the war. As for the aspect of confrontation, the absence of common understandings triggered so serious an inter-alliance dispute as to be dubbed the biggest diplomatic row since the Suez crisis (see Chapter 3). This confrontation appeared when the use of force option was discussed. While those countries that had already sent their own troops to the UN peacekeeping operation in Bosnia – especially Britain and France – were opposed to military action owing to the danger to their soldiers, those that had not, i.e. the United States, pushed for this tough-line policy. As a result, their contrasting claims led to a head-on clash among the same allies. These factors merely contributed to producing ineffective policies and resulted in public reprimands for failing to stop this ongoing humanitarian tragedy. This problem is now generally argued to have arisen from 'the lack of a [common] doctrine'.

> It had already been pointed out from various sides that peacekeeping and peace-enforcement operations carried out at the same time in one area engendered great risks. With their rigorous action against the Serbs [in Bosnia], NATO and the UN had in fact become party to the conflict, while the success of peacekeeping and humanitarian aid is dependent on strict impartiality.
>
> (De Wijk 1997: 112)[14]

Even if action with respect to foreign contingencies is demanded, it is not pre-organised at the international stage. Thus, an appropriate goal to stop humanitarian tragedy is not necessarily materialised under conditions where there is no interstate agreement on how to take action.

### *Agreeing in principle, disagreeing in practice: norm dilemmas*

Meeting normative expectations may constitute legitimate/appropriate state policy. However, this is not guaranteed because of the clash with other norms and interests and the lack of an interstate framework.

From a theoretical viewpoint, this poses an interesting question to constructivist research. Constructivists have contended that social norms shape appropriate state policy and, in turn, states reflect these in international politics. Such an argument is embodied in Finnemore and Sikkink's (1998) norm life cycle model – the emergence of new norms by entrepreneurs in domestic society, the adoption of the norms by states and the spread of the norms worldwide that acquire a taken-for-granted quality.[15] This tells us that the social legitimacy – or appropriateness – of state policy hinges entirely on how consistent it is with normative expectations.

Since Finnemore and Sikkink's exposition was published, researchers in this field have contended that norms are not necessarily accommodated in state policy in a linear process. Some have claimed that it requires some mechanism, such as social learning, to internalise norms (Checkel 2001), and learning and teaching by recipients and norm entrepreneurs (Gheciu 2005, also Finnemore 1996a); others have discussed how norms are incorporated under the public's social influence (Johnston 2001) and through common practices with other states in the politics of everyday life (Adler 2008; Adler and Pouliot 2011). Moreover, Amitav Acharya (2004) presents the concept of localisation, through which norms are modified and adjusted to local normative contexts, while Theo Farrell (2001) argues that norm transplantation is dependent on the match between international norms and domestic contexts.[16] In addition, recent studies have made clear that whether states accept or reject norms relies on how they manage their stigmas (Adler-Nissen 2014; Zarakol 2008), what self-images actors have in relation to the world (Cloward 2014), where negotiations take place (Coleman 2013) and in what social hierarchies states are placed in relation to others (Towns 2012).[17] These examinations have shown that norms are not straightforwardly absorbed in state policy but sometimes can generate friction with other existing norms and interests.[18]

This book also pays attention to conflicts caused by normative influence. In this respect, for example Alan Bloomfield (2016) expressly focusses on 'contestations' that norms generate. He discusses how adopting norms gives rise to countermovements by norm 'antipreneurs', who defend the status quo of the extant conditions, by examining the cases of the Responsibility to Protect and the anti-whaling campaign.[19] Likewise, Diana Panke and Ulrich Petersohn (2012, 2016) specify under what conditions older norms are replaced by new ones. Meanwhile, Wayne Sandholtz (2007, 2008) discusses how norms change through cyclical processes of conflict between their general rules and specific experiences, just as anti-wartime plundering norms emerged out of disputes over the pre-existing dominant norm of 'to the victor go the spoils' by contesting actors. He suggests how concrete action causes tensions with what is taken for granted.

In particular, Antje Wiener's expositions are significant to understand why norm contestation occurs. She argues that this is because norms that involve constitutional quality, such as 'the rule of law, democracy, human and fundamental rights, and equal citizenship' transcend the state and challenge others derived from the peace of Westphalia, such as the principles of respect for sovereignty and the rule of non-interference (Wiener 2008: 14). There is a 'legitimacy gap' (Wiener 2014: 10, 36–37) between what the former defines as appropriate in a territorially unconstrained context and what the latter preserves as conventional practices in an international political system. This gap provokes contestation, which is similar to what this book calls norm dilemmas.

Although Wiener (2008: 66; 2014: 36–37) sees that contestations occur because of different qualities of norms (fundamental norms, organising principles and standardised procedures), this book argues that they (or norm dilemmas) are caused because of different discussions at the general and practical levels, as already explained. To make clear its dynamics, this can be rephrased on a time axis.[20] At the time of ($t_0$), people may start to demand action after witnessing shocking images of tragedy, but at the next stage ($t_1$), the same people find themselves ambivalent towards conducting military engagements – furthermore, opinions are more likely to be divided over the need for deeper or limited commitment. Nevertheless, whatever difficulties dog the actual processes, governments are expected to end humanitarian crises immediately and, if the result is unfruitful, failure to conform to this normative requirement will be met with severe criticism.

How are state policymakers to respond to such circumstances? Given that a state's domestic legitimacy is constituted by its policy conforming to social norms, pursuing this aim triggers another conflict. In the case of Bosnia, while measures to address its humanitarian tragedy were demanded, it was also a requirement to conform to other incompatible demands. The next section explores how they tried to manage these dilemmas.

## From normative expectations to international security management

### *Responding to one norm while conforming to others*

Norms designate appropriate ideals to which states should aspire but, in the process of achieving them, conflict can be triggered by other demands. This is because different arguments are deployed at the levels of general and practical discussion. In the case of intervention, even if action on mass killings is implemented essentially for humanitarian reasons, it violates other social norms, such as the rules of non-intervention and non-use of force, which are prescribed in the UN Charter.[21] Moreover, if soldier casualties of the intervening state increase, voices reprimanding the policy of intervention and demanding withdrawal would be loudly raised. Consequently, while ignoring crises is regarded as improper, taking measures for this purpose also sparks off other criticisms.

This book argues that these dilemmas prompt states to lay out a whole series of institutional frameworks to manage security contingencies. More concretely, if they have well-established international security mechanisms, they are more likely to respond appropriately to normative social expectations, while avoiding, or at least mitigating, conflicts at the practical discussion level, and thereby maintaining their legitimacy. For this reason, states are motivated to develop institutions to enhance their governability. The flow of this discussion is summarised in Figure 2.1.

The reason why states develop international organisations derives from the rationale on which norm dilemmas are based. Normative concerns set appropriate goals to be achieved from a geographically unconstrained angle as there is a moral expectation that foreign tragedy will not be ignored. In contrast, state decisions are made individually and such an undertaking has not been traditionally assumed to be one of the state's duties. In order to permit an effective response to this internationally defined anticipation, states are propelled to set out their common views on security management and facilitate institutional building. In short, international 'governance' is demanded to manage different normative and interest-based claims at the same time.[22]

This understanding is different from the existing accounts that are investigated in the previous section. Which norm is selected through contestations between A and B has been discussed (norm entrepreneurs vs. antipreneurs by Bloomfield 2016; disappearance of norms by Panke and Petersohn 2012, 2016). Alternatively, how a new norm C emerges out of contestation between A and B has been analysed, just as Sandholtz (2007, 2008) reveals how pre-existent norms change to newer ones by specific instances; on the other hand, Wiener (2014: 36–39, 66–67) explains how a new intermediary norm (e.g. the Responsibility to Protect) emerged to bridge fundamental norms (e.g. non-intervention) and standardised procedures (e.g. United Nations Charter Articles 2 (4)). Instead, this book explores how states can meet certain normative demands while simultaneously conforming to other, conflicting ones. That is to say, there is a demand that norm A + norms B, C, D ... will be met at the same time, as it was anticipated not to ignore a humanitarian catastrophe, not to use force and not to endanger soldiers. To abide

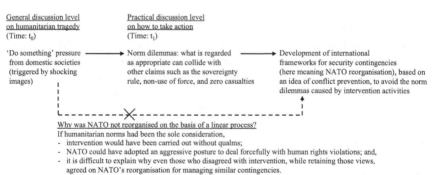

*Figure 2.1* How normative action in response to humanitarian tragedy was linked with the reorganisation of NATO

by these various and contrasting social expectations, states are propelled to develop international governance mechanisms.

Certainly, a new institutional design does not come into being spontaneously. It is activated by an idea that overarches different claims – which in this field can be thought of as 'conflict prevention' or 'preventive diplomacy'. This term is commonly used to urge prevention of or early response to crises, but its significance lies in the purpose for which it is discussed among nations: namely, avoid norm dilemmas.

In this respect, Thomas Risse (2000) provides insightful thoughts on how actors contending over different claims reach a reasoned consensus through truth-seeking discussions. States are, as explicated in his exposition, oriented to problem-solving to fulfil different sorts of social appropriateness in a more effective manner. This 'truth-seeking' urges states to generate an idea ('a mutual understanding', to use his words) by linking themselves to broader normative contexts. As an effective means of accommodating different claims, a new rationale will be attached to an international organisation.

It is almost impossible to proffer a generalised argument because a decision on humanitarian intervention as such is hugely influenced on an individual case basis, which would include issues such as the vicinity of conflicts, media coverage, the involvement of regional powers and so forth. Additionally, this argument relies on the condition that similar normative orientations are shared by several states. That means, when confronted by foreign humanitarian tragedies, domestic societies of different countries simultaneously demand their own governments to take action. Put differently, if action is pushed for in some countries while not in others, international coordination would not be needed. Thus, this condition should be articulated to clarify when the argument is likely to work.

## *From norm dilemmas to international security governance*

It appears plausible to assume that the normative outcry for action to the onslaughts against the civilians in Bosnia pushed for international intervention and, as a continuation, facilitated NATO's reorganisation for humanitarian purposes (see Kitchen 2009 and 2010). Against such a linear flow of normative influence reflected in NATO, this book raises three unresolved questions.

First, although NATO state leaders and their public broadly concurred that an emergent action was necessary for the ongoing humanitarian catastrophe, what impeded the smooth implementation of actual policy? If the humanitarian norm had been the sole consideration, all necessary means would have been promptly used to achieve the desired goal. In fact, solid support for the claim that 'something must be done' soon became fragmented when concrete action was discussed. Norm dilemmas need to be analysed because different debates were deployed over whether to intervene (at the general discussion level) and how to intervene (at the practical discussion level).

Second, if attention had only been paid to the humanitarian norm, a 'gung-ho' style NATO could have been conceived, at least hypothetically: one that was willing to intervene in all human rights violations, while caring little about sovereign integrity, the use of force, human casualties and other related costs.[23] In reality, however, it seems to have evolved as an organisation that lays emphasis on 'prevention', or early conflict management, to respond to emergencies before they deteriorate further, although it is a task of the following chapters to investigate. Even if normative expectations paved the path that the post-Cold War NATO should take, the reasons for its reorganisation in a *particular* form still demand explanation.

The third question is why even those who had opposed the intervention in the Balkans for cost-benefit reasons and on pacifist grounds pushed forward NATO's reform to enable it to deal with crises beyond the member states' borders. An ordinary constructivist understanding would tell us that having 'learned' the contents of the humanitarian norm, they changed their views (Checkel 2001). Nevertheless, do all people, at once and unanimously, change their views so easily? It is also feasible that, because they found themselves torn between the humanitarian normative pressure for action and their own preferences, they sought to develop international organisations so as to avoid clashes with each other. Thus, those who disagreed on the intervention also concurred on NATO's reorganisation for the purpose of preventive diplomacy (the gist is also summarised in Figure 2.1). These characteristics can be discovered in the preferences of British conservative politicians and German left-wing parties, who chose non-intervention for fear of involvement and for pacifist reasons.

This perspective, by focussing on norm dilemmas, illustrates a more nuanced view of NATO's reorganisation than could be achieved by considering humanitarian normative influence alone. NATO's institutional structure was drastically overhauled through the involvement in the Balkans. Particularly, those reforms were targeted to improve the capability for the 'non-Article five' missions, viz. activities other than collective defence, such as crisis response, peacekeeping and ceasefire monitoring. Hence, 'prevention' and coordinated 'conflict management' were more stressed for regional contingencies, although examination on how its reforms were concretely conducted is reserved for Chapter 3.

## Theory and case study

The following chapters explore how NATO states actually carried out the military intervention in the war in Bosnia and, through this experience, how they reconstituted the Alliance to meet post-Cold War challenges.

Chapter 3 shows there were no concrete (or even conflicting) views of the post-Cold War NATO within its member states in the early days and, by exploring Bosnia, analyses how the lack of shared understandings on international conflict response resulted in unfruitful policies and diplomatic confrontation among the

*Norms, dilemmas and governance* 33

members. Simultaneously, the rise of domestic criticisms and its intensification as the war was prolonged are assessed. Ultimately, the chapter discusses how this experience, in turn, pushed member states to redesign a new security framework in NATO.

Chapters 4–7 explore the policymaking processes of Britain, France, Germany and the United States. Paying attention to their state-society relations, documenting the upsurge of normative pressure for action against humanitarian tragedy and revealing the dilemmas governmental leaders faced in responding to this anticipation, they elucidate how these states finally gave NATO a new rationale as a security management institution. Taking this fact into account – that the Europeans (even among themselves) and the Americans saw the conflict differently and argued for different approaches – it is also puzzling how these different views were reconciled sufficiently to reach an agreement on establishing NATO's capability for conflict prevention.

Basically, the discussions of each chapter will be deployed by following the arrows shown in Figure 2.1. First, how the war was debated within these states is investigated. Next, the problems caused by each state's involvement are elucidated, while the question of how the reorganisation of NATO was facilitated by reflection on the experience in the Balkans is discussed.

## Notes

1 On the review of post-Cold War NATO in general, see Duffield (1994/95), Hellmann and Wolf (1993), Walt (1997, 2000), Webber et al. (2012: Chapter 2).
2 Quoted in Hellmann and Wolf (1993: 17). His testimony was made at Hearings before the Committee on Foreign Relations, 102nd U.S. Congress, November 1990.
3 In this line, Fred Chernoff's research also adds more accounts on the persistence of military alliances, cybernetic interaction to learn from past experiences, the role of hegemons and the perception of a common threat (1995: 2). From a more empirical perspective, see Chayes and Weitz (1996).
4 James Adams, John Davison and Michael Prescott, 'Ties that Unwind; NATO Alliance', *Sunday Times*, 4 December 1994.
5 From classical realism, Hans Morgenthau (1967) argues that intervention should be carried out only when tangible national interests are at stake, while Kenneth Waltz (1979) presents neorealist conventional views on state decisions based upon security interests. Also see Mearsheimer (1994/1995).
6 Quoted in David Binder, 'U.S. May Loosen Yugoslav Embargo', *The New York Times*, 1 October 1992.
7 There are many discussions on the CNN effect; e.g. see Robinson 1999. In particular, Gow et al. (1996) and Kent (2006) provide a full account of the role of the media in this war.
8 Like the reference of James Gow et al. (1996: 3) to 'the advent of the camcorder', the development of media technology, not to mention today's inexpensive communicative devices, is a significant element in spreading information.
9 David Chandler (2006: Chapters 1–3) argues, by intensively tracing historical discussions, that human rights abuses in foreign countries have become more likely to be taken up as important political agendas, especially since the end of the Cold War.
10 Also see Michael Barnett (2011: 22–32), who explains the development of humanitarianism in the world. N.B. one of the differences between Crawford and Finnemore is that the latter includes colonisation as one of the causes that expanded the concept

34  *Norms, dilemmas and governance*

of universal human rights, as colonisation was connected with enlightenment of humanitarian values (Finnemore 2003: 70).

11 As Inis Claude (1966) and Katherina Coleman (2007) contend, the legitimacy of military intervention relies heavily on whether it is backed by the United Nations. Certainly, its authorisation is not always guaranteed. Even if an agreement is reached in the Security Council, controversy over an intervention will ensue as long as it accompanies the use of armed forces and potential human casualties.

12 For instance, Aidan Hehir (2013) explains how interests and geopolitics affect decisions of intervention. Also see his argument (2012).

13 This relates to what Roland Paris (2014: 576–577) calls 'the end-state problem': 'how to disengage or withdraw without recreating the same threatening conditions that prompted military action in the first place'.

14 Also see Sloan (1998: 27).

15 Risse et al. (1999) proffer the 'spiral model' on how norms spread internationally, which sheds more light on strategic calculations of states to adopt norms. Given this difference, however, it also rests upon a similar assumption that norms are diffused through a linear process.

16 Similarly, Jeffrey Legro (1996, 1997) shows that whether norms are accommodated or not is determined by the match with domestic organisational culture, while Richard Price (1998) argues that their effects are 'grafted' with other existing ones.

17 Besides these instances, as important pieces, it is argued that norms are used to achieve states' strategic interests (Hurd 2005, 2007; Krebs and Jackson 2007; Schimmelfennig 2001, 2003, also see Acharya 2011).

18 Alexander Betts and Phil Orchard's edited volume (2014) also explores how norms are implemented through a variety of different processes and mechanisms.

19 Kenki Adachi (2013) conducted similar research by providing a concept of 'norm protectors'. Also see Bloomfield and Scott (2017).

20 For instance, Wiener characterises 'sovereignty' as an 'organising principle'. However, as sovereignty has diverse meanings (cf. Krasner 1999), this leaves room for different interpretations, as Ian Hurd (1999) finds in its more 'fundamentally constitutive' nature. To avoid this conceptual controversy, this book adopts the levels of 'general' and 'practical' discussion based upon a 'time axis'.

21 On this point, Bellamy (2009) explicates more detailed discussions.

22 This book adopts the concept of governance defined by Mark Webber et al. (2004: 4) as 'the coordinated management and regulation of issues by multiple and separate authorities' (also see Webber 2007: 63). What matters in this context is how to coordinate understandings of independent states on their response to humanitarian contingencies and establish security frameworks for this.

23 For example, David Chandler (2006) warns about armed interventions under the name of humanitarianism because they simply facilitate military action rather than peaceful negotiations in disregard of international laws (158) and only fall on the will of powerful states over the weak (133). This observation tells us about the danger of this type of intervention. In this sense, this book differs from the view of the 'solidarist' English School's argument about intervention to rectify human rights abuses, which is sometimes and more precisely expressed as 'coercive solidarism' (Hurrell 1998; cf. Kerton-Johnson 2009).

# 3 Reforming NATO through Bosnia

Addressing normative expectations beyond borders

## Introduction

It is argued that NATO's new role after the Cold War has emerged under the pressure of necessity, and the agenda has been driven by events, mainly in the Balkans (Asmus 2002: 124–125; De Wijk 1997: 109; Flockhart 2014: 81; Gordon and Shapiro 2004: 34–35; Ivanov 2011: 83; Kay 1998: 74; Kelleher 1995: 121; Lindley-French 2006: 74; Moore 2007: 28; Yost 1998: 190). When the war was terminated, which was described as 'having an electric effect on NATO',[1] the Western states' experiences in it seem to have been indispensable in accounting for the reorganisation of the Alliance.

The question is why and how this resulted in NATO's reorganisation in post-Cold War Europe. Seen from the conventional International Relations (IR) wisdom based around realism, alliance re/formation is explained in relation to external military threats that directly affect state survival. As has been and will be investigated, this strife within the Balkans was unlikely to directly imperil the security of NATO states, or the wealth and lives of their populations, as policymakers of these countries stated. Nevertheless, today it is argued that their involvement in this conflict became a critical juncture in defining NATO's new role and it was reorganised in order to cope with similar contingencies in a more efficient manner. How to explain NATO's reorganisation and what impact this had on its member states, occurring as it did outside their borders? These are the questions with which this chapter wrestles.

This chapter explains the restructuring of NATO by focussing on the difficulties of intervention that struck its members. With the occurrence of violence in Slovenia and Croatia in June 1991 and in Bosnia in March 1992, European states started mediation efforts. At that time, they shared no common understanding on the response to this sort of foreign contingency and, needless to say, on the use of military power. Therefore, their diplomacy lacked not only consistency but also decisiveness to make the local parties comply with what they had agreed upon at the table. As the war dragged on without showing any sign of improvement, forceful measures in the framework of NATO were gradually discussed after its inconspicuous presence at the beginning of the war.

However, NATO members were soon caught by another problem because of the absence of common assessments at the early stage. European states, having deployed their troops there, objected to military intervention for fear of exposing their soldiers to the retaliation of the local militias. On the other hand, the United States, which joined the international mediation efforts later, was more supportive of a tougher approach because it had no troops on the ground. This difference resulted in so severe a dispute among the member states that it was dubbed 'the greatest transatlantic rift since Suez'. Meanwhile, inaction due to this political confrontation generated criticism against the government leaders of each state for failing to take effective measures in response to this crisis.

After the end of the war, all these experiences led the members of NATO to initiate a new security system. In the post-Bosnia war summits in 1995 and 1996, its new missions were clearly defined, based on common understandings as to how they should react to such external crises that exploded in the Balkans to avoid the repetition of the same reprimands of the past four years.

These reforms were intended to address problems caused by normative influence. Irrespective of whether national security is threatened or not, humanitarian tragedy is brought to the political table. However, policy that conforms to this normative anticipation not only triggers another debate on the concerns of entanglement, human casualties and the use of force but also poses a question as to how to implement joint international action. Because state decisions are made literally on a state-by-state basis, while norms expand globally across states, there exists no international framework to deal with such issues effectively. For this reason, international governance beyond borders is demanded, from which perspective this chapter accounts for the transformation of NATO. Here can be seen a logic of the evolution of international institutions: the more state leaders try to meet *domestic* normative expectations, the more *international* organisations are developed.

This chapter is divided into five sections. First, it surveys the initial reaction of the Western states to the outbreak of war in the Balkans. This section argues that their diplomatic efforts lacked common understandings on the management of this sort of foreign crisis and on the role of NATO. The second section illustrates what kind of domestic pressure the countries involved faced and, additionally, why an inter-alliance dispute about the use of force was caused. The third section points out how unsuccessful international conflict management raised concern over the credibility of government leaders of these states in manoeuvring security issues. The fourth section reviews the discussions about the reorganising of NATO by exploring how the experiences in the past four years were reflected in this process. Finally, the conclusion makes clear the relationship between state-society relations and the reforms in NATO.

## European states' mediation efforts towards the Balkans

### 'The hour of Europe': the outbreak of the wars in Slovenia, Croatia and Bosnia (June 1991–July 1992)[2]

The first military clash erupted with the declarations of independence from Yugoslavia by Slovenia and Croatia on 25 June 1991. Soon after the conflicts occurred in these republics, the members of the European Community (EC) dispatched its 'troika' to Belgrade,[3] demanding suspension of the fighting, withdrawal of the federal army to its barracks, and a three-month moratorium on the independence of Slovenia and Croatia. For the EC, this was, in a sense, an opportunity not only to overcome the memory of its invisibility in the Gulf War but also, with the Maastricht Treaty looming at the end of the year, to establish its ability in crisis management by putting forward the nascent idea of the 'Common Foreign and Security Policy' (CFSP) (Gow 1996: 48). The now well-known phrase by Luxembourgian Foreign Minister, Jacques Poos: 'the hour of Europe, not the hour of [the] Americans',[4] precisely depicted the EC troika's determined will to solve the first post-Cold War security crisis in Europe using the EC's initiatives. In fact, according to Italian Foreign Minister Gianni de Michelis, Washington was 'informed, but not consulted' about the Community's activity.[5]

In contrast to active European engagement, the United States was rather silent. The inaction of the George H. W. Bush administration is now explained as caused by its fatigue in the Persian Gulf and ongoing engagement in Northern Iraq, concerns over the deteriorating relationship with Moscow for interfering with the Balkan issue and its intention to save its resources to deal with issues such as the Soviet Union and the Middle East peace processes (see Chapter 7). Among others, what made Washington reluctant was the decrease of the Balkans' strategic importance after the Cold War, as President Bush and his core advisers recognised (Guicherd 1993: 159; Halverson 1996: 1–8; Western 2002: 118). Against this background, it is said that inside the U.S. government, the EC's statement on 'the hour of Europe' rather relieved its political staff, because it would exempt the United States from involvement in the war.[6] Susan Woodward (1995: 158) summarises Washington's view as one where: 'The Europeanists' initiatives suited the U.S. position on Yugoslavia in many ways, for policymakers were unwilling to commit substantial U.S. resources or any troops to an area no longer of vital strategic interest'. For this reason, the initial approach to the war was broached by the European states only.

*Slovenia and Croatia*

In a series of secessions from the Yugoslav Republic followed by a military clash, Slovenia's case was solved immediately, where 90 per cent of the population constituted Slovenes. Owing to this demographic condition, the EC troika succeeded in gaining a ceasefire agreement in June and in establishing peace (the Brioni Agreement) on 7 July. Meanwhile, on Croatia, the EC held the European Community Conference on Yugoslavia in The Hague from 7 September, chaired by Lord Peter Carrington, former Secretary General of NATO and former British Foreign Secretary. The core principles of this international conference were 'no unilateral change of borders, protection of human rights, and the rights of ethnic and national groups'.[7] In the initial mediation, Lord Carrington elicited a joint statement from Croatian President, Franjo Tudjman, Serbian President, Slobodan Milosevic, and its Defence Secretary, General Veljko Kadijevic, on 17 September (Gow 1997: 54).

As it gradually emerged, however, mere signatures were not enough to obtain a genuine ceasefire in Croatia. In contrast to Slovenia, whose peace was almost restored by that time, it was more complicated as it contained ethnic diasporas, particularly the Serbian communities in the Krajina region. For them, secession would mean becoming 'national minorities' in the newly independent state from the status of majority in the entire Yugoslav Republic (Gow 1997: 57). During the aforementioned conference, assaults by Serbia and the Yugoslav People's Army (JNA) continued incessantly and spread out from Vukovar (August–September) to Dubrovnik (October) (Kaufman 2002: 71–72). Although the 'eighth' ceasefire had already been signed as early as the beginning of October,[8] no parties seemed to have actually decided to follow this agreement.

From the end of November 1991, however, the situations on the battlefield in Croatia changed to a stalemate, in which neither side was able to make any progress (Gow 1997: 62). Thanks to this condition, Cyrus Vance, former U.S. Secretary of State, dispatched as a UN special envoy and having worked with Lord Carrington from mid-November, succeeded in concluding a relatively durable ceasefire agreement on 2 January 1992 under the auspices of the United Nations. Following this truce, the UN Security Council authorised, on 21 February, the creation of the UN Protection Force (UNPROFOR) and deployed a 15,000-strong force, whose military mandate was limited to self-defence. Britain, France and the Netherlands sent their troops on this operation.

The circumstances in Croatia were still unstable: potential conflicts were endemic in Krajina in particular. Nevertheless, with this ceasefire agreement and the deployment of UNPROFOR, the focus of European states' crisis management moved on to Bosnia, where the ethnic configuration was more complicated and violence had sporadically but increasingly been occurring from the previous year.

*Bosnia Herzegovina*

Facing the wobbling situations in Bosnia where three ethnic groups, Serbs, Croats and Muslims, were intermingled, the EC Conference, with the initiative of Portugal, the country holding the EC Presidency from January 1992, opened talks on its future framework. The first session was convened on 21 February, in which they proffered the idea of three constituent units headed by a common central government: to divide Bosnia Herzegovina into three units according to the principle of ethnicity (Sloan 1998: 45). Before the second session scheduled on 7 March in Lisbon, however, the referendum on the independence of Bosnia was held from 29 February to 1 March, revealing that 99.7 per cent of the votes were pro-independence, while 25 Serbian-dominated municipalities boycotted it and even erected barricades.[9] Under these circumstances where the tensions between the ethnic groups had already been growing, it was difficult to produce any agreement and, before long, fighting broke out in several cities such as the Croat-dominated town of Bosanski Brod from late March 1992 and soon spread throughout Bosnia (Kaufman 2002: 78).

Against these deteriorating situations in Bosnia, the UN Security Council, on 8 June, passed Resolution 758 to expand UNPROFOR in Sarajevo airport to reopen it and make the distribution of humanitarian relief supplies possible. In this operation, Britain, France, the Netherlands and Spain participated from the West European side. *Inter alia*, France was the most active in providing the largest number of troops. To galvanise other reluctant European states and to manifest European initiative in this crisis management, President François Mitterrand suddenly visited Sarajevo just before its airport was to be opened (see Chapter 5).

Unlike traditional peacekeeping operations (PKO), however, the deployment of UNPROFOR (both in Croatia and Sarajevo) was not founded on the conditions where either a reliable ceasefire had been established or the consent of the parties had been obviously secured, as has been discussed in UN PKO studies.[10] In hindsight, the deployment of lightly armed forces later caused serious consequences that made the management of this conflict more tangled because the soldiers were not only exposed to the war but could also function 'as hostages, making the Western governments extremely reluctant to adopt any policies which might invite retaliation by the [Bosnian] Serbs against their vulnerable troops', says Noel Malcolm (1994: 247), with the Bosnian Serbs being the dominant fighters while receiving weapons from the Serbian Republic. Furthermore, this subsequently triggered a vehement dispute among NATO states; those European states which had the so-called 'men on the ground' problem were opposed to resorting to any kind of military action for fear of harm to their personnel, while the United States, which had not taken part in this UN operation, was more inclined to air strikes. The seeds of this contention were sown at this time.

## No agreement on the role of NATO: divisions among the European states on the deployment of monitoring forces in the Adriatic Sea

Tracing the discussions in the first two NATO summits in 1990 and 1991 indicates that the roles NATO should play in the post-Cold War world were still ambiguous at the time; the summits are both now considered to contain symbolic meaning for the members' search for a new *raison d'être* for NATO after the collapse of the Soviet Union. In the former summit in London in July 1990, the focus was placed on the renunciation of their adversarial relations and on the new relationship with the Warsaw Treaty Organisation; the 'London Declaration' did not refer to any concrete prospects on NATO's future tasks.[11] Taking into consideration that this summit was held before the outbreak of the Yugoslav War, this outcome was very much to be expected.

Even in the latter summit in Rome in November 1991, when the Conference on Yugoslavia in The Hague was concurrently being convened, little indication of its role in this war can be found. Although a new 'Strategic Concept' was issued in this summit, it briefly mentioned 'Ethnic and religious rivalries, territorial disputes' as one of the risks in the post-Cold War era but did not refer to any particular policy that NATO would launch.[12] A NATO specialist, David Yost (1998: 192), remarks that 'NATO did not then envisage participating in any crisis management or peacekeeping operations as they came to be understood in subsequent years; the mission remained collective defence against aggression affecting Alliance territory, not intervention beyond that territory'. In this summit, the proposal to engage in peacekeeping activity outside NATO as its new role, which came from Dutch Prime Minister, Ruud Lubbers, was not accepted by other members because it was regarded as 'not yet ripe' (De Wijk 1997: 54).[13]

High officials in NATO also stated that nothing was prepared for any new activities. For example, Secretary General, Manfred Wörner, saw in 1991 that 'many at NATO questioned whether the alliance should intervene militarily in a conflict within a country when its purpose always had been to defend its members from external attack and to prevent aggression among states'.[14] Likewise, the NATO spokesman, Jamie Shea, later mentioned in an interview conducted by Brendan Simms (2002: 102) that 'there was at the beginning a sense of unreality, when the Bosnian conflict first broke out, that this organization need do nothing'. Besides some quotations used in the 'Review of the existing literature' section of Chapter 2, these statements of those who were in responsible positions in NATO in the early 1990s are suggestive in that this military organisation was not ready to act, in contrast to the neoliberal institutionalist argument that NATO had sufficiently developed mechanisms to adapt itself to the new environment quickly (Wallander 2000; Wallander and Keohane 1999). In short, the understanding about NATO at that time was that 'The Alliance is purely defensive in purpose: none of its weapons will ever be used except in self-defence'.[15]

In reality, there was a tendency among European states to intentionally avoid employing NATO for fear of increasing the U.S. presence in Europe. France's attitude was the most vivid in this regard; Paris, having withdrawn from NATO's military structure by the decision of President Charles de Gaulle in 1966, objected to any movement in NATO to accept new activities. Instead, the French government, a core supporter of the European Security Defence Identity (ESDI) and the CFSP, claimed that the Western European Union (WEU), which consisted of European members and expected to be integrated into the EU in the future, should be utilised, aiming to establish a more independent European security policy (see Chapter 5).

In fact, the WEU's policy line became clear in its 'Petersberg Declaration' on 19 June 1992, in which its future tasks were set up as: (1) humanitarian rescue tasks, (2) peacekeeping tasks and (3) tasks of combat forces in crisis management including peacekeeping (Bloed and Wessel 1994: 142). At the same time, the WEU issued a 'Declaration on the Yugoslav Crisis' and reiterated that 'the WEU is prepared ... to contribute towards effective implementation of the UN Security Council resolutions' (Bloed and Wessel 1994: 148). As can be seen from these statements, it was the WEU that had the will to engage in new security crises occurring in the Balkans.

For sure, there was a change in NATO as the war in Bosnia proceeded. The NATO Oslo summit in June 1992, synchronising with the WEU, concluded in its final communiqué that the Alliance was 'prepared to support on a case-by-case basis in accordance with our procedures, peacekeeping activities under the responsibility of the CSCE [Conference on Security and Cooperation in

Europe] countries' and 'contribute to United Nations peacekeeping and other efforts'.[16] This opened the way for possible activity in NATO's 'out of area', but, compared with the aforementioned declaration by the WEU, the tone of NATO's communiqué is somewhat general and still ambiguous about the role it would play in this crisis.[17] In any case, what can be said is that NATO's possible operations and those of the WEU could overlap each other.

The different views among European states on the prospects of future European security came to the surface over the implementation of the UN mandate for monitoring arms embargoes, and economic sanctions on Yugoslavia (UN Security Council Resolutions 713 and 757). Concerning the deployment of monitoring forces in the Adriatic Sea, countries such as France, Germany, Italy, Belgium and the Netherlands demanded the WEU's role in this mission, while others, such as Britain, claimed NATO's priority over military issues and the importance of the connection with the United States. As a result of this unresolved discussion, the WEU began its monitoring activity 'Sharp Vigilance' on the River Danube from 10 July 1992; on the other hand, NATO also commenced its first foreign operation, Operation Maritime Monitor in the Adriatic Sea, sending ships from Standing Naval Force Mediterranean (STANAVFORMED), which resulted in the fact that 'two naval forces from many of the same nations [were] acting in competition' under the name of 'interlocking institutions' (Rees 1998: 69).

To summarise the argument here, there was no shared understanding on the management of the conflict in the early 1990s nor any clear expectation about what kind of activity NATO should launch even after the outbreak of the war. As a consequence, differing perspectives on future European security came into collision when members were actually required to take action.

## Setback of international mediation and discussion over military intervention

### *Domestic pressure and the stalemate of European mediation activity in Bosnia (August 1992–May 1993)*

This section considers how the war in the Balkans was perceived domestically in the Western states. Analysis on the rise of domestic pressure in each country is reserved for later chapters; here it focusses on the magnitude of the so-called 'do something' pressure against the catastrophic situations at the collective level.

Around the time when UNPROFOR in Bosnia and monitoring forces at the Adriatic Sea were deployed (from June to August 1992), it was said that the public outcry for action was becoming increasingly louder (Kaufman 2002: 78). The reason for this is attributed to the discovery of concentration camps in Bosnia. In fact, it is around this time when the term 'ethnic cleansing', which was artificially forged by a media company in July to express the atrocity in Bosnia, is said to have soon spread and been 'regularly [used] after the first week of August' (Kent 2006: 255).[18] The existing research on media studies tells us that this catchy term, in tandem with 'genocide', caught public attention and prompted

## 42  Reforming NATO through Bosnia

political pressure on governments to take action to halt the violence (Gow et al. 1996; Kent 2006).

Given the public attention to the Balkans, how much pressure was generated within Western societies? There is a broad consensus within the existing literature on the rise of this social pressure not to ignore this humanitarian catastrophe, as Woodward (1995: 273) says that 'the pressure from the media and the public acted as a moral campaign, reminding the world that international conventions and moral law were being violated and demanding that the major powers take decisive military action' (also see Gow 1997: 215–216; Simms 2002: 54; Strobel 1997: 147; Szamuely 2013: 137–140). But it is difficult to evince this intensity in a systematic manner, which has consequently left the issue on domestic pressure ambiguous.

To elucidate this, this study develops the following method: relying on the previous examination that the terms of ethnic cleansing and genocide were used as an expression to describe the seriousness of the situations in the Balkans, it can be expected that the more newspaper articles employing these strong expressions, the more pressure was brought to bear upon governments to stop the violence. Counterfactually, if the expressions were little used, the nature of the conflict was not considered in light of what these terms meant and not even considered as an important topic in the public sphere of the Western states. Based on this expectation, Figure 3.1 counted how many articles utilised these terms per month.

First, as the figure demonstrates, there was a dramatic upheaval in August 1992, mirroring the discovery of concentration camps in Bosnia. This confirms the account provided in the existing literature discussed earlier. Other notable findings from this figure are as follows:

- If the number rises beyond 30, one article on average appeared in each paper every day;

*Figure 3.1* The number of articles using the word 'ethnic cleansing' or 'genocide'

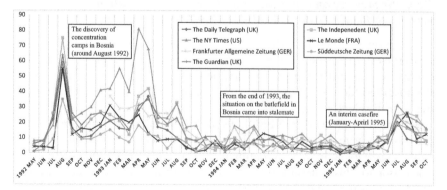

Method: Collecting numbers from each newspaper's digital archives. In order to exclude unrelated articles, the author confirmed the properness of content (due to a technical problem, *Frankfurter Allgemeine Zeitung* starts from 1993).

- Even after late1993, when the situation in Bosnia fell into a military stalemate, at least one article can still be found every four days on average, although it depends on the conditions on the battlefield;
- The deployment of the terms, 'ethnic cleansing' and 'genocide', can be used as proxies for identifying how much the war in the Balkans was discussed in the public realm of the Western states. Importantly, articles that discuss the conflict but do not employ these terms are excluded. Accordingly, were we to have included these articles this would provide further support for the argument being made here.

Under these circumstances where public attention was highly focussed on this crisis, the European states' diplomacy had been deployed. The London Conference was convened under the auspice of the United Nations and the EC on 26–27 August 1992, hosted by British Prime Minister, John Major. This meeting agreed to set up a UN-EC joint-run 'International Conference on Former Yugoslavia' (ICFY), chaired by Cyrus Vance (successively) and Lord David Owen, former British Foreign Minister.[19] The ICFY began mediation efforts from 3 September in Geneva and, in January 1993, submitted a new proposal known as the 'Vance-Owen Peace Plan' (VOPP) to divide Bosnia Herzegovina into ten provinces, in accordance with its ethnic configuration.

To describe the aftermath of the London Conference and the ICFY, neither international mediation produced fruitful results in reaching a ceasefire. Following the detailed account by James Gow (1997: 229–230), the crux of the consequences can be summarised by the fact that the implementation of the peace plans was not secured by enforcement using external military power. The London Conference issued a number of documents, including the handover of all heavy weapons of the Bosnian Serb camp under UN supervision, the lifting of the sieges of towns and the delivery of humanitarian assistance. The lack of a monitoring mechanism for its implementation, however, failed to make the ethnic militant groups abide by what they had concurred with on the negotiating table and resulted in just watching artillery pieces being fired at Sarajevo; ultimately, it lost effectiveness by the beginning of January 1993. Gow (1997: 231) concludes that

> Had implementation of that agreement been secured, as well as the introduction of monitors on the Serbian-Bosnian border as Milan Panić [the Federal Prime Minister of Yugoslavia] had said his country would permit, then the history of the Yugoslav War of Dissolution, and in particular its Bosnian phase might have been irrevocably changed for the better.[20]

The same problem was also true of the long negotiation process of the VOPP by the ICFY – the absence of external enforcement revealed the limitation of this talk. Although the VOPP itself was criticised even at that time for possibly stimulating a variety of irredentism because minority groups would be created in each province,[21] one of the possible solutions was to conclude the war by convincing minority groups to accept a political framework in Bosnia. Indeed, the representatives of the three parties in Bosnia – Serbs, Croats and Muslims – indicated acceptance of the plan. First, the Bosnian Croat leader Mate Boban agreed to the whole package and, despite initial reluctance, the Bosnian Serb leader, Radovan Karadzic, and the Bosnian President (i.e. the representative of the Bosnian Muslims), Alija Izetbegovic, signed the final part of the VOPP at the beginning of May 1993. However, as Gow (1997: 239) discusses, the lack of 'direct involvement by international bodies' to monitor all three ethnonational groups made the implementation of the agreement almost impossible.[22] Ultimately, the Bosnian Serb Assembly in Pale voted against ratification, after receiving the result of a referendum in May 1993, in which 96 per cent of the voters rejected the map of the VOPP.[23]

After the setback of the VOPP, Lord Owen and Thorvald Stoltenberg (former Norwegian Foreign Minister), who succeeded to the position after Vance's resignation in April 1993, continued the mediations and proposed a 'three-part confederation' of mini-republics under the Union of Republics of Bosnia and Herzegovina (Malcolm 1994: 253). Although the negotiations came near to closing an overall deal by the end of September, again, the outcome resulted in the rejection by the Bosnian Parliament (i.e. the Bosnian Muslim side). Lord Owen and Stoltenberg carried on further mediations under the framework of the ICFY; however, diplomatic efforts were stalled at the end of late December 1993. All detailed negotiation processes thus far are summarised in Table 3.1.

## *On the use of force: NATO's gradual engagements (1993–1994)*

The failure of the negotiations on the VOPP provoked severe criticism against the governments of the European states. For example, it was argued that the

*Table 3.1* The war in the former Yugoslavia and international mediations (1991–1993)

| | |
|---|---|
| **1991** | |
| Jun: | Declaration of independence by Slovenia and Croatia |
| Jul: | The Brioni Agreement (ceasefire in Slovenia) and the introduction of EC Monitoring Mission (ECMM) |
| Sep: | Mediations initiated by the European Community (EC) Conference on Yugoslavia led by Chairman Lord Carrington |
| **1992** | |
| Feb: | Lisbon Conference by the EC: the three-unit plan for Bosnia |
| Mar: | Declaration of independence by Bosnia Herzegovina |
| Aug: | London Conference (convened by British Prime Minister John Major): discussions about a ceasefire plan for the conflict in Bosnia and the creation of an International Conference on the Former Yugoslavia (ICFY) |
| Sep: | ICFY started negotiations (led by Cyrus Vance and Lord David Owen) |
| **1993** | |
| Jan: | Vance-Owen Peace Plan (VOPP): a ten-province plan |
| May: | Rejection of the VOPP |
| Jun: | ICFY posed the Owen-Stoltenberg Plan: a tri-partite ethnic division plan |
| Nov: | EU Action Plan (modification of the previous plan) |

Source: Summarised from Gow (1997: Chapters 4–5). For a more detailed chronology, see Kelleher (1995: 126–135).

crisis demonstrated 'the impotence of the West to put an end to the conflict';[24] that 'since Western statements on Bosnia now enjoy almost as little credibility as those of Slobodan Milosevic, the answer can be provided only by deeds, not words';[25] and that 'Europe failed ... the United Nations failed; the Vance-Owen plan is dead; the Serbs have won',[26] while a consensus summed up the damning verdict that Bosnia was a 'debacle for the West: preventive diplomacy failed in the Balkan test'.[27] In addition, the European states' non-military approach was also condemned. Principal newspapers increasingly advocated a tough policy such as 'only force will do in Bosnia',[28] 'no choice but to act'[29] and 'no half measures'.[30] Additionally, they claimed that 'the failure of European policy in Bosnia is to be blamed on the absence of a fully integrated European military strategy'.[31]

Faced with the political impasse, the expectations on NATO to take military action were eventually increased and, concomitantly, some changes appeared in NATO. The first sign was seen in the integration of NATO and WEU monitoring activities in the Adriatic Sea. Through the 'Joint Session' of the North Atlantic Council and the Council of the WEU on 8 June 1993, agreement was reached for 'a WEU contingent [to be] placed inside NATO's Southern Command in Naples' and for the two bodies to start a new activity known as 'Operation Sharp Guard' (De Wijk 1997: 69; Gow 1997: 130–131; Rees 1998: 69). At the time, the French government explained this decision by arguing that 'Western countries must put a halt to the absurd battle pitting NATO against [the] WEU'.[32] This indicates not only that the views of the states on the role of NATO were gradually converging but also that a more pragmatic approach was starting to receive greater emphasis.

Moreover, in the June and August meetings of the North Atlantic Council in 1993 (the latter one was specially convened to discuss Bosnia), the Alliance officially announced that it would offer protective airpower in case of attacks on UN peacekeepers, UNPROFOR, abiding with the UN Security Council Resolution 836, which authorised the use of force on 4 June 1993.[33] This was the first time that the Alliance concretely made public its willingness in principle to carry out military action.

It is true that European states' views converged on NATO with the realisation on the limits of a non-forceful approach and with the increase of criticisms from domestic societies over the lengthening of humanitarian disasters in Bosnia, and NATO, an organisation that includes the United States. Baroness Pauline Neville-Jones, then political Director for the Foreign Office in Britain, recalled that 'our ability to actually have influence on Milosevic, following the efforts like that of Lord Owen, was going to require more international support. It was necessary to bring the U.S. in'.[34]

## *Inter-alliance debate: the greatest transatlantic rift since Suez (1993–1994)*

As Chapter 2 discussed, intervention is certainly not unconditionally permitted in the sovereignty-based world. States try to secure UN endorsement to make their action legitimate – in the case of Bosnia, the use of military forces was granted on a mission-by-mission basis, such as UN Security Council Resolutions 770, 781, 816, 819 and 824.[35] The existence of these conditions, backed by public support and the United Nations, would seem to indicate that intervention would be carried out swiftly.

However, NATO members were struck by the problem of 'something must be done – but what?'.[36] In fact, strong consensus on the use of force was not yet created at that time. European states were reluctant to use air power because they (especially Britain, France and the Netherlands) had deployed their troops on the ground in Bosnia under the UN operations. On the other hand, the United States, having no troops on the ground, advocated air strikes. The different political circumstances between European states and the United States emanating from this so-called 'men on the ground' problem caused a serious dissonance in the transatlantic relationship.

Despite its initial attitude of distancing itself from the Balkans, the United States was gradually dragged into Bosnia in accord with the rising push from domestic society. In particular, the presidential election campaign in 1992 added fuel to the debate, which consequently boosted the pressure on the government to take action over the crisis in Bosnia (Halverson 1996: 10; Western 2002: 127).

From Congress, both Democrats and Republicans pushed President Bill Clinton to lift the UN arms embargo on Bosnia and launch a round of air strikes (see Chapter 7). This policy was called 'lift and strike', which was planned first to remove the arms embargoes in order to improve the situation of the Bosnian Muslims, which was inferior to that of the Bosnian Serbs who had inherited stockpiles of arms from the Yugoslav People's army as well as having their own arsenal and, once they became able to defend themselves from attacks by the Serbs, to carry out aerial bombardment in order to create a military balance on the battlefield.[37]

The lift and strike policy placed the United States and the European states in a head-on confrontation. The Europeans feared that lifting the embargo would facilitate the inflow of new weapons to any party in Bosnia and, furthermore, air strikes would antagonise the Bosnian Serbs and risk retaliation against their own troops (Daalder 2000: 32; Simms 2002: 69). Their claim can be summarised as: "'What would happen if the arms embargo was lifted … ?' … the Bosnian Serbs would go on a killing spree and slaughter all opposition', said British Foreign Secretary, Douglas Hurd.[38]

From mid-1993 to the end of 1994, these different political stances triggered a serious dispute among Alliance members, which was symbolically depicted as 'the biggest diplomatic row … since the Suez crisis of 1956'.[39] Numerous examples of the harshly worded exchanges between the representatives of the United States and Europe are enumerated by Ivo Daalder (2000: Chapter 1), Brendan Simms (2002: Chapter 3) and Wallace Thies (2009: 276–280). Some examples are enough to indicate this, such as the heated disputes between the Chairman of the U.S. Joint Chiefs of Staff, General Colin Powell, and Britain's Air Chief Marshal Sir Peter Harding (April 1993); the repeated clashes at the UN Security Council between Britain's permanent representative, Sir David Hannay, and the U.S. Ambassador, Madeleine Albright (late November 1994); and the ferocious attack in the *Washington Post* (mid-October 1993) on Europe by President Clinton and his Secretary of State, Warren Christopher, an attack that was particularly directed against Britain. Other examples include French public condemnation of the U.S. policy of 'lift and strike' (January 1994); the discord among the Alliance members during and after the January 1994 NATO summit in Brussels; and the vehement arguments between British Defence Secretary, Malcolm Rifkind, and Senators Robert Dole and John McCain (late 1994). Thus, it was claimed that the 'transatlantic relationship reached an all-time low' (De Wijk 1997: 111).

It would sound rather strange if seen from the conventional IR perspective, which emphasises hegemon/super power's influence over junior partners – the United States compromised. Although the details of how these compromises were made will be considered in Chapters 4 and 7 from the British and American perspectives, leaders in Washington could not pursue claims prioritising the unity of the Alliance members in the face of strong resistance.

In sum, although the necessity of military power was increasingly discussed, the contrasting political backgrounds of European states and the United States made conflict management more complicated. Consequently, the political staff on both the American and British sides expressly concurred that Bosnia 'had begun to adversely affect everything' (Holbrooke 1999: 84) and 'was starting to threaten the fabric of the NATO alliances'.[40] Corresponding to the decision makers' view, the argument within the public space was that 'What the Bosnian failure demonstrates is not so much the failure of the alliance as the penalty of evasion. It poses ... all these questions: Is the alliance still important?'[41] Thus, as Chapter 2 discussed, what was socially regarded as appropriate was not realised smoothly; in this case, the results were deteriorating relations among the Alliance members.

## Credibility of NATO and military intervention

### Dilemmas of intervention

'To pull out would be a disaster; to stay would be a tragedy'.[42] This expression by French President, François Mitterrand, aptly depicted the situation of international involvement in Bosnia. In the circumstances where negotiations came to an impasse and UN peacekeepers' casualties increased,[43] withdrawal from Bosnia was gradually discussed within the European states. Nevertheless, it was difficult to 'pull out without doing huge damage to their own credibility' because 'they are too deeply involved'.[44]

Indeed, the ceasefire was largely pronounced to halt the military offensive in Bosnia. However, when it came to the question of how to realise this goal, opinions were more divided. In particular, this became more obvious as the degree of military involvement deepened. The opinion polls in Table 3.2 reveal these ambivalent circumstances and where the Western states were placed on these

*Table 3.2* European attitudes towards intervention in Bosnia, 1994 (in percentage)

|  | Britain |  |  | France |  |  | Germany |  |  |
|---|---|---|---|---|---|---|---|---|---|
|  | 25 Feb | 25 Mar | 29 Jun | 25 Feb | 25 Mar | 29 Jun | 25 Feb | 25 Mar | 29 Jun |
| *(a) Let things go on as they are now* | | | | | | | | | |
| Favour | 11.5 | 28.4 | 15.7 | 8.0 | 14.5 | 11.0 | 20.0 | 17.1 | 20.3 |
| Oppose | 80.3 | 65.6 | 78.3 | 89.3 | 79.9 | 84.6 | 78.8 | 77.4 | 71.8 |
| Don't Know | 8.2 | 6.0 | 5.0 | 2.7 | 5.6 | 4.4 | 1.3 | 5.5 | 7.9 |
| *(b) Fight when necessary to get humanitarian convoys through* | | | | | | | | | |
| Favour | 84.4 | 83.5 | 77.6 | 90.2 | 89.2 | 85.1 | 59.4 | 64.8 | 57.8 |
| Oppose | 11.8 | 10.3 | 17.1 | 7.1 | 7.0 | 9.9 | 39.4 | 30.1 | 36.1 |
| Don't Know | 3.8 | 6.3 | 5.3 | 2.8 | 3.9 | 4.9 | 1.2 | 5.0 | 6.2 |
| *(c) Withdraw all troops* | | | | | | | | | |
| Favour | 24.7 | 26.7 | 28.3 | 23.5 | 26.8 | 30.7 | 27.7 | 25.0 | 27.1 |
| Oppose | 67.1 | 68.4 | 65.7 | 71.9 | 67.5 | 62.0 | 70.5 | 70.8 | 65.5 |
| Don't Know | 8.1 | 4.9 | 5.9 | 4.6 | 5.8 | 7.3 | 1.7 | 4.2 | 7.5 |
| *(d) Lift the arms embargo against Bosnia* | | | | | | | | | |
| Favour | 28.2 | 26.4 | 25.6 | 32.1 | 29.9 | 35.5 | 30.1 | 30.0 | 33.9 |
| Oppose | 55.5 | 58.9 | 58.1 | 57.6 | 58.7 | 53.8 | 67.2 | 62.9 | 57.8 |
| Don't Know | 16.3 | 14.7 | 16.3 | 10.3 | 11.4 | 10.7 | 2.8 | 7.2 | 8.4 |
| *(e) Launch air strikes* | | | | | | | | | |
| Favour | 38.9 | 55.2 | 43.0 | 53.1 | 58.4 | 48.3 | 43.2 | 49.5 | 39.8 |
| Oppose | 51.7 | 37.3 | 47.3 | 40.6 | 33.4 | 45.8 | 55.5 | 44.8 | 50.4 |
| Don't Know | 9.4 | 7.5 | 9.7 | 6.4 | 8.2 | 5.9 | 1.4 | 5.7 | 9.9 |
| Number | 506 | 507 | 501 | 497 | 502 | 502 | 1,576 | 1,580 | 1,573 |

Question: 'Are you for or against the following actions being taken by European states concerning the conflict between Serbs, Muslims, and Croats in Bosnia?'

Source: *Flash Eurobarometers* 24: 2/25/94; 25: 3/25/94; 29: 6/29/94 (also see Sobel 1996: 179). Questionnaires are slightly modified for grammatical reasons and order is also changed.

questions (data taken in 1994 when international negotiations were deadlocked, and the war in Bosnia had also reached an impasse).

Question (a) suggests that the majority of people considered it undesirable for the war to continue; by implication, it can be assumed that stopping the war was regarded as the necessary outcome. Meanwhile, Question (b) implies support for limited military action to assist humanitarian relief activity despite Germany's nuanced attitude. As the German exception indicates (cf. Chapter 6), people's opinions were nevertheless more divided when it came to concrete options. As mentioned, international peacekeeping activity under the United Nations had already started in Bosnia; bearing in mind that Question (c) was asked against this background, whilst it is true that pulling out the already deployed troops was rejected, it is also true that some people opted for this choice. Furthermore, forceful action was more controversial. Questions (d) and (e) are about the lift and strike policy. Question (d) uncovers ambivalence towards lifting the arms embargo, while it was not so strongly supported, but opinions were more or less divided. Question (e) shows us a clear division over possible air strikes.[45]

In short, whereas ending the war was generally anticipated by the public, concrete action would cause friction of different views as to how to approach this conflict practically. Whatever option was to be chosen (or even if no action was to be taken), they were unlikely to get away from public criticism not only for failing to stop the crisis but also for endangering their troops and so on. In other words, they were forced to face such a dilemma of action because of the foreign war occurring outside of their borders.

In fact, failure to stop the war was severely reprimanded. For example, it was said in Britain that 'Western credibility and long-term European security have already suffered grave damage from Nato's posturing and vacillation in Yugoslavia'[46] and that 'If Nato does not [carry out its threat], it will lose what little credibility it still has and might as well pack its bags and admit that it has no further role to play as an effective security organisation in a post-cold war Europe';[47] it was also contended in Germany that 'the credibility and self-confidence of the Alliance, which regards itself as the only workable military coalition of the world, is now being endangered',[48] and in France that 'the failure in the former Yugoslavia undermines the ambitions of the Twelve [here, meaning the EU members] as much as the credibility of Atlantic Alliance'.[49] Similarly, in the United States *The Washington Post* said, just after the assault against the Sarajevo market by the Serb militia: 'Let's see if NATO can act, the challenge is clear',[50] while after the aggression in Bihac, *The New York Times* commented that 'NATO's credibility, and very likely its raison d'être, died under Serbian assault on the town of Bihac in Bosnia'.[51]

Therefore, the problem had become 'Not only to preserve Bosnia, but also to restore some respect for international institutions, for principles ... and for something called the Western alliance', according to Senator Dole.[52] This concern was overshadowing NATO and political leaders on both sides of the Atlantic. President Clinton also stated that 'the alliance risked losing its credibility if cannot make good on its threats to use force in Bosnia'.[53] From the European side, Sir Richard Vincent, the British chairman of NATO's Military Committee, recalls that the West was 'blowing its credibility' over Bosnia.[54] In addition, although Germany had not sent any troops to the ground in Bosnia because of the unsolved constitutional debate (cf. Chapter 6), in October 1993, the German Defence Minister, Volker Rühe (1994: 103–104), expressed his concern by saying 'the process of the Bosnia-conflict has brought NATO into an extremely difficult situation', while in France, President Mitterrand, who had previously stuck to the Gaullist policy of keeping a distance from the Alliance, also called for 'action to NATO'.[55]

Against this background, in February 1994, NATO embarked on the first military action in its history since 1949, shooting down four Bosnian Serb fighter planes violating the no-fly zone as a countermeasure to the assault on the

Sarajevo market, which was mentioned at the opening of Chapter 1. Thereafter, NATO carried out limited air strikes against Serb targets both in Bosnia and in the Serbian Republic, responding to their attacks in Gorazde (April 1994) and Bihac (November 1994), respectively. Of course, every military decision caused vehement arguments over the safety of the troops on the ground of those dispatched. This concern was realised when the Bosnian Serbs captured and used UNPROFOR hostages as a human shield, which resulted in stopping the air strikes in November 1994 (De Wijk 1997: 111).

In addition to this problem, emanating from the absence of internationally shared understandings on the use of force, there was another procedural confusion. Even if NATO states could reach an agreement on military action, the authorisation of the United Nations Secretary General, or his representative, was also required as force would be used under the UN auspices. The so-called 'dual key' problem forestalled international operations, which frustrated the United States in particular (Chapter 7) as every NATO decision had to go through this process and could be overturned. This also suggests that the international response to foreign contingencies was not ready at that time. Despite this operational problem in the actual process, pressure on the governments of the Western states mounted as the war lingered on because their policy was judged on whether it could successfully halt the war in the Balkans or not.

## *To the Dayton Accords*

While Alliance members were in discord over the use of force, international diplomacy entered a new phase in 1994. Britain, France, Germany, Russia and the United States formed the Contact Group with their representatives in April, replacing the previous mediation activity by the ICFY. From this time, Russia officially began to commit itself to the conflict management process. Carrying over the basic position of the Owen-Stoltenberg Plan, the Contact Group posed a new proposal to divide Bosnia into two units: 51 per cent of the territory for the Muslims and the Croats and the remaining 49 per cent for the Serbs (Malcolm 1994: 258; Szamuely 2013: 208).

Meanwhile, the situations on the battlefield of Bosnia gradually changed from the beginning of 1994, owing to the military deadlock on both the Bosnian Serb and the Muslim-Croat sides (Gow 1997: 261–262). As shown in Figure 3.1, the decrease in the use of the words 'ethnic cleansing' and 'genocide' in newspapers is more or less related to these military circumstances. This certainly did not mean that the war had ended, but it became less intense and continuous than before. Furthermore, in late 1994, an interim ceasefire was achieved by former American President, Jimmy Carter, who voluntarily travelled to Pale, where the Bosnian Serb Assembly existed, and successfully brokered a four-month ceasefire from 1 January to 30 April 1995.

As its expiration approached, however, military clashes again escalated, especially the assaults from the Bosnian Serbs.[56] Faced with this situation, on 22 May NATO carried out air bombing of Serb ammunition dumps. In response, the Serb forces detained more than 350 UN peacekeepers and placed them where the bombings were likely to occur. To this hostage-taking, the newly inaugurated French President, Jacques Chirac, called for the creation of a Rapid Reaction Force (RRF) designed to protect UNPROFOR. He mentioned that 'the crisis must not just be defused but used to force a breakthrough in diplomacy and peacekeeping'.[57] This also became a 'turning point' for the United States to take tough measures with a strong recognition that 'its policy was failing' (Asmus 2002: 126). With the endorsement of the Contact Group, the RRF, consisting of 14,000 well-equipped British and French troops together with a small Dutch contingent, was dispatched to Bosnia, which consequently made 'the crucial difference on the ground' by rectifying the vulnerability of the UN peacekeeping troops (Sharp 1997: 52–54).

In July 1995, the infamous massacre of Srebrenica, which was described as 'a horror without parallel in the history of Europe since the Second World War' (United Nations General Assembly 1999: 108), served to accelerate the movement of NATO's military action. On 21 July, an international crisis meeting was convened in London with the representatives of the UN, the EU and the countries contributing to UNPROFOR, in which a more concrete plan on military operation was discussed. British Defence Secretary (Foreign Secretary from 1995) Rifkind describes the situations at that time by stating that 'the problem was doing nothing'.[58]

Finally, in response to a mortar attack on Sarajevo by the Serbs on 29 August, the Alliance commenced a comprehensive military campaign 'Operation Deliberate Force', which consequently lasted until mid-September. Concerning NATO's decision, *The New York Times* stated 'After 40 months of awkward hesitation, NATO today stepped squarely into the midst of the Bosnian war',[59] and in Britain *The Financial Times* argued that 'Western policy in Bosnia would not have had a shred of credibility left if there had not been a tough response to the latest gratuitous slaughter of civilians',[60] while *The Times* stated that 'there was no alternative to launching comprehensive air strikes if the NATO and UN missions in Bosnia were to retain any credibility'.[61] Similarly, the German news magazine, *Der Speigel*, mentioned that 'the West seized the last chance to recover its credibility',[62] while *Le Monde* remarked that 'the international community finally releases itself from the image of impotence'.[63] These expressions suggest how the international conflict management was assessed within the domestic societies of NATO states.

This intensive air bombardment contributed to creating a military-political balance on the ground between the Bosnian Serbs and the Muslim-Croats and to paving a way for diplomatic talks; 70 per cent of the territory that the Bosnian Serbs had held since the summer of 1992 was reduced to almost half that size, which was consistent with the plan posed by the Contact Group (Aybet 2000: 218). Additionally, in Croatia, on 4 August, approximately four weeks before NATO's military operation, the Croatian government suddenly started an offensive against the Serb-controlled Krajina in its territory, which not only resolved the diaspora problem in the republic but also reduced the Bosnian Serb's military dominance as the link with Krajina weakened and helped NATO's air strikes to be effective. By the end of September, the situation in the former Yugoslavia changed promptly and the war went into its final phase.[64]

Grounded in the agreement of each ethnic group to start peace negotiations and the announcement of a general ceasefire by President Clinton on 5 October, the proximity talks started, chaired by U.S. Assistant Secretary of State for European and Canadian Affairs, Richard Holbrooke, and co-chaired by the representatives of the EU, the UN and Russia. Thereafter, the presidents of Serbia (Milosevic), Croatia (Tudjman) and Bosnia (Izetbegovic) gathered with the Contact Group countries in a U.S. Air Force base in Dayton, Ohio, and the peace agreement, with which Bosnia Herzegovina was to be constituted by the Muslim-Croat Federation and Republika Srpska, while holding unity as a single state, was signed. Following this Dayton Agreement, NATO's first-ever ground activity – the Implementation Force (IFOR) – was deployed under the 'Operation Joint Endeavour', consisting of 60,000 heavily equipped troops and the participation of the U.S. forces (20,000) and other non-NATO states, including Russia; the operation therefore became the first NATO-Russia joint military activity. To avoid the experiences of UNPROFOR, IFOR's missions were limited to peacekeeping but entitled with authority to achieve calm by the use of force. Gülner Aybet (2000: 219) states that the dispatch of fully armed soldiers under NATO's operation gave it 'a prominence in Europe security unprecedented since the end of the Cold War'.

## After Bosnia: reorganising NATO for effective crisis management

### *Defining new role of NATO: changes at the international level*

After the engagement in Bosnia, the argument about European security moved onto a more concrete and pragmatic terrain, away from the ambiguous ideas in the early 1990s and the antagonistic debates in the past years. During the war, one of the main causes of the intra-alliance tension was whether to lift the arms embargo. In the end, this confrontation was not solved until 11 June 1996 when the embargo was eventually lifted.[65] Because this problem emanated from the absence of a common approach and assessment, NATO states were propelled to reorganise it for the sake of joint conflict management.

In the North Atlantic Council summits of December 1995 and June 1996, much stress was put on how to deal with new security problems in a more effective way. In the first of these summits, held in Brussels immediately after Bosnia, NATO's position on European security was explicitly defined in its final communiqué in these terms: 'the Alliance is preparing itself for implementation of the military aspects of the peace agreement for Bosnia Herzegovina ... This confirms the key role of the Alliance in ensuring security and stability in Europe'. [66] In addition, the 'Statement on Bosnia Herzegovina', specially issued during the summit, also reiterated that NATO would 'fulfil its new missions of crisis management and peacekeeping in addition to its core functions as a defensive Alliance'.[67] These statements reveal that an alliance originally organised against the Soviet threat had changed into a new one that addressed security contingencies outside its area, by making clear that it would embark on these activities, i.e. known as the 'non-Article 5' missions, in addition to collective defence.

In 1996, the reorganisation of European security system advanced with remarkable speed, and the Secretary General of NATO, Javier Solana, (1996a) stated that '1996 could be the year in which practice finally replaces theory and the pieces of a new European security architecture can begin to come together'. The June 1996 NATO summit in Berlin announced that 'we have taken a major step forward in shaping the new NATO' and 'we have taken decisions to carry further the ongoing adaptation of Alliance structure so that the Alliance can more effectively carry out the full range of its missions'.[68]

Moreover, the Berlin summit officially concluded the completion of the Combined Joint Task Force (CJTF),[69] which was designed to realise WEU-led operations by permitting the European members to utilise NATO's infrastructure during situations when the United States would not participate. Admittedly, the CJTF has the meaning that the United States put forward this concept to make it possible for European members to utilise NATO's infrastructure, without the need for U.S. involvement. Nevertheless, from the American side too, it was argued that 'CJTFs [sic] will allow NATO assets to be used more flexibly, and especially in operations outside traditional patterns involving different mixes of contributors. CJTFs will likely provide the mechanisms for the most probable NATO contingency operations', by Under Secretary of Defence for Policy, Walter B. Slocombe.[70] Accordingly, its purpose is defined as follows: 'By permitting a more flexible and mobile deployment of forces, including for new missions, this concept will facilitate the mounting of NATO contingency operations'.[71] This development helped to establish and advance the chief objective – an efficient response to a crisis such as Bosnia. The so-called 'Berlin agreement' became the basis of future European security (Rynning 2005: 33).

On the CJTF, Solana (1996b: 5) remarks that 'CJTF was conceived mainly as a means to improve NATO's ability to manage a complex peace support operation'. Likewise, it is characterised as 'part of the restructuring of NATO's integrated military structure' (De Wijk 1997: 128) 'intended to be capable of carrying out multiple missions in a flexible manner' (Yost 1998: 204), while it is also argued that 'CJTF was intended to give NATO' forces improved mobility and flexibility' (Ivanov 2011: 117). Reforms in NATO through Bosnia are epitomised in Table 3.3.

54  *Reforming NATO through Bosnia*

*Table 3.3* NATO's main reforms

| 1994 | |
|---|---|
| Jan | Proposition of the *Combined Joint Task Force (CJTF)* in the Brussels summit |
| Apr | Chiefs of Defence Staffs started the Long-Term Study (to revise MC 400*) |
| 10 May | *Provisional Policy Co-ordination Group (PPCG)* was created for CJTF Missions |
| **1995** | |
| May | The new *Ministerial Guidance 1995*** (decided by the ministers of defence), based on the outlines produced by the Long-Term Study |
| 28 Nov | The new MC 400/1 *** was announced |
| Dec | The creation of a *Combined Joint Planning Staff* (1) for the two Major NATO Commanders at SHAPE, and the establishment of a *Capabilities Co-ordination Cell* (2) at NATO headquarters in Brussels |
| **1996** | |
| Jun | The Berlin summit set up the *Policy Coordination Group (PCG)* (PPCG was upgraded) (3) |
| Dec | The NATO Military Command Structure (based on MC 400/1) |

\* MC 400 was made public soon after the Cold War as general guidance on NATO's new direction.
\*\* This is a review of Article 5 missions: collective defence and non-Article 5 missions (conflict management).
\*\*\* MC 400/1 shows basic principles of the future command and forces structures.

Source: Summarised from De Wijk (1997: 99–105) and Rynning (2005: 52–54). Italics with (1), (2) and (3) are newly introduced programmes and institutions, which are discussed later.

To accomplish the objectives of the CJTF, three new institutions were established:

(1) A Capabilities Coordination Cell within the International Military Staff (IMS) at NATO headquarters in Brussels 'to provide staff support to the Military Committee on contingency-related matters and assist the Military Committee in providing guidance to the Major NATO Commanders';
(2) A Combined Joint Planning Staff at Supreme Headquarters Allied Powers Europe (SHAPE) in Mons, Belgium, to 'perform centralized CJTF headquarters planning functions and co-ordination with all relevant headquarters, as well as with forces that might serve under a CJTF headquarters, and as appropriate with the WEU planning cell'; and
(3) A Policy Coordination Group (PCG) at NATO headquarters in Brussels to 'provide politico-military advice to assist the North Atlantic Council in managing and ensuring timely overall direction of Alliance military operations, particularly crisis management operations'.[72]

As a series of institutional reforms to improve crisis response capability, the number of headquarters was reduced from 65 to 20 for the purpose of simplifying the command structure (Yost 1998: 207). In addition, the NATO 'Standardization Organization' was established in January 1995, 'aimed at improving the co-ordination of allied policies and programmes for material, technical, and operational standardization'.[73] As a former British diplomat, Baroness Neville-Jones sees the characteristics of current NATO as a 'framework organisation' arranging 'standard operating methodologies … standardisation of weapons and capabilities and so on';[74] it can be said that reforms were intended to enable flexible joint response to regional crises.

The experiences in Bosnia surely provided the momentum for NATO's transformation, as Sean Kay (1998: 83) remarks that 'after four years of futile institutional activity, it had moved from theory to practice in terms of its post-Cold War role'. Solana (1996a) also argues that 'it is the Bosnian crisis, for so long a bone of contention, that has given new impetus to drawing the pieces together'. From this, it is possible to conclude that, by reviewing activities in the Balkans, in which the lack of a common assessment aroused crucial criticism against their credibility, the members of the Alliance tried to construct a new NATO in order to avoid a repeat of the same experiences.[75]

## NATO reforms: security governance to manage norm dilemmas

This examination suggests that Bosnia became a critical juncture for NATO states to launch new undertakings. To be sure, the normative pressure for action in response to the humanitarian tragedy in Bosnia played an important role in their policymaking. Here a question arises as to whether the same normative influence also furthered NATO's reforms. As Chapter 2 discussed, if this were the only driving force, three points defy explanation: (1) why military intervention was not conducted smoothly despite public support for action; (2) in its reorganisation, why an aggressive posture of NATO was not conceived to deal forcefully with foreign human rights abuses; and (3) why even those who disagreed with NATO's intervention agreed on its reorganisation after the war.

Concerning the first, this chapter has made clear that even though taking measures to address a foreign tragedy was considered socially appropriate, an international response was not readily available. In reality, divided opinions became more obvious as the degree of military commitment deepened, and as the danger of entanglement and human casualties loomed. That is to say, norm dilemmas were caused over the course of action. Moreover, under the circumstances where no internationally shared understanding on joint action existed, confusion, as well as friction, was triggered at the practical discussion level over how to approach the war. It can be contended that these past experiences prompted NATO members to create security governance capability to avert these problems and thereby meet public anticipation not to ignore a humanitarian tragedy.

On the second point too, concrete reforms in the Alliance were rather more intended to cope with regional emergencies at an early stage, not to eagerly undertake military interventions in response to other countries' human rights abuses. Counterfactually, if international mechanisms had existed that would help states to deploy a unified and swift approach, NATO states could have addressed the crises in the Balkans in a more efficient manner and complied with what was socially regarded as appropriate. Therefore, reforms were intended to coordinate their policy and enable conflict prevention, as Chapter 2 proposed.

It is premature to answer the third point, which requires examining each state's policymaking process. Thus far, this chapter has explained, at the international level, how the experiences in Bosnia propelled members of NATO to reorganise it for the purpose of coping with foreign crises. Questions are left unexplored as to what each member state thought about this. The following chapters analyse the cases of Britain, France, Germany and the United States, with a special focus on how their unique political conditions generated different types of norm dilemmas and, through their involvement, what they thought of NATO's reorganisation.

## Conclusion: from an anti-Soviet alliance to a security governance framework for humanitarian contingencies

This chapter has examined, through the involvement in Bosnia, how NATO, an international organisation originally created as an anti-Soviet alliance, changed. As this case revealed, given that action to address a humanitarian catastrophe was demanded, effective policy was not necessarily guaranteed because there was a gap between what is normatively considered desirable and the scope of each state's policymaking. Whereas normative influence not to ignore humanitarian tragedy attracted public attention, concrete action inevitably collided with other social demands, such as the fear of entanglement in a foreign war with the possibility of human casualties for the intervening states' personnel. Therefore, the support for action dwindled in accordance with the deepening degree of military involvement. Additionally, no effective measures were readily available to meet such social expectations. The European states began their mediation efforts, but their non-forceful approach did not make major progress and failed to induce strong commitment from the local parties in Bosnia. Furthermore, after the United States came into the process, an intense diplomatic row broke out because it advocated military bombardment, while the Europeans, having already deployed their own troops, were strongly opposed. After all, the international response was confronted by harsh criticism for failing to put an end to the war.

These experiences pushed the Western states to create new rationales for NATO in the post-Cold War period. As discussed, its reform was intended to develop security governance mechanisms that would help states to solve external crises before intervention became unavoidable. In other words, normative anticipation is not always straightforwardly reflected in international organisations; instead states design their institutional arrangements to avoid norm dilemmas.

Here, the discussion has been deployed at the international level, in particular, concentrating on how the war in the Balkans was treated by the Western states. The following chapters move on to the debates at the individual state level and ask how Britain, France, Germany and the United States reacted and how they reached the idea of reconstructing NATO. These questions will be investigated by examining their state-society relations.

## Notes

1 Quoted in Asmus (2002: 125), originally from an article by Ian Davidson, 'Unwrap the Package: The Political Effects of the Bosnian Peace Plan Should Force a Rethink of the Agenda for the Intergovernmental Conference', *Financial Times*, 29 November 1995.
2 As the purpose of this book lies in examining the international response to this war, it is difficult to explicate the process of the break-up of Yugoslavia, including such topics as how its political system granting autonomy to each republic (as well as Kosovo and Vojvodina) had worked to facilitate separatism after the death of Josip Broz Tito, how nationalist sentiments were boosted by democratic elections, and how political leaders used them as a means to gain popularity. For more detailed explanations from the inside of the former Yugoslavia, the following expositions are among those that should be referred to: Almond (1994), Donia and Fine (1994), Gagnon (2006), Glenny (1996), Malcolm (1994), Ramet (1996), Silber and Little (1995), Thompson (1999).
3 The EC troika is constituted by the foreign ministers of the countries holding the past, current and upcoming presidencies. At that time, the members were Gianni de Michelis (Italy), Jacque Poos (Luxembourg) and Hans van den Broek (the Netherlands). NB, the words 'the EC' and 'the EU' (before and after the effectuation of the Maastricht treaty) are used interchangeably.
4 Annika Savill, Donald Macintyre and Andrew Marshall 'EC Dispatches Peace Mission to Belgrade', *The Independent*, 29 June 1991 and 'EC Troika Sets Out to Halt Balkan Collapse', *The Guardian*, 29 June 1991. Also see Glaurdić (2011), Guicherd (1993), Szamuely (2013: 71–75).
5 David Usborne, 'Europeans Lay a Ghost and Hold Back a Balkan Nightmare', *The Independent*, 30 June 1991.
6 Richard Perle, former Assistant Secretary of State for Defence, commented in the interview conducted by Brendan Simms (2002: 54). Additionally, Thomas Halverson (1996: 6) adds that 'Washington happily let the EC and its appointed mediator, Lord Carrington, take the diplomatic lead'.
7 Sarah Lambert and Leonard Doyle, 'EC Tells Serbs to Stop War or Face Sanctions: Federal Forces', *The Independent*, 29 October 1991.
8 Philip Sherwell and Michael Montgomery, 'Turmoil in Yugoslavia: Eighth Ceasefire is Signed in Croatia', *The Daily Telegraph*, 9 October 1991.
9 Michael Montgomery, 'Croatians in Secret Talks over Bosnia', *The Daily Telegraph*, 29 February 1992. Gow (1997: 84–85), Sharp (1997: 15). Germany's unilateral recognition on the independence of Bosnia is discussed in Chapter 6.
10 For instance, Ramsbotham and Woodhouse (1996: 178–179).
11 'Declaration on a Transformed North Atlantic Alliance' (the London Declaration), Paragraph 6, www.nato.int/cps/en/natohq/official_texts_23693.htm (Accessed on 1 July 2018).
12 'The Alliance's Strategic Concept', Paragraph 9, www.nato.int/cps/en/natolive/official_texts_27433.htm (Accessed on 1 July 2018).
13 The Netherlands again presented this plan in the brainstorming sessions of the ambassadors in NATO on 17 February 1992, but it was again rejected; France and Belgium showed the most scepticism (De Wijk 1997: 54). Similarly, the then chairman of the Military Committee NATO, General Vigleik Eide, recommended the dispatch of 40,000 NATO troops in early 1992 but was 'blocked at the political level' (Simms 2002: 102).
14 Quoted in Chayes and Weitz (1996: 391).
15 'The Alliance's New Strategic Concept', Paragraph 35, www.nato.int/cps/en/natohq/official_texts_23847.htm (Accessed on 1 July 2018).
16 Ministerial Meeting of the North Atlantic Council in Oslo, 4 June 1992, 'Final Communiqué', Paragraphs 11 and 13, www.nato.int/docu/comm/49-95/c920604a.htm (Accessed on 1 July 2018).

17 On this point, see Simms (2002: 102).
18 On public relations firm Ruder Finn Global Public Affairs' media campaign, see Szamuely (2013: 137).
19 With the initiation of the ICFY, Lord Carrington's EC Conference on Former Yugoslavia was closed and replaced by this new international diplomacy.
20 Panić showed a more cooperative attitude to the West than any other politicians but was defeated by Milosevic's re-election when Panić ran for Serbian President in late 1992. See Gow (1997: 229–230).
21 For example, Marcus Tanner, 'Bosnian Serbs "ready to agree peace": Karadzic Calls Halt to Fighting after Referendum Rejects Vance-Owen Plan by 96 per cent', *The Independent*, 20 May 1993.
22 As one of the lessons of the Balkans, Lord Owen (1966: 375) also touches upon credible military commitment including peacekeeping forces for immediate deployment.
23 Tanner, *op. cit.*, 20 May 1993.
24 Alan Frachon, 'L'impuissance des Occidentaux à mettre fin au conflit Les divergences sur la Bosnie s'aggravent entre Américains et Européens', *Le Monde*, 13 May 1993.
25 'Leading Article: The Test of the Bosnia Deal', *The Independent*, 24 May 1993.
26 Ian Davidson, 'Failure on Every Front', *The Financial Times*, 19 July 1993.
27 Michael Strümer, 'Debakel des Westens: Die vorbeugende Diplomatie ist bei ihrer Reifeprüfung auf dem Balkan durchgefallen', *Frankfurter Allgemeine Zeitung*, 28 July 1993. See other similar articles, e.g. Dominique Mosi, 'Britain's Failure, or All Europe's?: Amid Final Preparations for the Edinburgh Summit', *The Independent*, 11 December 1992; Annika Savill and Giles Elgood, 'Lord Owen Admits His Peace Plan Has Failed: Mediator Urges Bosnian Muslims to Consider Three-Way Carve-Up of Yugoslavia Proposed by Presidents of Serbia and Croatia', *The Independent*, 18 June 1993; 'Leading Article: Toothless Allies', *The Financial Times*, 10 June 1993; Robert Mauthner, '"Reality" Buries Vance-Owen Plan', *The Financial Times*, 18 June 1993; Philip Stephens and Lionel Barber, 'EC Concedes Bosnia Plan is in Tatters: Izetbegovic to Meet Ministers on Drive for New Settlement', *The Financial Times*, 21 June 1993; Marie Colvin and Geordie Greig, 'Serbs Triumph as West Abandons Bosnia', *Sunday Times*, 23 May 1993; 'Le conflit dans l'ex-Yougoslavie Après l'abandon du plan Vance-Owen sous la pression serbe et croate Avis de décès', *Le Monde*, 19 June 1993; Claire Trean, 'Les missions de l'ONU ex-Yougoslavie: les dérobades', *Le Monde*, 25 September 1993; 'Schwierige Suche nach gemeinsamer Position zum Balkankrieg', *Frankfurter Allgemeine Zeitung*, 22 June 1993; 'Wir sind nicht feige. Wir wollen aber einen Fehlschlag vermeiden', *Die Zeit*, no. 19, 7 May 1993.
28 'Leading Article: Only Force Will Do in Bosnia', *The Independent*, 23 April 1993.
29 'Leading Article: No Choice Now But to Act', *The Independent*, 7 May 1993.
30 'Leading Article: No Half Measures', *The Daily Telegraph*, 4 August 1993.
31 Dominic Lawson, 'Laying Down Their Lives for the UN', *The Financial Times*, 17 July 1993.
32 Grant (1996: 76), fn. 25, originally from a Comment by the Rassemblement pour la République deputy Jacques Baumel, Vice President of National Assembly's Defence Commission. For more detailed accounts, see Chapter 5.
33 Ministerial Meeting of the North Atlantic Council in Athens, 10 June 1993, 'Final Communiqué', Paragraph 3 (www.nato.int/docu/comm/49-95/c930610a.htm) (Accessed on 1 July 2018); the Special Meeting of the North Atlantic Council in Brussels, 'Press Statement by the Secretary General', 2 August 1993, Paragraphs 3 and 5 (www.nato.int/docu/comm/49-95/c930802a.htm) (Accessed on 1 July 2018).
34 Interview with the author (12 September 2013).
35 Cf. Gow (1996: 92).
36 '"Something Must be Done" – But What?', *The Daily Telegraph*, 5 August 1992.

37 Concerning the lift and strike policy, see Gow (1997: 212–222), Sharp (1997), Daalder (2000). In fact, the application of an arms embargo throughout Bosnia was originally proposed by the Serbian Republic which, it is now said, seemed aware that this sanction would produce favourable conditions for the Bosnian Serbs (Sharp 1997: 40, also see Gow 1996: 93–94). Hence, Richard Holbrooke (1999: 30), U.S. Assistant Secretary of State for European and Canadian Affairs, remarks that

> this seemingly neutral position [the arms embargos against the entire Yugoslavia] was a gift to the Serbs, since almost all the armaments and weapons factories of Yugoslavia were located in Serbia. To the Croats and especially to the Muslims of Bosnia, this was a huge blow.

38 Quoted in James Adams, John Davison and Michael Prescott, 'Ties That Unwind; Nato Alliance', *Sunday Times*, 4 December 1994, which depicts the conversation between American Senator Dole and the British counterparts, including Hurd, Malcolm Rifkind (Defence Secretary) and Field Marshal Sir Peter Inge (Chief of the Defence Staff).

39 Bruce Clark and George Graham, 'Wide Relief over Arms Embargo: Bosnian Moslems Accept Delay in Ending Ban', *The Financial Times*, 28 September 1994. Also see Andrew Marr 'A Special Relationship? Don't Mention It', *The Independent*, 24 February 1994. See Kaplan (2004: 116–120), Theis (2009: 276–279), Webber (2012: 60–61).

40 Sir Robin Renwick's (British Ambassador to Washington) remark, quoted in Simms (2002: 101).

41 Henry Kissinger, 'Expand NATO Now', *The Washington Post*, 19 December 1994.

42 Quoted in 'Leading Article: We Must Not Abandon Bosnia', *The Independent*, 21 January 1994.

43 Until the end of the war, 117 members of UNPROFOR were killed only in Bosnia and 167 in the former Yugoslavia (United Nations General Assembly 1999: 6).

44 'Leading Article: Only Force Will Do in Bosnia', *The Independent*, 23 April 1993.

45 Public opinion data on the American case are analysed in Chapter 7.

46 'Leading Article: Options in Bosnia', *The Daily Telegraph*, 25 April 1994. Also see 'Leading Article: Rationale for the Alliance', *The Daily Telegraph*, 10 February 1994; 'Leading Article: The Limits of Balkan Military Intervention', *The Daily Telegraph*, 29 January 1994.

47 Robert Mauthner, 'Sarajevo Ultimatum: West Creates New Uncertainties', *The Financial Times*, 11 February 1994. Also see Robert Mauthner, 'Sarajevo Deaths Revive Debate Over Response', *The Financial Times*, 8 February 1994; Lionel Barber and David White, 'Clinton Warns of Threat to Credibility', *The Financial Times*, 11 February 1994; Bruce Clark, 'Nato Tries to Play Down Serbia Row: Dispute with UN a "communications mismatch"', *The Financial Times*, 25 April 1994. From other newspapers, see Joel Brand, 'Untidy War Tests Nato Credibility', *The Times*, 25 November 1994; Andrew Marshall, Robert Block and Tony Barber, '10-day Deadline for Serbs', *The Independent*, 10 February 1994; 'Leading Article: At Last, the UN Draws a Line', *The Independent*, 1 March 1994; Christopher Bellamy and Tony Barber, 'West Left in Disarray over Gorazde Siege', *The Independent*, 18 April 1994; Andrew Marshall, 'Nato Divided on Use of Bosnia Airstrikes', *The Independent*, 7 October 1994; Rupert Cornwell, 'Dole's Trip Likely to Sow More Seeds of Disunity', *The Independent*, 26 October 1994; Richard Dowden, '"More strikes", Dole Tells Downing Street', *The Independent*, 1 December 1994; Andrew Marshall, 'Time to Consider Bridging a Once Great Divide', *The Independent*, 5 December 1994; Michael Prescott, Peter Millar, Andrew Hogg, Stuart Wavell, Geordie Greig, Colin Smith and Louise Branson, 'No Choice: How Britain was Bulldozed into Line on Air Strikes', *Sunday Times*, 13 February 1994; Michael Evans, 'Nato Struggles to

Win Credibility after Moscow's Revenge', *The Times*, 21 February 1994; Joel Brand, 'Untidy War Tests Nato Credibility', *The Times*, 25 November 1994.
48 Stefan Kornelius, 'Frieden schaffen – mit Konfusion und Waffen. Im Bosnien-Konflikt: Zwischen UNO und NATO gibt es Misstrauen und Verdruss', *Süddeutsche Zeitung*, 13 October 1994. Also see Josef Joffe, 'Diplomatie der gepanzerten Faust', *Süddeutsche Zeitung*, 11 February 1994; indem, 'Der zweite Bosnische Krieg', *Süddeutsche Zeitung*, 21 November 199; Theo Sommer, 'Der Westen zeigt die Zähne', *Die Zeit*, No. 10, 4 March 1994.
49 Parenthesis added, Claire Trean, Jean La Gueriviere, 'Emergence de l'Europe, ou désengagement des Etats-Unis?', *Le Monde*, 9 January 1994. Similar articles are, e.g. 'L'ultimatum de l'Alliance atlantique aux Serbes de Bosnie La peau de l'ours', *Le Monde*, 22 February 1994; Florence Hartmann, 'La percée serbe sur Gorazde: "C'est l'échec total de la communauté internationale. Bravo!"', *Le Monde*, 19 April 1994.
50 'Let's See If NATO Can Act—The Challenge is Clear', *The Washington Post*, 9 February 1994.
51 Anthony Lewis, 'Abroad at Home: The End of NATO?', *The New York Times*, 28 November 1994. Also see John Darnton, 'British Worry That U.S. is Slighting Them Now', *The New York Times*, 4 February 1994; Craig R. Whitney, 'Clash on Bosnia Creates Strain in NATO', *The New York Times*, 26 November 1994; Michael R. Gordon, 'Conflict in the Balkans: The Policy Colliding Missions – A Special Report; U.S. and Bosnia: How a Policy Changed', *The New York Times*, 4 December 1994; Michael R. Gordon, 'U.S., in Shift, Gives Up Its Talk of Tough Action Against Serbs', *The New York Times*, 29 November 1994; William Drozdiak, 'U.S. and Europe in Serious Rift over Bosnia War; Allies Resent GIs' Absence as Americans Call for Action', *The Washington Post*, 27 November 1994; Jim Hoagland, 'When the World Won't Behave; Clinton Learns the Limits and Lessons of Gunboat', *The Washington Post*, 4 December 1994; Ruth Marcus and John F. Harris, 'Behind U.S. Policy Shift on Bosnia: Strains in NATO', *The Washington Post*, 5 December 1994; and Charles Forrest, 'The Coward's Way Out', *The Washington Post*, 12 December 1994.
52 Quoted in James Adams, John Davison and Michael Prescott, 'Ties That Unwind; Nato Alliance', *Sunday Times*, 4 December 1994.
53 Quoted in Douglas Jehl, 'The NATO Summit: In NATO Talks, Bosnia Sets Off a Sharp Debate', *The New York Times*, 11 January 1994.
54 Quoted in the interview conducted by Simms (2002: 104).
55 'Le treizième sommet de l'Alliance atlantique à Bruxelles M. Mitterrand appelle l'OTAN à "l'action" en Bosnie', *Le Monde*, 11 January 1994.
56 One of the reasons which provoked the Bosnian Serbs' attack was that Bosnian Muslims used the ceasefire to import arms and train their forces, which means that the ceasefire, as a consequence, worked in favour of the Muslims (Daalder 2000: 37–40, also see Szamuely 2013: 220).
57 Charles Bremner, 'Paris Drums Up Support for Tougher Mandate', *The Times*, 29 May 1995.
58 Interview with the author (8 September 2013).
59 Roger Cohen, 'Conflict in the Balkans: The Overview; NATO Presses Bosnia Bombing, Vowing to Make Sarejvo Safe', *The New York Times*, 31 August 1995. Also see Rick Atkinson, 'NATO Air Raids: Step toward Peace or a Wider War? Raid on Serbs is Biggest since Alliance's Founding', *The Washington Post*, 31 August 1995, which stated that 'NATO finally went to war today, more than 18 months after the world's most powerful military alliance fired its first shot in anger in Bosnia'.
60 'Leading Article: Belated action in Bosnia', *The Financial Times*, 31 August 1995. In other newspapers, expressions are also very alike: 'NATO's Bosnian Policies Would Have Lost All Credibility If the Alliance Had Failed to Keep Its Promise, Made Last Month, to Respond with Massive Force to Bosnian Serb Attacks in the UN

"safe areas"', *The Independent*, 31 August 1995; and 'If the Serbs Were Allowed to Demonstrate That Potential Aggressors Had Nothing to Fear from the Alliance, Then Its Deterrent Capability Would Be Limited in the Future', *The Daily Telegraph*, 4 September 1995.
61 Michael Evans, 'Military Chiefs Given Free Rein: NATO', *The Times*, 31 August 1995.
62 'Peitsche und Zuckerbrot', *Der Spiegel*, vol. 36, 1995: 26.
63 Alain Frachon and Claire Trean, 'Un pari franco-américain pour la paix', *Le Monde*, 1 September 1995.
64 Another important factor to end the war, according to Daalder, was the fact that Milosevic, as the President of Serbian republic, secured the control of the Bosnian Serb military and political leadership by agreements with Bosnian Serb leader Radvan Karadzic and the military commander, General Ratko Mladic, which consequently facilitated political negotiations to end the war (Daalder 2000: 127–129).
65 The details are shown in the Royal United Service Institute for Defence Studies (1998: 1220).
66 Ministerial Meeting of the North Atlantic Council held at NATO Headquarters, Brussels, 5 December 1995, 'Final Communiqué', Paragraph 2. www.nato.int/docu/comm/49-95/c951205a.htm (Accessed on 1 July 2018).
67 'Press Communiqué M-NAC-2 (95) 119 For Immediate Release, Statement on Bosnia-Herzegovina', www.nato.int/docu/pr/1995/p95-119.htm (Accessed on 1 July 2018).
68 'Ministerial Meeting of the North Atlantic Council Berlin: Final Communiqué', Paragraph 2, 3 June 1996, www.nato.int/docu/pr/1996/p96-063e.htm (Accessed on 1 July 2018).
69 The concept of the CJTF originally appeared after the end of the Cold War, but its concrete contents were set out in the Brussels NATO summit 1994. On this point, see Chapter 7.
70 Quoted in Yost (1998: 204).
71 'Final Communiqué', Ministerial Meeting of the North Atlantic Council, 3 June 1996, www.nato.int/cps/en/natohq/official_texts_25067.htm?mode=pressrelease (Accessed on 1 July 2018).
72 Quoted in Yost (1998: 205). Originally, the document from 'Final Communiqué of the Meeting of the North Atlantic Council in Defence Ministers Session', June 13, 1996, Paragraphs 6 and 9, www.nato.int/docu/pr/1996/p96-089e.htm (Accessed on 1 July 2018). Regarding more detailed examples of NATO reforms, see Yost (1998: 378), fn. 41. The PCG was replaced by the Operations Policy Committee in 2010. See www.nato.int/cps/en/natohq/topics_69312.htm (Accessed on 1 July 2018).
73 'NATO Council Agrees to Set Up New Alliance Standardization Organization', Press Release, 95 (4), 24 January 1995, available at www.nato.int/docu/pr/1995/p95-004.htm (Accessed on 1 July 2018). Also see Mayer (2014: 322).
74 Interview with the author (12 September 2013).
75 Additionally, such orientations were reflected in NATO's updated Strategic Concept in 1999, which places emphasis on crisis management, available at www.nato.int/cps/en/natolive/official_texts_27433.htm (Accessed on 1 July 2018). Also see Herd et al. (2013: 25).

# 4 Beyond intervention or non-intervention
## Britain's view on the reform of NATO through Bosnia

### Introduction

During the war in the Balkans, an article in *The Daily Telegraph* referred to the 'moral' and 'realistic' traditions in British foreign policy: the former is in the line of Milton, Cromwell and Gladstone, and the second is reminiscent of Disraeli and Lord Salisbury. This article asserts: 'What is actually happening is that the government is trying to contain and harmonise the two attitudes'. That means, 'Yugoslavia, from a British point of view, does not matter. That is why [Foreign Secretary] Mr Hurd has constantly resisted calls for military intervention'. However, in the face of the atrocities 'seen on television from the Balkans', 'Mr Hurd cannot stand up and say: "The death of thousands of Yugoslavs makes no difference to Britain, so we shall let them get on with it"'.[1] The article aptly characterises the government's changing attitude on the pendulum of these two considerations.

Britain's reaction to Bosnia began with this 'realistic' tradition; it was quite reluctant for fear of getting involved in what its political leaders considered a quagmire historically and ethnically complicated situation. Nevertheless, confronted by the public outcry for taking measures against this tragedy, John Major's government gradually steered towards the other 'moral' tradition. As the opposition parties, Labour and the Liberal Democrats, as well as the public, increased pressure on the government for not doing enough to stop this humanitarian catastrophe, it commenced its engagement by sending its troops to the UN peacekeeping operation in Bosnia. This participation, however, in triggered a fierce backlash against the government from inside of the Conservative Party itself, for being dragged into a war where 'No important British national self-interest' was implicated.[2]

Moreover, the government was confronted by another problem on the international stage. As the war was prolonged, military options were increasingly discussed, primarily by the Americans; however, London was vehemently opposed because it would endanger soldiers that it had already deployed in Bosnia, by triggering reprisals from the local militias. It had to undergo head-on clashes with the United States and their relationship deteriorated significantly. As a consequence, because of this foreign war occurring far away from their homeland,

London decision makers were placed under siege not only domestically from those pushing for more action and reprimanding its involvement but also internationally from those attacking its policy.

This chapter reveals that this experience led the British government towards a rearrangement of the European security framework, with particular regard to the reorganisation of NATO. At the beginning of the 1990s, Britain saw its role exclusively as collective defence and found no reason to embark on new activities beyond its border. Having gone through Bosnia, nevertheless, the necessity of NATO reorganisation was contended to coordinate inter-state understandings on how to carry out crisis response properly and thereby avert repetition of the experience. Through this process, the country that showed reluctance and wariness of its involvement in Bosnia prompted the reorganisation of the Alliance for the sake of responding to foreign humanitarian crises.

It is not because British policymakers had altered their views of non-intervention but because they sought a way to make compatible their original claim – that armed forces should be employed only to save material British interests – with social normative anticipation. This is why they preferred NATO capability for conflict prevention to that of intervention in other countries' domestic affairs. This case study tells us that normative effects are injected into international organisations not necessarily through a unanimous consensus but through creating a governance mechanism for responding to contrasting social demands at the same time.

This chapter proceeds in five parts. The first section reviews Britain's initial attitude to the war in the Balkans, while the second examines how it increasingly began its commitment – here the rise of domestic normative pressure is assessed. The third section contemplates the predicament of the John Major administration. The fourth section investigates why, after the war, political leaders in Britain agreed on the reorganisation of NATO to address humanitarian contingencies. The conclusion discusses what can be inferred from studying the British case and considers the connection between normative influence and international security governance.

## Britain and Bosnia: its first reaction

### *The British government's view*

Britain's response to the war in the Balkans was consistent with (neo)realist thinking (cf. Chapter 2). By observing from the vantage point of cost-benefit calculations, it preferred to distance itself from this conflict, because 'the John Major government … saw no vital British interests at stake – no vital resources, investments or citizens to protect' (Sharp 1997: 8). Even long after the end of the war, this point was still clearly and even blatantly being reaffirmed by the then Foreign Minister, Douglas Hurd, who said: 'There was no serious British national interest involved. No strategic. No commercial'.[3] Moreover, as will be discussed later, throughout the war a number of Conservative Members of Parliament (MPs) were frustrated by Britain's involvement and frequently asked, 'what is the British national interest in Bosnia?'[4] and claimed that 'no obvious British national interest' was implicated.[5]

In addition, there were also other reasons that made political leaders cautious. It is now said that they saw the war through 'historic and ethnic lenses' (Gow 1997: 175) as they were afraid of becoming bogged down in a 'Vietnam-like' quagmire (Sharp 1997: 7; Simms 2002: 4–5). Indeed, this crisis was often compared to other intervention precedents, such as 'the danger of dragging the United Kingdom into another war in a region of historically unresolved conflict', or 'a European Vietnam',[6] and 'we should learn the lessons of the Americans in Vietnam and the Russians in Afghanistan'.[7] Needless to say, as some researchers point out, the experience in Northern Ireland also worked to make the decision makers wary about a possible entanglement (Gow 1997: 175; Lucarelli 2000: 190; Simms 2002: 9). From the British perspective, it was difficult to find any incentive to start an intervention.

Of course, the Major government was not completely silent on the ongoing war. It appointed Lord Carrington, former Foreign Secretary and former NATO Secretary General, as the chairman of the diplomatic talks on the break-up of Yugoslavia in 1991. Even within the Conservative Party, some MPs, such as Patrick Cormack and Quentin Davies, argued for a more active policy for humanitarian reasons.[8] According to Brian Rathbun's research, however, these politicians belonged to a minority group, as Cormack himself acknowledges that supporters for pro-intervention were 'very, very, very few indeed' and that he was 'on occasion the sole voice in [his] party' (Rathbun 2004: 57–58). It is also true that the former Prime Minister, Margaret Thatcher, had been one of the strongest proponents of taking tough action, including air strikes.[9] Nevertheless, since she had already retired from the political stage at that time, her voice came mainly from the outside of the party through the media, not from the inside.

The Tory government's cautiousness became obvious when military deployment was internationally discussed. As early as August 1991, when the focus was placed only on violence in Croatia, Britain soon opposed the French proposal to dispatch interposition troops under the Western European Union's activity. Likewise, in the emergency meeting of EC foreign ministers in The Hague, Hurd warned his colleagues that sending their troops would be a dangerous first step leading 'Europe into a quagmire without exit'.[10] Subsequently, the Foreign Office Minister, Douglas Hogg, stated that 'There is no military solution to this problem, let alone one imposed from outside'. He rejected the possibility of peacekeeping operations, saying that 'In the present circumstances "peacekeeping" is not a policy option – because there is no peace to keep'.[11] In short, Britain's commitment was limited to applying 'political pressure' (including the EC's mediation and the dispatch of British monitors) and 'economic and other measures'.[12]

On the government's view on 'non-intervention', Defence Secretary (later Foreign Secretary) Malcolm Rifkind states that 'the main anxiety in the Parliament was not that Britain was doing too little, but it was doing too much', and what was feared at that time was 'mission creep, that gradually we will become involved in combat operations'.[13] Similarly, his successor as Defence Secretary, Michael Portillo, also recalls that 'the expression that was used a lot by the military was being worried about putting your hand in a mangle'.[14] From a broader perspective, a former British diplomat, whose name was agreed not to be disclosed, reveals that 'There was also a very strong sense from our military experts and political leaders that people would not understand it if we went almost immediately from one operation in Iraq [i.e. the Gulf War] to another operation in the Balkans'.[15] From today's perspective, when it is known that a massive military intervention was actually carried out in August 1995, the British attitude at the beginning shows how long a distance there was to reach the actual use of force.

On NATO, although the Foreign Office made clear in the early 1990s that the organisation was 'a defensive alliance' and 'none of its weapons [would] ever be used except in self-defence',[16] London proposed the idea of establishing an Allied Rapid Reaction Corps (ARRC) in the November 1991 NATO summit.[17] Despite such a flexible view, it was not thought that this military alliance was to be employed to cope with the ongoing crisis in the Balkans because the government was cautious of being entangled in it.

### *Opposition parties' view: Labour and Liberal Democrats*

The existing literature tells us that 'Labour policy and rhetoric was indistinguishable from that of the Major administration' (Simms 2002: 298) – at least at the earliest phase, this account is correct. For example, in mid-1992, referring to his personal conversation with the Israeli prime minister, the Shadow Foreign Secretary, Gerald Kaufman, warned of the danger of military involvement in the former Yugoslavia, by saying: 'military action is more easily entered into than got out of'.[18] Owing to its complexity, he supported the Tory approach as he remarked: '[the government] has not mentioned the use of force and I welcome that'.[19] Likewise, Kaufman's successor, Jack Cunningham, also argued that 'The Foreign Secretary rightly ruled out military solutions to these complex problems',[20] while the Shadow Defence Secretary, David Clark, added that 'British military involvement must not be allowed to escalate into such a quagmire'.[21] Furthermore, George Robertson, the Labour European Affairs Spokesman, also said that 'It would be utterly wrong to contemplate sending young soldiers into a war zone when economic sanctions are being flouted daily'.[22]

During the course of the war, as will be debated later, the Labour Party, in tandem with the Liberal Democrats, produced strong interventionist arguments. However, what can be said from these findings is that Labour's initial attitude was as wary as that of the Conservatives; Labour MP, Clare Short, who had been vocal on international action, later recalled that 'Labour frontbench spokespeople did not make any particularly strong criticism' against the government.[23] The difference from the government's posture was at best that this party advocated comprehensive economic sanctions and a more direct UN involvement a bit more clearly.[24]

The party that had been consistently calling for a more active engagement from the early days was the Liberal Democrats. This party, which takes a pro-European and liberal stance stressing human rights issues, perceived the Yugoslav problem, according to its party leader, Paddy Ashdown, not only as 'the first example of the threats that will affect Europe's peace and stability' after the end of the Cold War,[25] but also as 'a challenge to the new world order, to the political will of the European Community, and to our common humanity which we will dodge at our peril'.[26] In fact, he visited Bosnia and Croatia in early August 1992 and, in his letter to the Prime Minister, accused Major of his '"weakness" and failing to set a lead' in conflict management.[27] Furthermore, he urged the establishment of 'safe havens' for Bosnian refugees and the use of 'air power', if necessary, to halt further attacks by the Bosnian Serbs.[28] In Parliament, the Liberal Democrats were the sole collective voice pushing for a stronger commitment in the Balkans.

## Britain's incremental engagement

### *The government's policy change and the public debate*

Despite its very cautious early considerations, Prime Minister John Major announced in mid-August 1992 an offer of 1,800 troops to UNPROFOR in Bosnia to protect its aid convoys and to ensure that food and medicine would get through to the victims of Serbian aggressors. Why did the government agree to this? *The Daily Telegraph* explained: it was the result of its 'Having been pushed into this decision by the weight of public sentiment',[29] while *The Times* also stated that 'To prove that his government is "doing something", John Major has offered to send up to 1,800 ground troops'.[30] To account for this policy change, it seems pertinent to investigate the public debate in Britain at that time.

August 1992, when this announcement was made public and which was recalled as 'the darkest period in Europe since the Holocaust',[31] was the time when media pressure became so intense because of the discovery of the Serb-run detention camps (borrowing a media expression, 'Nazi-style concentration camps') as well as the escalation of the war in Bosnia.[32] The news relating this conflict had rapidly permeated British society. As examined in the previous chapter (see Figure 3.1), in August 1992 alone, 59 articles in the conservative *Daily Telegraph*, 64 in the liberal *Guardian* and 75 in the liberal *Independent* newspapers used the terms 'genocide' or 'ethnic cleansing' to describe the conflicts in the Balkans.[33] This means, on average, more than two articles per day in each paper did not merely report this foreign war but also described its fierceness by utilising such terms as genocide and ethnic cleansing. These newspapers actually referred to 'the most vicious fighting in Europe since the Second World War',[34] 'Shame of Camp Omarska',[35] 'Death-camp scoop made the world sit up',[36] 'They must be stopped'[37] and 'A test of Europe's conscience'.[38] Certainly it was said that 'N[othing] better illustrates the power of television to affect foreign policy than ITN's [Independent Television News] film of a Serbian-run detention camp in Bosnia'.[39] Vivid television images facilitated the so-called 'something must be done' pressure on the government.

The British media was highly critical of the government's inaction and its uncooperative attitude. For example, the major newspapers unanimously attacked Britain's closed door to Yugoslav asylum seekers. When it became clear that the Germans took in more than 200,000 refugees, the Austrians and Hungarians took in 50,000, and the Swedes took in 44,000, but the British government accepted only 1,300, British newspapers all reprimanded this stance by arguing that 'B[ritain]'s failure to respond adequately to the Yugoslav refugee crisis is a failure of will and a failure of common sense',[40] and 'Britain gave the disturbing impression that it was only willing to take a limited number of refugees'.[41] This public reaction, calling for more acceptance of the victims of the war rather than showing a fear of an influx of refugees, indicates that normative concerns dominated the public debate.

In addition, in the face of the atrocities in Bosnia, these British newspapers pushed for more direct measures just as they said: 'We need a more urgent response'.[42] It is claimed that Britain is a country where public opinion has 'less resistance' to the use of armed forces than other countries like Germany (Lucarelli 2000: 188; Sharp 1997: 4; Towle 1994: 94), and the content of 'urgent response' was directly linked with military action. In this regard, it can be seen that 'unexpected allies' formed between right and left wingers.[43] The conservative paper, *The Daily Telegraph* (also *Sunday Telegraph*), strongly urged the use of force to halt the ethnic cleansing in Bosnia. While criticising 'The current Foreign Office response' as 'gesture politics', it asserted that 'only full-scale military intervention can make a difference'.[44] This paper backed Liberal Democrat leader Ashdown's plan to use 'Nato air forces' to 'impose a ceasefire'.[45] From the liberal strand, *The Independent* (also *Independent on Sunday*) articulated humanitarian concerns that 'It is time to try the language of air power'[46] and 'it would be very dangerous for the future of Europe if [the Bosnian Serbs] were allowed to complete [the takeover of Bosnia-Herzegovina] without suffering heavy retribution at the hands of the international community'.[47] This paper had been supporting military action since the outbreak of the first clash in Slovenia and Croatia to contain the violence.[48]

Meanwhile, although some articles in *The Times* (also *Sunday Times*) and *The Guardian* (also *The Observer*) were not so emphatically advocating military options at that time because of the ethnic complexity of the war, both papers were, as with the aforementioned two papers, very critical of the government's inaction and called for direct involvement, including armed measures. For example, in the article entitled 'Europe's bloodstained lies', *The Times* reprimanded the West's reluctance by arguing: 'The West bears considerable responsibility for the Balkans tragedy'.[49] Likewise, *The Guardian* accused the government of having a lack of 'political will to determine action'[50] and remarked, by referring to the attacks by the Bosnian Serbs: 'Can [the] new world order … really accept such a murderous solution?'[51]

The opinion polls taken in August 1992 underpin the presence of public pressure. First, 68 per cent of those questioned said that they were following events in Yugoslavia (very closely: 16 per cent and fairly closely: 52 per cent), thus suggesting that a large number of people were aware of what was happening in this foreign country. Second, nearly twice as many people were dissatisfied as satisfied with the government's handling of the crisis (satisfied: 27 per cent; dissatisfied: 53 per cent), which indicates that the government's attitude was not generally supported by society. Third, 86 per cent agreed to the sending of British troops as part of a limited UN force to protect food and medical aid convoys to Bosnia, while only 11 per cent disagreed.[52] Hence, despite the government's concern not to get dragged into the war, the rising social awareness made remaining silent on this war impossible and prompted the government to take more action including the use of force.

Under those circumstances, the Tory government's hesitant attitude was regarded as socially inappropriate and was criticised for its inadequacy in responding to this humanitarian tragedy. Given that the Labour Party's views were not so different at that time (its full-scale attack started from 1993 as revealed in the next section), public outcry exerted no small influence in making it difficult for the Major government to keep up its non-intervention policy.

## *Difficulties in humanitarian intervention*

When it came to which measures should be adopted, however, people's opinions were divided. Even if halting the violence had been demanded, and even if Britain's foreign policy had been relatively open to military activity, extensive military involvement would not likely have been unanimously accepted.

Opinion polls reveal the ambivalence towards taking concrete measures. Although the British participation in UNPROFOR to assist humanitarian aid activity was highly supported (as shown earlier, 86 per cent), the level of support decreased as the degree of military involvement deepened. For example:

1 Dispatching British troops as part of an intervention force to help keep Bosnian and Serbian troops apart (agree: 61 per cent; disagree: 30 per cent);
2 Not dispatching British troops as the Balkan situation does not justify putting British lives at risk (agree: 51 per cent; disagree: 38 per cent);
3 Sending the Royal Air Force to bomb Serbian artillery positions (agree: 37 per cent; disagree: 50 per cent);
4 Rearming Bosnians to help them to fight Serbia by sending weapons and ammunition (agree: 13 per cent; disagree: 79 per cent).[53]

Referring to the first and second results, *The Guardian* remarked that

> A contradictory ... opinion poll showed 51 per cent of people opposed to putting British lives at risk in Yugoslavia and 61 per cent favouring British forces to be sent as part of an international force to keep the Serbs and Bosnians apart.[54]

Although contradictory, it nevertheless precisely uncovers the intrinsic problem of humanitarian intervention. Society claimed the government should not only stop the violence but also not endanger its soldiers. On the basis of the study in this book, this situation suggests that a norm dilemma was caused by the different discussions at the general and practical levels.

Whereas *The Times* and *The Guardian* urged a more immediate response, there can also be found some opposite opinions (in the former) or careful observations (in the latter) – it is difficult to find such opinions in *The Daily Telegraph* and *The Independent*.[55] For instance, *The Times* stated that 'military intervention would only deepen and extend their sufferings, and add to them those of our own soldiers, dying in vain'.[56] Likewise, it was argued that 'The military cannot solve the political problem because it is too complicated'.[57] Meanwhile, *The Guardian* questioned the simultaneous deployment of peacekeeping and forceful action because, quoting one diplomat's statement: 'It is almost inconceivable to run a negotiation/peacekeeping role when there is military intervention', as it would deprive UNPROFOR of the role of 'impartial arbitrators'.[58]

Even where there is a consensus that grave humanitarian catastrophes must be stopped, and especially when their frightening images are pervasive, people's opinions on the 'how' questions – such as how to take action (military or non-military approach), how to intervene (air strike or the use of ground force) and how many troops should be dispatched – are likely to be divided. The analysis of an article in the *Independent on Sunday* concisely pointed out the difficulty with which the government would be confronted:

> The dilemma for John Major and the Foreign Secretary, Douglas Hurd, boils down to this. If they are seen to resist moves to intervene on the ground, they risk being criticised by voters here for inaction. ... Yet if [they] do send troops as part of a UN operation to protect aid convoys, and if that operation goes wrong, then the government may well be blamed for sending servicemen to their deaths.[59]

The subsequent British policymaking faced exactly this dilemma, as Defence Secretary Rifkind stated 'It's fairly easy to say "something must be done", [but] not for someone who has to take decisions'.[60]

## The John Major government's steering under the attacks from the inside and the outside

### Domestic debates in 1993–1995: more intervention or withdrawal

*The media discussion: after the stalemate of the international mediation efforts*

Britain, holding the EC Presidency at that time, convened the London Conference, co-chaired by the United Nations Secretary General, Boutros Boutros Ghali (on 26 August 1992). Meanwhile, Lord David Owen, former Foreign

Secretary, was appointed, together with Cyrus Vance (former American Secretary of State), as EC and UN co-chairmen of the Conference for the Former Yugoslavia. Despite their efforts, their Vance-Owen Peace Plan was rejected as Chapter 3 discussed, which resulted in a harsher tone of critiques against the government.

For example, *The Independent* argued: 'Time to show our anger',[61] and 'Only force will do',[62] while *The Daily Telegraph* claimed that 'the West has an obligation to ensure that a humanitarian disaster of unimaginable enormity is not allowed to occur in its own backyard' and that 'the West had the means to stop it, but not the will'.[63] Meanwhile, by that time, *The Times* and *The Guardian* had clearly taken on an interventionist stance. The former criticised the lack of military support in the international mediation efforts by stating that 'Vance-Owen will not work without force'.[64] This paper declared: 'Diplomacy has been exhausted in the Balkans. It is time for Western generals to don their helmets'.[65] Additionally, *The Guardian* asserted that 'Despite mounting public disquiet on the Bosnian tragedy, Britain remains opposed to military intervention in Bosnia'.[66] The brunt of this accusation was directed at the government because 'Britain's special responsibility to the Balkan challenges arises from our high diplomatic standing, and from our unusual degree of military readiness and competence, together with the fact that we held the [European] Community presidency during a critical period in the Bosnian war'.[67] After the setback of the international mediation efforts became evident, forceful measures were broadly discussed in the British public sphere.

*Attacks from the left: pressure to 'do something' more*

In Parliament, the opposition parties made relentless attacks against the Major administration's failure to resolve the war. With the stumbling of the Vance-Owen Peace Plan, the voice for action became louder and the government was denounced by the group of MPs branded as the 'something must be done' school.[68]

By that time, Labour had already broken ranks with the Conservatives and demanded a more direct and stronger approach.[69] For example, the Labour Shadow Foreign Secretary Cunningham reprimanded the government's policy by arguing: 'The use of air power is never ruled out, but it is never ruled in … The war is continuing in Bosnia, but no action, even limited action, is taken'.[70] Likewise, the Shadow Defence Secretary Clark stated: 'It is important to remember that the use of the military is a means to an end. … If we can use the military to force the warring factions to sign a peace agreement … that would be the first step along the path'.[71] Active support for air strikes and deployment of ground forces came mainly from such Labour MPs as Short, who claimed that 'if there had been limited use of air strikes [earlier], it might have turned back the Serbian aggression',[72] and Ken Livingstone, known as 'Red Ken', who called for ground troops to be sent in, 'as many as it takes for as long as it takes'.[73]

The Liberal Democrats' attack was more straightforward. Party leader Ashdown condemned the government's policy by arguing that 'the failure of judgement and action' had allowed 'tragedy to be heaped on tragedy'.[74] He contended that Bosnia was not merely catastrophic for the Bosnian people but had also led to 'the humiliation of the United Nations and the weakening of its international standing, and to the humiliation of our own troops on the ground',[75] while the party's Shadow Foreign Secretary, Sir Menzies Campbell, said 'not enough' to the government's decision to send 900 extra troops to Bosnia; the party demanded a full-intervention.[76]

For the government leaders, however, the Opposition's demands to dispatch more troops were nothing but military adventurism, because the situations in Bosnia had never guaranteed any safety. Foreign Secretary Hurd refuted these demands by making clear that 'We could not agree to action which would put British forces at serious risk'.[77] Instead, the Tory government emphasised the British contribution, which had 'helped to keep alive hundreds of thousands who might otherwise have perished this winter from cold and hunger'.[78] To be sure, the number of the British troops, which had incrementally risen from 1,800 troops to 3,600 at the final stage, was the second largest in UNPROFOR next to France.

Furthermore, until the massive military operation in August 1995, Britain sent '£271 million in aid to the former Yugoslavia' and 'incurred net costs of £292 million' for UN peacekeeping and 'the Sarajevo airlift'.[79] Despite these enormous contributions, it was also said that 'The House of Commons should show that it recognises the scale of Western failure in Yugoslavia, rather than waste time on ritual praise for the British soldiers performing a thankless, and now increasingly fruitless, task'.[80] Put differently, irrespective of how much the government contributed – let alone what problems were entailed in the actual intervention process – policy is judged only on whether violence is stopped. As Chapter 2 indicated, the difficulties in responding to foreign humanitarian disasters can be observed here.

*Attacks from the right: pressure to pull out of Bosnia*

As it became increasingly evident that international conflict management had stalled and British troops taking part in the UN peacekeeping were endangered by the local militias, a question appeared: 'For what noble cause could our troops die in Bosnia?'[81] This sort of argument came from 'a true Tory view' – according to a Conservative MP Nicholas Budgen – that 'British soldiers should risk their lives only in upholding the British national interest'.[82]

In fact, the Major administration's other tough opponents were in its own party backbenches (Rathbun 2004: 57–58). The call for withdrawal could be heard as early as the beginning of 1993. At the initial stage, Peter Viggers, Sir Nicholas Bonsor and Sir Peter Tapsell, respectively, demanded pulling out British soldiers, 'should they come under fire',[83] 'should circumstances change and an attack on Serbian artillery positions be contemplated'[84] or 'if the present battalion is not safe with its present support'.[85] As time went by, however, these 'conditional clauses' were removed and withdrawal was outspokenly demanded. For example, Sir Archibald Hamilton stated, 'I hope that we will consider withdrawal seriously, before we suffer some ghastly disaster, as the Americans did in the Lebanon',[86] and Terry Dicks added that

> some of us said at the beginning that it was a mistake for British forces to be in Bosnia under any circumstances. We have now lost four British lives. ... People are sick and tired of having British forces at risk when there is no British interest there at all.[87]

Concomitantly, confronted by the repeated rejections of the peace plans by the local Bosnian groups, the tone of some newspapers' opinions gradually changed to urge withdrawal. Among others, *The Daily Telegraph*, one of the vocal proponents for full-intervention, published an article in late December 1993 entitled 'Let's get our troops out', which concluded that '[many senior British officers on the ground] see no point in continuing to risk the lives of their men, when the warring parties seem so reluctant to accept the help they offer or accept any of the countless chances to find a peace settlement presented to them by the international community'.[88] It is true that this sort of argument did not appear very often,[89] but in any case, the brunt of criticism was directed at the government's failed policy.

Facing such pressure, Defence Secretary Rifkind countered with the argument that 'In practice, [it] would mean pulling out the 2,500 British forces who have taken thousands of tonnes of aid to rescue many Bosnians, from all communities, from the starvation that they would have faced over the winter months'.[90] Of course, the government hinted that 'if the risks become unacceptable, the troops should be withdrawn'.[91] Realistically, however, this option was difficult because it would count as an 'abject failure' according to the criticisms expressed by the opposition parties, and would also mean that the government admitted the failure of the entire activity.[92] Moreover, unilateral withdrawal would significantly damage Britain's international reputation as it was said that 'officials were ... conscious of the tragic consequences a pull-out could have' in relation to other countries working together.[93]

In the course of duty in Bosnia, 18 soldiers lost their lives and 41 others were seriously injured in total.[94] A generalisation cannot be made as to whether the number is high or low but, from the perspective of what was claimed as 'a true Tory view', losing British troops in an operation such as Bosnia was not ideal. From this angle, the government met with several expressions of severe condemnation as well.

## Discussion inside Britain

Confronted by the contrasting claims of intervention and non-intervention, the government was trying to maintain a 'balance' between the two (Rathbun 2004: 59). Foreign Secretary Hurd accounted for Britain's political stance as follows:

> It would be possible for us in Britain to say ... that none of these conflicts are anything to do with us: that ... no specific British interest exists. ...

Alternatively, we could take the view ... that, wherever there is injustice or intolerable suffering, it is part of our duty as a nation to do our best to bring it to an end. ... Somewhere between those two extreme answers ... lies the policy that any British government would in practice seek to follow.[95]

Nevertheless, this policy eventually led the government into a dilemma. The Opposition group Hurd dubbed 'The school of something must be done' blamed the Major administration's failure to manage this humanitarian crisis, whereas those Conservatives dubbed, again by Hurd, 'the school of "let them fight it out"',[96] reprimanded the administration for the risks faced by the British soldiers. Consequently, the government was surrounded by criticisms emanating from the dissatisfaction of both sides, which led to Hurd stating that 'Over the years, I have had a bit of impatience with both those powerful bodies of opinion'.[97]

Opinion polls also suggested strong dissatisfaction with the government's policy. Table 4.1 shows that there existed a clear contrast between 'very satisfied' and 'very dissatisfied'. The former is constantly in single figures (ranging from 2 to 8), while the latter ranges from 17 to 25. Even when the figures of 'very satisfied/dissatisfied' and 'somewhat satisfied/dissatisfied' are added, the satisfied rates are lower than those of the dissatisfied, particularly as the war became prolonged.

Do these figures represent a dissatisfaction with the government not doing enough or not withdrawing the British troops from Bosnia? Table 4.2 helps to answer this question.

*Table 4.1* Support for the British government's policy towards Bosnia (in percentage)

|  | Feb 93 | Sep 93 | Jan 94 | 1–6 Jun 95 | 8–13 Jun 95 | Aug 95 |
|---|---|---|---|---|---|---|
| Very satisfied | 5 | 4 | 7 | 4 | 8 | 2 |
|  | (38) | (32) | (33) | (30) | (35) | (22) |
| Somewhat satisfied | 33 | 28 | 26 | 26 | 27 | 20 |
| Neither satisfied nor dissatisfied | 19 | 21 | 16 | 19 | 19 | 20 |
| Somewhat dissatisfied | 26 | 27 | 25 | 27 | 25 | 30 |
|  | (43) | (46) | (49) | (49) | (46) | (55) |
| Very dissatisfied | 17 | 19 | 24 | 22 | 21 | 25 |
| Don't Know | 5 | 0 | 2 | 1 | 8 | 2 |

Question: Taking everything into account, are you satisfied or dissatisfied with the government's handling of the situation in Bosnia, part of the former Yugoslavia? Very or only somewhat?

*Figures in brackets are the amount of 'very' and 'somewhat' 'dis/satisfied' (added by the author).
Source: *Gallup Political & Economic Index*, report no. 423, November 1995: 27 (order changed by the author).

74  *Beyond intervention or non-intervention*

*Table 4.2* Public opinion on policies towards Bosnia (in percentage)

|  | Apr 93 | Jun 93 | Sep 93 | Jan 94 | 1–6 Jun 95 | 8–13 Jun 95 |
|---|---|---|---|---|---|---|
| A. Pull them out | 32 | 39 | 36 | 32 | 38 | 39 |
| B. Continue to limit to fighting back only when attacked | 17 | 17 | 16 | 16 | 16 | 14 |
| C. Reinforce | 43 | 34 | 41 | 43 | 35 | 38 |
| Don't Know | 8 | 10 | 6 | 8 | 11 | 9 |

Question: If the British troops protecting the aid convoys suffered serious casualties, should we pull them out, continue to limit them to fighting back only when they are attacked, or take steps to reinforce them?

Source: *Gallup Political & Economic Index*, report no. 423, November 1995: 27 (order changed by the author).

This table uncovers ambivalence in the minds of the British population on the whole – similar figures are shown in responses A and C. It can be supposed that for those who thought of withdrawal as desirable, the government's decision to carry on British engagement was unacceptable. Meanwhile, for those who thought that it was necessary to reinforce the British troops, its policy not to take further steps was unsatisfactory. Therefore, presumably, groups preferring A or C were frustrated by the government's balancing attitude; undoubtedly, failing to improve the situation in Bosnia while endangering British soldiers would boost the 'dissatisfied' rate as well.

In short, the calls to take action against the Balkan crisis strongly pushed the reluctant government to commence its engagement. As the danger to British troops became clear, however, other calls for withdrawal also came to surface. As a consequence of the collision between the different discussions at the general and practical discussion levels, the government was forced into difficult manoeuvring.

### *Attacks from the outside: diplomatic row with the United States*

In the international sphere, the British government was struck by another difficulty. London's political stance to reject the use of military forces for the safety of its troops was countered by that of the Americans to start air strikes. Eventually, this damaged the Anglo-American relationship so gravely that it was said that 'Bosnia has led to the most serious transatlantic split'.[98]

As explicated in Chapter 3, this problem was triggered by the different opinions over the way to solve the war, which gradually appeared after Washington got involved in the international conflict management process. At the outset, the American government had also tried to keep itself away from the Balkans for exactly the same reason that the British political leaders had held back, i.e. the lack of a significant interest to preserve. With the growing voices for action among the public and the stagnation of European mediations, however, the United States took part in this international conflict management, which is why its participation was a little delayed.

This different background between the European and the Americans made London's decision more complicated. The United States asserted forceful measures: namely, the 'lift and strike' policy (see Chapter 3). From the British perspective, however, such a policy, to remove the UN embargo to arm the weaker Bosnian Muslims and then to launch an air bombardment, would merely endanger its deployed soldiers by pouring oil (i.e. weapons) on the local battles and inducing retaliation against them. London was vehemently opposed as Foreign Secretary Hurd argued that 'it would create a "level killing field"',[99] and Defence Secretary Rifkind claimed that 'British soldiers [would end] up being killed by those who had been provided with weapons by the international community'.[100]

On the rejection of the American policy, there was an almost non-partisan consensus in Parliament. For example, Sir Nicholas Bonsor (Conservative) remarked, 'We have many troops sitting under the barrels of Serbian artillery, and I have no doubt that they would be the subject of retaliation the moment that any air attacks were launched'.[101] Opposition MPs were also against lifting the UN arms embargo. As their argument was to reinforce UN activity, including military action, there was absolutely no need to facilitate the free influx of weapons and add more risks to the local peacekeeping operation. The Labour Party leader, John Smith, criticised the lift and strike policy as it would 'merely intensify the conflict',[102] while the Liberal Democratic Party leader Ashdown 'also vigorously opposed the lifting of the arms embargo as "the single action best calculated to ensure the widening of the war"'.[103]

On the other side of the Atlantic, the Bill Clinton administration had been under heavy pressure from Congress, even before the Republicans took the majority in the Senate in 1994. For instance, Secretary of State Warren Christopher was questioned in May 1993 'by a Congressional committee on his failure to convince allies of the need for military intervention'.[104] This diplomatic confrontation gradually started in the middle of the war around May 1993, and was initially expressed as: 'A whiff of Suez'.[105] Ultimately, the debate heated up drastically and Clinton publicly reprimanded the Europeans, particularly the British government.[106] Secretary Christopher pronounced the '"Special relationship" with Britain and the primacy of the Atlantic alliance to be dead'.[107]

From the British side, harsh words were also expressed as Sir Anthony Grant, a Conservative politician, said, 'the government are absolutely right to resist the military ambitions of some American and other television armchair warriors. ... there is no question in future of British troops being further embroiled in a mad adventure'.[108] Former Prime Minister Sir Edward Heath stated that 'The new [American] President has no experience of international affairs. He has no military knowledge. ... So why should we risk being pushed into military action by the President of the United States?'[109] Likewise, Labour Shadow Defence Secretary Clark remarked that 'We and the French are certainly entitled to say to the Americans and others, "You are not on the ground and we are. Do nothing to make the position worse"'.[110] Liberal Democrat leader Ashdown also condemned Washington for refusing to 'put US troops on the ground, while promoting a hawkish agenda that puts those who are there at greatest risk'.[111]

In the British media too, *The Daily Telegraph* wrote: 'If the Americans want to have a voice in policy making, they will have to send ground forces, too'.[112] Struck by London's firm objection, President Clinton revealed that '"John Major told me he wasn't sure he could sustain his government" if he approved the [lift and strike] plan. "No government is going to risk falling, even to the most intense pressure by the United States"',[113] which suggests how strong its objection was.

Eventually, Anglo-American relations were described as reaching 'the lowest ebb since Suez'.[114] This tension was accelerated because they could not adopt any concrete action despite the repeated declarations at international summits in NATO that aerial bombardments would be launched, while being called a mere 'bluff'.[115] Thus, the problem had now become, Hurd remarked, not only to 'end suffering and save lives' in Bosnia, but also not to 'allow the strains created by Bosnia to disrupt the transatlantic partnership';[116] Clinton had also said that 'What is at stake is not just the safety of the people of Sarajevo and any possibility of bringing this terrible conflict to an end, but the credibility of alliance itself'.[117]

What broke this deadlock was the unexpected change when the Bosnian Serbs captured UN personnel and soldiers, including 33 members of the Royal Welsh Fusiliers and a Royal Air Force (RAF) officer in May 1995, to utilise them as human shields to deter NATO's air strikes. Facing this 'qualitative change' in the conflict situation,[118] London agreed on the plan from Paris to form a Rapid Reaction Force, a heavily armed regiment, to protect UNPROFOR, and sent 6,000 more troops to Bosnia for this activity. After this, the war in Bosnia moved to the final phase, as Chapter 3 has already explicated: namely, NATO's massive military campaign from late August 1995. With the end of the war, international discussion moved to a new dimension, the reorganisation of NATO.

## From intervention to prevention: Britain's view on the reorganisation of NATO

This final section explores what motivated the British government to reconstruct NATO through Bosnia. First, it considers how British policy in the past years was assessed by the decision makers. Prime Minister Major (1999: 549) wrote in his autobiography that 'As a leader of one member of the international community I accept the blame that must fall on all our shoulders for the inadequacy of the outside world's response to the crisis both then and in subsequent years'. Foreign Secretary Hurd (2003: 476) acknowledged that 'I have admitted mistakes and misgivings'. Likewise, Defence Secretary Rifkind stated that 'Of course, I accept that, if one measures success or failure by our aspirations, clearly the UN can be said to have failed'.[119] In each case before or after these remarks, they added the conjunction 'however' or 'yet' and touched upon British troops' enormous contribution to help many Bosnians who 'would have been slaughtered in the conflict, or would have died from starvation, or from a lack of medical supplies'.[120]

Certainly, the Opposition's views are more critical. The new Labour leader, Tony Blair (succeeding after John Smith's sudden death), said that 'there have been errors of judgement and there has been indecision at almost every turn by the international community', which resulted in 'a profoundly unhappy experience for the international community'.[121] Meanwhile, Ashdown argued that 'Europe is failing to tackle its own problem on its own doorstep' and that 'There is no question ... that the problem is Europe's failure. ... it is a particular failure of Britain. We had the duty of leadership through our presidency [of the EC in 1992], in the key months of the campaign'.[122] Beyond simply criticising the government, Labour's new Shadow Foreign Secretary, Robin Cook, noted that 'This is not a failure for which we can pass the parcel of blame between the political parties. We all have a share in the responsibility for the failure of the international community'.[123] As these quotes indicate, the opposition parties also shared the same negative assessment about the handling of the war.

Second, concerning what the British decision makers thought had caused confusion in their international crisis management, they unanimously stated that it was an absence of international mechanisms to address such emergencies. Major (1999: 549) said that

> It was a tragedy for the people of Bosnia that the crisis occurred when it did, at a time when NATO, the EC, and America were all unsure of their international roles, and the art of peacekeeping in the post-Cold War world was still unborn.

The opposition parties also agreed on this point. Blair indicated that 'We were too slow to recognise the need to deter the Serbian army and we were too hesitant when we did recognise it'.[124] Ashdown remarked, in the middle of the war, that 'The best that can be said about the tragedy in Bosnia is that it is a tragedy which arrived before Europe was ready to cope with it', and that '*Unless we are prepared* to cope with it [problems like Bosnia] ourselves, more problems will arrive to threaten our peace'.[125]

As it was contended that 'the lack of *co-ordinated* action on security and foreign affairs is one of Europe's current weaknesses',[126] it was regarded as the cause of failure in their crisis response to the Balkans. Hence, it is natural to expect that a movement emerged that was concerned with the reorganisation of NATO in order to avert a repetition of this experience.

This point was precisely summarised by Foreign Secretary Hurd when he was asked: 'What lessons have we learned from [the involvement in the Balkans]?'

> I think the lesson that we learn not just from Bosnia but from the other trouble spots, the other places where there's no television but people are slaughtering each other in even greater numbers ... is that the international

community should be quicker to try to prevent these tragedies. This means poking your nose into other people's affairs, getting involved in the internal affairs of other countries in a way which would have been thought *inconceivable even ten years ago*. But I think we have to do that and that's why we and the French have put forward ideas for *preventative diplomacy*, for helping countries resolve their disputes whether in Europe, or whether in Africa, *before they reach this tragic stage*.[127]

Without the normative pressure for action, he would not have admitted that 'we have to do' what was 'inconceivable even ten years ago'. However, such an 'inconceivable' engagement provoked new problems: domestically, the government was placed in a dilemma between the pressure not to ignore humanitarian crises and not to endanger British soldiers; internationally, it took issue with the United States because of their contrasting preferences. Thus, to pre-empt these problems, political leaders were motivated towards the idea of 'preventive diplomacy'.[128] In this regard, Prime Minister Major also made a similar remark, in September 1994, that 'Britain wants to develop new mechanisms to head off conflicts before they become unstoppable'.[129]

Undoubtedly, the need 'to develop new mechanisms' led the British government towards the reconstitution of NATO. For example, when Hurd touched upon the result of the 1994 NATO summit, he said that 'There was agreement and a strong feeling that NATO should be ready and equipped out of area to handle situations which the member states thought NATO could contribute to helping to resolve'.[130] As for the concept of the Combined Joint Task Force (CJTF) (Chapter 3), the Minister of State at the Defence Ministry, Nicholas Soames, made public that 'The UK has participated fully in the development of the [CJTF] concept', which 'will provide NATO with a capability to form deployable headquarters, from within existing fixed headquarters, to provide the command and control of multinational and multi-service forces deployed on contingency operations'.[131] Additionally, the newly appointed Defence Secretary Portillo, succeeding Rifkind, also agreed that 'we want [CJTF] to give the Alliance a more ready-made and effective way of mounting its new missions, using the existing command structure'.[132]

Why did the government prefer international organisational development, instead of redefining its own policy alone? In this respect, David Heathcoat-Amory, then Minister of State at Foreign and Commonwealth Office, explained the necessity of inter-state coordinated frameworks as follows:

> Security is coming to be seen as dependent on the effective use of *a broader range of instruments* in order to avoid the emergence of new threats to British interests. ... the simple fact is that the more we can contribute to stability through peaceful, preventative means, the less we risk having to pay subsequently for remedial military measures. ... This means that we have to be prepared to involve ourselves in *crisis management and preventive diplomacy* (Heathcoat-Amory 1994: 3, emphasis added).

Additionally, he continued that 'we cannot defend ourselves alone. We need to work with allies and through the international institutions, and the primary ones among those must of course be the United Nations and NATO' (Heathcoat-Amory 1994: 3).

Social normative contexts anticipate that crises should be addressed properly even if they occur in foreign territories. However, because this is beyond what each state can deal with individually, decision makers are propelled to set up 'a broader range of instruments'. Therefore, the British government tried to get 'prepared to involve ourselves in crisis management and preventive diplomacy'.

In a similar respect, reflecting on the clash with the United States, Rifkind remarked that

> One of the lessons we should learn is that the United States and western Europe should decide *jointly from the very beginning* what their common course of action should be. The US at first was not involved at all. Then it became involved in the air, and that led to very severe problems with decision-making ... We must try to ensure that doesn't happen in the future.[133]

For precisely this reason, Britain aimed to redevelop the Alliance, through which they could work out countermeasures against humanitarian disasters.

Considering the views pronounced by the British decision makers, and especially Conservative politicians, it is hard to find evidence that they supported NATO's reinvigoration because they had converted their views of non-intervention and agreed to perform interventions for the sake of human rights protection. As they clarified, it was not because they became more inclined to meddle with other countries' domestic affairs but because they needed an international mechanism to pre-empt intervention before it would become inevitable. For this reason, the concept of preventive diplomacy was particularly stressed in the context of NATO reforms.

In sum, normative anticipation was surely a driving force to turn Britain to the Balkans at the level of general discussion. On concrete measures at the level of practical discussion, nevertheless, its policymakers were struck by norm dilemmas because the response to humanitarian catastrophes was expected to be conducted without entanglement and risking the lives of soldiers. To enable international security governance, the British government agreed to give NATO new roles in out-of-area regions.

## Conclusion

After assessing Britain's policy towards Bosnia, it can now be argued why the government voluntarily sought the reorganisation of NATO, despite the fact that London initially showed strong reluctance and a fear of being bogged down. During the war, domestically, the Major government faced intense criticisms not only from the opposition parties for its insufficient reaction but also from

## 80  *Beyond intervention or non-intervention*

within the Conservative Party for sending soldiers to a place where no British interests were involved. Internationally, Britain's refusal of military enforcement because of the risk to its deployed troops collided with the Americans arguing to start bombardment. As a result, and because of this foreign conflict occurring some distance from Britain, its political leaders found themselves in a political predicament being attacked from within and without. To avoid the repetition of this experience, they moved towards the construction of a new security system, which would enable them to cope with regional emergencies before intervention would be required. Through this process, Britain attached to NATO a new rationale for the purpose of effective security governance.

Britain's policy to Bosnia was surely shaped under normative influences; without the bottom-up pressure for action, the government would have remained silent by the weight of the intervention's cost. Given this point, the assumption can be made that its decision makers were prompted to reorganise NATO in order to redress foreign human rights abuses. This chapter contended, however, that this account alone does not fully illustrate what concrete form of NATO they actually envisioned. There remains a question as to why those Conservatives, who firmly disagreed with intervention, voluntarily put forward its reforms. As discussed, it is difficult to find any sign that they changed their original conviction of non-intervention after the war. Instead, norm dilemmas facilitated their reorganisation of it, so that they could avert intervention while meeting the social demand to not ignore a humanitarian tragedy. Hence, more emphasis was placed on establishing conflict preventive capability. In other words, they found a new rationale for NATO as a governance mechanism for conflict management.

One of the pathways the British case reveals is how normative influences are absorbed into international organisations. Even if action was genuinely required for humanitarian moral reasons, intervention gave rise to conflicts with other social claims because it put lives of soldiers in danger and generated concerns around fear of involvement. That is to say, because humanitarian norms transcend the boundaries of the state, but policy is made within those boundaries, dilemmas are caused by this discrepancy; furthermore, when different approaches are adopted by each state, confusion and collision among states are liable to be triggered. To rectify these problems and establish security governance, states (re)design the structures of international organisations. Through this process, normative effects were reflected in the concrete reforms of the Alliance.

## Notes

1 Charles Moore 'Can Britain do well by doing good in the Balkans?', *The Daily Telegraph*, 20 August 1994.
2 Sir Peter Taspell (Conservative), *Hansard*, 31 May 1995, col. 1053.
3 Quoted in Brian Rathbun's interview in his monograph (2004: 58).
4 Nicholas Budgen (Conservative), *Hansard*, 19 April 1993, col. 30.
5 Quoted in Simms (2002: 278), originally from *Hansard*, 31 May 1995, cols. 1077–1079. Also see other statements by Conservative members shown by Rathbun (2004: 54).

6 Jacqui Lait (Conservative), *Hansard*, 18 April 1994, col. 646.
7 Sir Archie Hamilton (Conservative), *Hansard*, 18 April 1994, col. 649. In addition, there was also a concern over the influence of Britain's involvement on 'one of the top priorities of British foreign policy', i.e. 'the continuing improvement of relations between Russia and the United Kingdom', John Taylor (Ulster Unionist), *Hansard*, 12 April 1994, col. 27. On these grounds too, it was assumed that non-commitment was preferable to meddling with a former Eastern bloc country.
8 For example, Cormack's statements in *Hansard*, 7 December 1994, col. 316 and Davies's in *Hansard*, 1 March 1994, col. 792. N.B. Davis moved to the Labour Party from the Conservative Party in 2008. His affiliation, shown in this chapter, was at that time.
9 See Thatcher's open letter in *The Times*, 14 August 1992. Regarding her statements during the war, see Simms (2002: 49–50).
10 Quoted in Simms (2002: 4; the original source is in *The Independent*, 6 August 1991).
11 *Hansard*, 14 October 1991, col. 40.
12 *Ibid*.
13 Interview with the author (4 September 2013).
14 Interview with the author (8 September 2013).
15 Interview with the author (4 September 2013).
16 Quoted in Simms (2002: 101), originally from FCO memorandum, 'Recent developments in Eastern Europe with special reference to Yugoslavia', 6 November 1991, House of Commons Foreign Affairs committee, vol. II, CE 17.
17 *Hansard*, 12 November 1991, col. 901. On the linkage of this topic with the French case, see Chapter 5.
18 *Hansard*, 2 July 1992, col. 989.
19 Quoted in Simms (2002: 297), originally from *Hansard*, 2 June 1992, col. 715.
20 *Hansard*, 25 September 1992, col. 132.
21 *Ibid*., col. 180.
22 Patrick Wintour, 'Rift grows in Britain on sending in troops', *The Guardian*, 14 August 1992. Indeed, it is somewhat unfamiliar to hear such a statement from Robertson, who in 1999 took the initiative in the military campaign in Kosovo as Defence Secretary of the Tony (Blair administration).
23 Telephone interview with the author (15 August 2013).
24 For example, see Labour's support for the arms embargo by the UN Security Council, *Hansard*, 14 October 1991, col. 41.
25 Paddy Ashdown in *Hansard*, 20 November 1991, col. 302.
26 Ashdown's statement in Matthew d'Ancona and Michael Binyon, 'Debate on Yugoslav military option links unexpected allies', *The Times*, 3 August 1992.
27 Alan Philips, 'Bosnia "relief zones" urged for refugees', *The Daily Telegraph*, 31 July 1992.
28 Paddy Ashdown, 'When will you act?', *The Guardian*, 13 August 1992. Also see 'Leading Article: The use of air power', *The Daily Telegraph* 4 August 1992 and 'Leading Article: The dangers of inaction', *The Independent*, 7 August 1992.
29 'Leading Article: A high risk', *The Daily Telegraph*, 20 August 1992.
30 'Leading Article: Balkan reality', *The Times*, 19 August 1992.
31 Ian Traynor, 'War that has rewritten Europe's rules', *The Guardian*, 22 December 1994.
32 Con Coughlin and Philip Sherwell, 'Focus: Death in the Balkans: The week the world woke up', *Sunday Telegraph*, 9 August 1992.
33 See Figure 3.1 in Chapter 3. Owing to a technical problem, it is impossible to count the number in *The Times*.
34 '"Something must be done" – But what?', *The Daily Telegraph*, 5 August 1992.

82  Beyond intervention or non-intervention

35  Ed Vulliamy, 'Shame of Camp Omarska', *The Guardian*, 7 August 1992.
36  Jonathan Miller, 'Death-camp scoop made the world sit up', *Sunday Times*, 9 August 1992.
37  'Leading Article: They must be stopped', *The Financial Times*, 6 July 1992.
38  'Leading Article: A test of Europe's conscience', *The Independent*, 15 July 1992.
39  'Leading Article: Calling the shots', *The Daily Telegraph*, 10 August 1992. Also similar remarks are in *Independent on Sunday*, 9 August 1992 and *The Times*, 26 August 1992.
40  'Leading Article: Save their skins – let the Bosnians in', *Independent on Sunday*, 2 August 1992.
41  'Leading Article: no room in the in-tray', *The Guardian*, 14 August 1992. Similar articles which criticise the government's limited refugee acceptance are: Robert Fox, 'Europe facing refugee crisis not seen for half a century', *The Daily Telegraph*, 30 July 1992; Gordon Martin and Christopher Lockwood, 'EC nations shut doors to Yugoslavia's war victims', *The Daily Telegraph*, 30 July 1992; Robert Shrimsley, 'Britain eases curb on refugees', *The Daily Telegraph*, 13 August 1992; Helia Pick, 'Refugees "need political solution"', *The Guardian*, 30 July 1992; Adrian Bridge, 'Britain attacked for ignoring Bosnia refugees', *The Independent*, 27 July 1992; Heather Mills, 'Britain deports Yugoslavs: Home Office ignores United Nations appeal to relax asylum regulations and steps up expulsions of would-be refugees', *The Independent*, 12 August 1992 and Alan McGregor and James Bone, 'Britain refuses to open the door to refugees', *The Times*, 30 July 1992.
42  'Leading Article: We need more urgent response', *The Guardian*, 14 July 1992.
43  Matthew d'Ancona and Michael Binyon, 'Military option links unexpected allies', *The Times*, 3 August 1992. Godfrey Hodgson, 'We must fight to save Europe', *The Independent*, 12 August 1992 also referred to this cooperation with the term 'strange bedfellows'.
44  Edward Stourton, 'Why Britons must be ready to die for Balkans peace', *The Daily Telegraph*, 30 July 1992.
45  Quoted in Alan Philps, '"Relief zones" urged for refugees', *The Daily Telegraph*, 31 July 1992. Also see, Susannah Herbert, 'UN approves force to back aid to Bosnia: Decision threatens the Serbs but stops short of immediate action', *The Daily Telegraph*, 14 August 1992 and Robin Lodge, 'Weasel words let war rage', *Sunday Telegraph*, 16 August 1992.
46  'Leading Article: Yugoslavia', *The Independent*, 5 August 1992.
47  *Ibid.* Also see Godfrey Hodgson, 'We must fight to save Europe', *The Independent*, 12 August 1992. Cf. 'Leading Article: The dangers of inaction', *The Independent*, 7 August 1992 and 'Leading Article: The crossing of a Rubicon', *The Independent*, 11 August 1992.
48  For example, Tony Barber, 'Army hamstrung by ethnic differences', *The Independent*, 27 June 1991. In fact, *The Independent* says: 'Just over a year ago The Independent urged European military intervention to prevent the crushing of Slovenian and Croatian independence by the Serb-controlled Yugoslav federal army', *The Independent*, 5 August 1992.
49  'The West's shame', *Sunday Times*, 16 August 1992. Also see Daniel Johnson, 'Europe's bloodstained lies', *The Times*, 5 August 1992 and Mark Almond, 'Will the West dare to fight?', *The Times*, 26 August 1992.
50  Hella Pick, 'Refugees flee, diplomats dither', *The Guardian*, 1 August 1992.
51  'Leading Article: When the children die', *The Guardian*, 3 August 1992. Also see Michael Simmons, 'Millions at risk as winter nears', *The Guardian*, 20 August 1992.
52  The data are quoted in Peter Kellner and Donald Macintyre, 'Don't risk UK troops in Bosnia, says poll: As more refugees head for this country, a survey shows little enthusiasm for offering them a haven here', *Independent on Sunday*, 16 August 1992, and Patrick Wintour and David Fairhall, 'Sanctions to be tightened', *The Guardian*,

17 August 1992. Wybrow (2003: 38–41) considers these results more comprehensively. Originally, this poll was conducted by NOP, 15 August 1992.
53 Data is shown in Wybrow (2003: 40–42).
54 Patrick Wintour and David Fairhall, 'Sanctions to be tightened', *The Guardian*, 17 August 1992.
55 As far as the author could tell through his research, there are only two articles that adopted a cautious view: Auberon Waugh, 'Way of the world: A rare opportunity', *The Daily Telegraph*, 1 August 1992 and John Casey, 'We must not sink in the Balkan quagmire', *Sunday Telegraph*, 9 August 1992.
56 Conor Cruise O'Brien, 'Only fools step in', *The Times*, 6 August 1992.
57 Edward Gowan, 'Should we intervene?', *Sunday Times*, 9 August 1992.
58 Ed Vulliamy, 'Aid corridor raises backlash fears', *The Guardian*, 11 August 1992. A similar view was posed by Tim Judah, 'Warring groups seek to exploit peace force as Serbs widen gains', *The Times*, 12 August 1992.
59 Peter Kellner, 'British do not want troops in a Balkan war', *Independent on Sunday*, 16 August 1992.
60 Interview with the author (4 September 2013).
61 'Leading Article: Time to show our anger', *The Independent*, 19 April 1993.
62 'Leading Article: Only force will do in Bosnia', *The Independent*, 23 April 1993.
63 Patrick Bishop, 'Witness to a nightmare that will haunt us all for years', *The Daily Telegraph*, 1 July 1993. Also see 'Leading Article: No half measures', *The Daily Telegraph*, 4 August 1993.
64 Rosemary Righter, 'Vance-Owen will not work without force', *The Times*, 11 May 1993.
65 Roger Boyes, 'Now for a short sharp war', *The Times*, 7 May 1993.
66 Ian Black, 'Britain opposes intervention', *The Guardian*, 7 April 1993.
67 Martin Woollacott, 'Shameful anniversary in Bosnia intervention', *The Guardian*, 20 March 1993.
68 This term was first used by Foreign Secretary Douglas Hurd, see *Hansard*, 14 July 1993, col. 972.
69 Undoubtedly, the Labour Party's move towards interventionist policy and the Conservative Party's unchanged attitude, despite their similar views at the beginning, are explained by how much political parties lay emphasis on social and humanitarian values in their ideology, as Rathbun's research examines (2004). Although he argues as if Labour's policy had been consistent from the start, it is difficult to be empirically upheld.
70 *Hansard*, 14 July 1993, col. 972.
71 *Hansard*, 29 April 1993, col. 1242.
72 *Hansard*, 23 April 1993, col. 1237. Short also stated that 'if there'd been a stronger mandate, … the whole thing could have been stopped much earlier, much less suffering', telephone interview with the author (15 August 2013).
73 Livingstone's remark in *The Guardian*, 30 April 1993 and *Hansard*, 29 April 1993, col. 1219. Other Labour MPs calling for intervention were Tony Banks and Dawn Primarolo, see 'Leading Article: Time to break into the holidays', *The Guardian*, 24 August 1992. It is true that there were some comprehensive anti-militarist Labour politicians, who objected to any use of armed activity. For example, Tony Benn, in particular, argued for non-intervention and withdrawal of British troops. See *Hansard*, 18 April 1994, col. 646, *The Times*, 30 April 1993 and *The Independent*, 8 February 1994.
74 *Hansard*, 29 April 1993, col. 1189 (also quoted in *The Guardian*, 30 April 1993). Concerning the Liberal Democrats' view, see Ashdown's letter in 'Abandoning Bosnia to its fascist fate: European disinterest is hastening a final crisis in former Yugoslavia', *The Guardian*, 17 December 1993.
75 *Hansard*, 29 April 1993, col. 1189.

84  *Beyond intervention or non-intervention*

76 *Hansard*, 12 April 1994, col. 24.
77 *Hansard*, 29 April 1993, col. 1174.
78 Douglas Hurd, *Hansard*, 19 November 1993, col. 118. Similar statements are, for instance, in *Hansard*, 29 April 1993, cols. 1168 and 1245 and 10 March 1994, cols. 399–401.
79 In addition, on Britain's commitments to NATO's operation to support UN activities (£34 million), the EC's monitoring mission (£10.9 million) and international conference on former Yugoslavia (£1 million), see *Hansard*, 5 July 1995, cols. 262–263.
80 *The Daily Telegraph*, 31 May 1995.
81 Andrew Robathan, *Hansard*, 31 May 1995, col. 1079.
82 *Hansard*, 14 July 1993, col. 967.
83 Peter Viggers, *Hansard*, 12 January 1993, col. 762.
84 Sir Nicholas Bonsor, *Hansard*, 14 April 1993, col. 832.
85 Sir Peter Tapsell, *Hansard*, 14 January 1993, col. 1060.
86 *Hansard*, 18 April 1994, col. 649.
87 *Ibid.*, col. 651. Similarly, Bernard Jenkin (Conservative) said that 'we shall have to look seriously at withdrawal', *Hansard*, 18 April 1994, col. 651. Also see David Howell (Conservative) *Hansard*, 7 December 1994, col. 315.
88 Tim Butcher, 'Let's get our troops out', *The Daily Telegraph*, 23 December 1993.
89 Also see Anne Applebaum, 'When peace-keepers clash: it's time we all got out', *The Daily Telegraph*, 29 November 1994.
90 The number is at that time, *Hansard*, 14 April 1993, col. 839.
91 Douglas Hurd, *Hansard*, 7 December 1994, col. 314.
92 Robert Block, 'Europe sounds a rash retreat: A Bosnia pull-out would spell abject failure', *Independent Sunday*, 2 January 1994.
93 Bruce Clark and Laura Silber, 'UK holds back from Bosnia withdrawal', *The Financial Times*, 9 December 1994.
94 Quoted in Royal United Service Institute for Defence Studies (1998: 1199), originally from House of Commons *Official Report*, 12 December 1995, cols. 835–836.
95 *Hansard*, 23 February 1993, col. 774, this statement is also used in Rathbun (2004: 59).
96 *Hansard*, 3 May 1995, col. 330.
97 *Ibid.*
98 Alan Philps, 'Nato's in-fighting over Bosnia gives no comfort to Russia', *The Daily Telegraph*, 29 November 1994.
99 Stephen Robinson and George Jones, 'US anger erupts against Britain: Frustration over Bosnia leads White House to question historic ties', *The Daily Telegraph*, 18 October 1993. The same term was also used by Prime Minister Major, *Hansard*, 1 December 1994, col. 1329.
100 *Hansard*, 29 April 1993, col. 1246.
101 *Hansard*, 14 April 1993, col. 832.
102 John Smith, *Hansard*, 29 April 1993, col. 1147. Labour Shadow Defence Secretary Clark stated that the lifting of embargo is 'a dangerous escalation of the Bosnian conflict' and 'It is like pouring oil on to a burning fire', *The Financial Times*, 12 November 1994.
103 Quoted in Simms (2002: 296), originally from *Hansard*, 29 April 1993, col. 1196. The political stance taken by the Opposition did not change significantly till the end of the war; see John Smith's successor, Tony Blair, *Hansard*, 3 May 1995, col. 1009, and Paddy Ashdown, *Hansard*, 3 May 1995, col. 1013. It is true that some Labour politicians underpinned the lift of the UN arms embargo for the purpose of the Bosnian Muslims' self-defence, simultaneously claiming for beefing up UNPROFOR to pursue its mission, see Clare Short, *Hansard*, 29 April 1993, col. 1236, Max Madden, *Hansard*, 10 November 1992, and Jim Marshall, *Hansard*, 19 April 1993, col. 32.

104 Stephen Robinson, 'The dithering over Bosnia, Americans blame Europe: Major is "Mr Wobbly"', *The Daily Telegraph*, 12 May 1993. Also see Owen (1996: 174).
105 'Leading Article: A whiff of Suez', *The Times*, 12 May 1993 and Marie Colvin, 'Row over Bosnia leaves a "whiff of Suez"', *Sunday Times*, 16 May 1993. Also see Stephen Robinson, 'The dithering over Bosnia, Americans blame Europe: Major is "Mr Wobbly"', *The Daily Telegraph*, 12 May 1993.
106 Ann Devroy and R. Jeffrey Smith, 'Bosnia – excessive rhetoric had haunting echo', *The Washington Post*, 17 October 1993. On this point, also see Gow (1997: 175), Simms (2002: 71).
107 Stephen Robinson and George Jones, 'US anger erupts against Britain: Frustration over Bosnia leads White House to question historic ties', *The Daily Telegraph*, 18 October 1993. Also see Simms (2002: 95). Other numerous examples were enumerated in Chapter 3.
108 *Hansard*, 24 May 1993, col. 575.
109 *Hansard*, 29 April 1993, col. 1188.
110 *Ibid*. 1993, col. 1233.
111 Quoted in Simms (2002: 296). Originally from Paddy Ashdown, 'Too little, too late, too bad for all our Bosnians', *Observer*, 27 November 1994. In addition, an anti-militarist Labour MP, Tony Benn, also criticised the U.S. policy, *Hansard*, 31 May 1995, col. 1021.
112 Robert Fox, 'Commentary: Time for a tougher UN stance', *The Daily Telegraph*, 3 September 1993.
113 See fn. 112 (*The Washington Post*, 17 October 1993), also see Owen (1996: 240).
114 John Keegan, 'He doesn't understand: With Bihac crumbling, Senator Dole has been criticising the Anglo-French policy in Bosnia', *The Daily Telegraph*, 2 December 1994. Also see Andrew Marr, 'A special relationship? Don't mention it', *The Independent*, 24 February 1994.
115 Newspaper articles include, e.g. 'Leading Article: Serbs call NATO bluff', *The Daily Telegraph*, 26 November 1994; David Buchanan, 'Friction with UN fails to deter French: Despite the "waltz of the generals" Paris is determined to keep troops in Bosnia', *The Financial Times*, 21 January 1994; Robert Block, 'Serbs write another "deal" in the sand', *The Independent*, 10 February 1994; Patrick Brogan, 'Clinton may regret first foray abroad', *Observer*, 9 January 1994; and 'Leading Article: How much longer?', *The Times*, 26 March 1993.
116 Hurd, *Hansard*, 17 November 1994, col. 134. David Clark remarked that 'first, to stop the killing of innocent civilians in the United Nations safe area of Bihac. ... Secondly, we believe that it was necessary to maintain the reputation of the United Nations and NATO', in *Hansard*, 21 November 1994, col. 342.
117 William Drozdiak and Daniel Williams, 'NATO warms to East, splits on Bosnian action', *The Washington Post*, 11 January 1994.
118 Prime Minister Major, *Hansard*, 31 May 1995, col. 1001.
119 *Hansard*, 9 May 1995, col. 645.
120 *Ibid*.
121 *Hansard*, 31 May 1995, col. 1008.
122 *Hansard*, 29 April 1993, col. 1191.
123 *Hansard*, 19 July 1995, col. 1746.
124 *Hansard*, 31 May 1995, col. 1008.
125 Emphasis added, *Hansard*, 29 April 1993, col. 1189. Likewise, he added that 'One of the major flaws in the whole Bosnian operation is the fact that military action on the ground has seemed consistently to have neither *co-ordination* nor even connection with diplomatic action being taken', emphasis added, *Hansard*, 31 May 1995, col. 1015.
126 Emphasis added, Nick Raynsford (Labour), *Hansard*, 29 May 1995, col. 1003. Although this statement was made in the discussion of the EU's Intergovernmental

## 86  *Beyond intervention or non-intervention*

Conference in 1996, because it is meant not only in the context of the EU itself but also in European security in general including NATO, it is quoted as a piece of relevant evidence.
127 Emphasis added, 'On the Record: Recorded from Transmission: BBC-1', 4 December 1994, www.bbc.co.uk/otr/intext94-95//Hurd4.12.94.html (Accessed on 1 July 2018). Also see his similar statement in 27 June 1993 in the same site.
128 Hurd also mentioned that 'The emphasis is now on preventive diplomacy followed if only necessary by intervention', email interview with the author, 23 October 2013.
129 Quoted in Cottey (1996: 183).
130 *Hansard*, 10 February 1994, col. 455.
131 Royal United Service Institute for Defence Studies, *Documents*, p. 310. Originally from *Hansard*, 20 May 1996, col. 55.
132 Quoted in Royal United Service Institute for Defence Studies (1998: 311) (original source is 'Speech by the Defence Secretary, Mr. Michael Portillo, to the senior British Officers' Conference, *The future of NATO*, London 8–9 November 1995').
133 Emphasis added, quoted in Royal United Service Institute for Defence Studies (1998: 1179). Originally from an interview by the Foreign Secretary, Mr Malcolm Rifkind, with *Newsweek*, 4 December 1995: 60.

# 5 Rapprochement with NATO
## France's attempt to construct a new European security order

### Introduction

In December 1995, French Foreign Minister, Hervé de Charette, announced at the North Atlantic Council that France would henceforth participate fully in NATO's Military Committee and, accordingly, the French Defence Minister would also 'be able to regularly take part in the work of the Alliance, alongside his colleagues'.[1] This statement is regarded as one of the examples of France's rapprochement with NATO after the break in 1966, when France's President, Charles de Gaulle, withdrew from NATO's military command (Grant 1996: 58). Since the mid-1990s, France has not only returned to NATO's main decision-making bodies but also tried to take the initiative in the construction of the European security system from *within* NATO. However, this political shift in French diplomacy would never have been expected at the beginning of the 1990s. Even after the end of the Cold War, withdrawal from NATO still remained as 'the sacred cow' of French policy (Vernet 1992: 661) and, in fact, President François Mitterrand articulated that France had 'no intention of changing [its] particular position with regard to NATO's integrated command'.[2] How can this change in French foreign policy be explained?

This volte-face through the early 1990s, which is expressed as a 'revolution' in the words of Frédéric Bozo (1997: 39), a French foreign policy scholar, has been chiefly discussed as a change in the way of attaining Gaullist goals, i.e. a pursuit of 'grandeur' as a global player in international politics. According to this explanation, during the Cold War, grandeur meant keeping an autonomous position by distancing itself from the U.S.-Soviet confrontation and maintaining its national independence by rejecting integration into NATO's military structure and American dominance. Therefore, the withdrawal from NATO had been a symbolic act reflecting its status. However, confronted by post-Cold War challenges such as the war in Bosnia, political leaders in Paris, realising the importance of cooperation with the United States through NATO, steered their policy towards the Alliance and aimed to play a vital role from within. This was initiated because half-hearted participation would not only isolate France from the international sphere, but France would also lose out on the chance to have a say in European security. In short, while searching for an independent position in the bipolar bloc constituted the 'grandeur-ness' of its diplomacy during the Cold War, finding a leading place in the security reorganisation process in Europe became more significant in meeting Gaullist objectives in a more uncertain environment after 1989. In this respect, the changes in the government (March 1993) and the Presidency (May 1995) – from Socialists sharing the traditional Gaullist vision to Conservatives promoting the understanding – are said to have facilitated this new orientation (Bozo 1997; Gordon 1993; Grant 1996; Gregory 2000; Howorth 1996; Lepick 1996; Menon 1995, 2000a, 2000b; Treacher 2003).

Such an account, founded on what is sometimes dubbed a 'neo-Gaullist' model (cf. Bryant 2000) to pragmatically reinterpret the French diplomatic tradition, seems to have given an impetus for French leaders to make a historic turn towards NATO, on which this chapter also concurs. Strictly speaking, nevertheless, the first steps were initiated under the Socialist government and President Mitterrand, namely, before the elections in 1993 and 1995. In addition, France's return did not mean a full reintegration.[3] Importantly, it stopped short of re-entering NATO's International Military Staff (IMS), Defence Planning Committee (DPC)[4] and the Nuclear Planning Group (NPG), whereas Paris was actively committed to other bodies. What explains these different preferences? Relying solely on this neo-Gaullist (re)interpretation might blur the reason for its new preference towards NATO. Moreover, there is a danger of explaining both scenarios, of returning and not returning, at the same time. When it returned, it would be illustrated as a result of the reinterpretation of Gaullism; when it did not, it would be justified as the robustness of traditional Gaullism.

This chapter claims that France's new partnership with NATO should be understood in the context of international institution building for humanitarian crisis management, which its decision makers found necessary through Bosnia. In France, action was hugely upheld in the face of repeated images of the critical conditions conveyed through the media, while the Paris decision makers were also driven towards it by their ambition to capitalise on European security initiatives. Given the general support for action, however, a different question gradually emerged of how to produce a policy to effectively cope with a foreign war in another country. As the stalemate of the international mediation efforts became evident, severe criticisms were hurled against the government for failing to halt the crisis. Moreover, as French personnel were killed in actual operations, the outcry pushing for their dispatch gradually turned to voices for withdrawal and attack against the government's mishandling. Decision makers were caught in a norm dilemma because of the different discussions at the general and practical levels. To address foreign contingencies swiftly and thereby to meet social expectations appropriately, the French government shifted its policy to come closer to NATO. In this process, its new cooperation with the Alliance was redefined, which accordingly propelled France voluntarily to set out a series of institutional frameworks for crisis management.

Since its focus was directed at building a post-Cold War security arrangement, France did not go back to bodies that it regarded as 'far too unyielding to cope with new, non-Article 5 types of mission' (Bryant 2000: 30, also Grant 1996: 64), such as the IMS, the DPC (a decision-making body on matters relating to the integrated military structure) and the NPG (which deals with nuclear topics, irrelevant to conflict management). As Foreign Minister de Charrette stated that its return was based upon 'the question of its renovation, i.e. of its missions, its role and its organisation',[5] it was aimed at the establishment of a new security arrangement. Thus, meeting domestic normative expectations prompted the French policymakers to develop international institutional capability for security governance.

This chapter analyses the processes through which political leaders in Paris moulded a new French attitude towards NATO by investigating their reaction to Bosnia. The first section reviews general characteristics of French diplomacy and contemplates how they were reflected even after the end of the Cold War. The second section investigates French reaction to the crisis in the Balkans by focussing upon the rise of bottom-up pressure from French domestic society. The third section illustrates how France's historic turn to NATO was made by exploring the stagnation of the international mediation efforts in the Balkans and the criticisms against the government. The fourth section discusses the consolidation of the new French partnership with NATO, while clarifying that its reconciliation was intended to build an international system for conflict management. The conclusion sums up the entire debate and examines the implications drawn from the observations of this chapter.

## Gaullist legacies and French security policy

### Franco-NATO relations: during and after the Cold War

The nature of French diplomacy has been characterised by the Gaullist model. Philip Gordon (1993: 3, emphasis in original, parentheses added) concisely portrays its features in the following five points: 'the absolute need for independence in decision making; a refusal to accept subordination to the United States; the search for grandeur and *rang* [rank]; the primacy of the nation-state; and the importance of national defense'. As this widely accepted definition indicates,[6] the quest for freedom to enjoy its defence policy and the strong will to play a major role in international politics constitute the core elements of Gaullism. Additionally, it is broadly agreed among researchers that French policies expressed in Gaullist terms bear considerable resemblances to those of the preceding eras, even before Charles de Gaulle (cf. Gordon 1993: 5–6; Menon 2000a: 8). In short, Gaullism is not only the *grandes lignes* laid down by the General himself but also an epitomisation of the legacies of French defence attitudes.

One of the typical incidents which symbolised these traits is France's withdrawal from NATO's integrated military command in 1966. The process by which the government leaders reached this decision was comprised of various factors. But without fear of oversimplification, these might be summarised shortly as: dissatisfaction with the dominance of the United States in NATO (for example de Gaulle's proposal to set up a tripartite organisation within NATO in which France, America and Britain would share decision-making authority was callously rejected in 1958); hence, by implication, the relatively small influence which France could bring to bear through its formulation; the possibility of France being drawn into a war caused by excessive American belligerence; and the lack of solidarity provided to France over Suez and Algeria (Bryant 2000: 21–23; Menon 2000a: 8–9). It is true that French withdrawal did not mean a concomitant decision to leave the Alliance permanently. In practice, it kept its presence in the Military Committee as an observer (with no right to vote, only to answer questions) and continued to attend the North Atlantic Council (a regular state leaders' summit). Simultaneously, diverse bilateral contacts between NATO and France supplemented its half-hearted attitude. Nevertheless, one consequence of its withdrawal was the removal of allied troops and military installations from its soil in the midst of the Cold War, while NATO headquarters was moved from Paris to Brussels.[7]

What is notable here is that France's 1966 decision later acquired so stable a position in its diplomacy as to be called a political 'taboo' that 'no one dared to question', i.e. 'the sacred cow', as mentioned earlier (Vernet 1992: 661–662). The change of international circumstances after 1989 made evident how deeply the withdrawal from NATO had been rooted in political leaders' thinking. In addition to Mitterrand's statement (cited at the beginning of this chapter), Foreign Minister Roland Dumas affirmed that there could be 'no question of France rejoining, covertly or more overtly, NATO's military organisation that it had left in 1966',[8] and Defence Minister, Jean-Pierre Chevénement, likewise remarked that 'nothing could make France go back on its 1966 decision to quit [NATO's] military structures'.[9] Although Chevénement's successor, Pierre Joxe, suggested in late 1991 that the Franco-NATO relationships 'should be revised',[10] he stated on a different occasion that 'the autonomy achieved by the decision of 1966 fulfils France's goal of a political consensus and is part of the basis of national attachment to our defence systems'.[11]

Even the Gulf War, despite its enormous impact on the French military system, did not affect the basic lines of its stance. As French commanders had to rely on information coming from the United States, its advanced military operation systems revealed 'serious shortfalls in French intelligence, reconnaissance, surveillance and tracking capabilities' (Bryant 1996: 83). Consequently, this experience made French officers consider the problems of updating their technical, logistical and manpower systems. However, it went no further than raising questions of the French military structure. Rather, another implication drawn from its involvement was more important for Paris. It is said that many French officials thought that 'the Gulf War demonstrated that France could fight alongside the Americans ... and that the ad hoc cooperation can be as effective as anything else'.[12] They recognised that if interoperability between the two states was to be improved, military coaction would be possible through independent political choices. The experience in the Persian Gulf did not urge France to think of its security policy beyond bilateral relationships with other states or of the necessity to reconsider its foreign policy principles.

## French attitude towards European security: NATO and the EC/EU

In terms of the debate over the Alliance, France's anti-NATO posture was explicit. Despite the cooperation with the United States, Paris immediately took a dismissive attitude when NATO's assets, such as its forces, equipment, commanders and doctrines, were used in the Persian Gulf, for fear that this would increase further American influence over the Alliance (Gordon 1993: 171).

In the discussion on NATO's reform, moreover, France made clear its unchanged stance. At the London NATO summit of July 1990, President Mitterrand announced that 'France would not participate in discussions of the Alliance's new strategy',[13] and that there was 'no question of changing [its] particular position with regard to NATO's integrated command'.[14] Subsequently, in May 1991, Paris vigorously opposed Britain's plan, developed through NATO's DPC, to create an Allied Rapid Reaction Corps (ARRC) within the Alliance. This plan, originally presented as one of the ideas on the future utilisation of NATO, was designed to consist of 70,000–100,000 troops, allowing more free command to Supreme Allied Commander Europe (SACEUR). The French government saw that this would not only deepen further military integration in NATO but also strengthen Anglo-Saxon initiatives before Europe had a chance to develop its own defence planning.[15] At the Rome summit in November 1991 (which is now, together with the London summit, regarded as one of the momentous summits of the early 1990s), France disapproved of any attempt to formulate new missions in NATO other than as a guarantor of collective defence. It is said that Mitterrand 'stormed' out of this summit 'in a fury' at the trend towards adapting political roles to include a flexible response to crises and possible enlargement towards East European states (Menon 1995: 23).[16]

## ESDI, CFSP and Eurocorps

Beyond its simple aversion to military integration in NATO, France's adamant objection came from its ambition to construct a more Europeanised defence system, independent of U.S. military predominance. As early as the beginning of the 1990s, France, in tandem with Germany, had already proposed a series of blueprints for future European security. On 6 December 1990, the Kohl-Mitterrand statement to the President of the European Council expressed the idea of European Security Defence Identity (ESDI), advocating that 'political union [here meaning the European Community: EC] should include a genuine security policy that would lead in the end to a common defence' and that the Western European Union (WEU) be 'part of the political union' (Kramer 1994: 34). France stressed that the ESDI should be realised *within* the framework of the EC. In the same context, nearly ten months later on 14 October 1991, Paris and Bonn argued for the creation of the Common Foreign and Security Policy (CFSP), suggesting that the WEU 'progressively develop the European Common Security Policy on behalf of the Union' – notably, this idea later became one of the three pillars of the Maastricht Treaty in December 1991.[17]

In addition, the proposal in October 1991 contained another idea, i.e. the concept of the 'Eurocorps'. Although it was only hinted at in two sentences in a footnote of the proposal, Paris and Bonn soon reached an agreement to develop the existing Franco-German brigade into a complete European army corps. The Eurocorps itself came into existence at the La Rochelle meeting, with its missions laid out as peacekeeping, peacemaking interventions and humanitarian tasks as well as the defence of Western Europe.[18] No doubt, these were the same missions Paris had strongly objected to when proposed in the scheme for NATO. French leaders contended that these tasks should be undertaken in a Europeanised context. For this reason, they were greatly angered when confronted by the plan for an ARRC because they saw it as an effort by Britain and the United States to obstruct French initiatives (Gordon 1993: 174).

In sum, French security policy at the beginning of the 1990s was aimed at the realisation of an authentic European defence structure, not at reconsideration of Franco-NATO relations. Apart from this aspiration, it should be addressed that the French tried to consolidate European security cooperation for two other reasons: the unification of Germany and a possible pull-out of the United States from the European continent. First, the problem of the so-called 'German obsession' had been a major concern for the French leaders, i.e. how to anchor a reunified Germany in a multinational context under a European roof (Gordon 1993; Kramer 1994; Menon 1995; Vernet 1992).[19] Second, although it did not want a further increase in the U.S. presence, the government was worried about potential American 'inwardness' in years to come, as Washington had already implied a reduction of its soldiers in Europe after the end of the Cold War. These factors also prompted the leaders in Paris to seek for an autonomous defence structure, which would enable European states to prepare for future problems in America's absence, especially potential issues caused by the instability of the former Soviet Union (Gordon 1993: 176). Nevertheless, for the French government, such a framework had to be rooted in a Europeanised background, and not result in the reinforcement of the pre-existing military Alliance.

## France and the war in Bosnia

### *French engagement at the initial stage*

As the EC troika viewed the crisis in the Balkans as 'the hour of Europe' (Chapter 3), the French government, a vocal supporter of the Maastricht Treaty, the conference which was due to be held at the end of 1991, thought of it as 'a test for the CFSP' and 'an opportunity to demonstrate the community's ability to hold a common line' (Lepick 1996: 77). French leaders aimed to build the Community's political and security system by dealing effectively with the conflicts in the Balkans.

In July 1991, less than one month after the outbreak of the first military clash in the former Yugoslavia, Paris set forth the idea of a WEU interposition force to

Slovenia and Croatia for the purpose of ceasefire monitoring (Lucarelli 2000: 168) and, in September 1991, France, as chair of the UN Security Council, also proposed the creation of a WEU emergency force under Chapter 7 of the UN Charter, a plan which reflected President Mitterrand's intention to involve the WEU directly in this crisis. On this occasion, France declared that it was 'prepared to bear the lion's share of the military burden' (Treacher 2003: 73).

After all, these French plans did not come to fruition because of Danish and Netherland objections in a WEU meeting and British objection in the UN Security Council, but it should be noted that France's vision to evolve European security and to lead conflict management in the Balkans was reflected from the start. Indeed, Sonia Lucarelli's (2000: 173) words are no exaggeration: 'what Yugoslavia did offer was an opportunity that the French had been waiting for, to create a working operational European security structure that could undertake peace-keeping operations independently of the United States'.

After the war broke out in Bosnia and the situation rapidly deteriorated, it was decided to deploy a UN peacekeeping operation (UNPROFOR) in Sarajevo from June 1992. The French government immediately agreed on the dispatch of its troops, showing a clear contrast with other reluctant/cautious countries such as Britain, Germany and the United States. Its strong will to lead the international response was symbolised when President Mitterrand suddenly visited Sarajevo on 28 June under the ongoing siege. This trip was aimed to galvanise other European states by highlighting France's presence in this war (Lepick 1996: 80), in which the government's initiative was appreciated by the public (Morjé Howard and Morjé Howard 2003: 112). Furthermore, in the following month of July 1992, the UN mandate to monitor the embargo against the former Yugoslavia in the Adriatic Sea (United Nations Security Council Resolutions 713 and 757) was set in motion. France contended that this mission should be undertaken under the scheme of the WEU, whose post-Cold War rationale had just been outlined by the Petersberg Declaration of June 1992 as peacekeeping and tasks of combat forces in crisis management.[20] As this UN mission was explained in Chapter 3, some other countries (especially Britain) affirmed NATO's role in consideration of their relationship with the United States; consequently, this unresolved discussion ended with not only WEU troops but also NATO contingents being dispatched to the same area despite almost all countries' dual membership.

France's European security vision was vividly imprinted in the actual conflict management and there was no room for the revision of Franco-NATO relations in this context. At that time, the likelihood that it would voluntarily take part in the discussion of NATO's new role was not conceived of at all.

## Public reaction to the government's policy

In France, as in other European countries, the war in the Balkans caught public attention from the outset (Howorth 1994: 113–114; La Balme 2001: 191–194; Wood 1994: 142). Especially the discovery of the Serb-led concentration camps around July–August 1992 caused a strong reaction, as did the argument that 'Bosnia Herzegovina is transformed into a concentration camp';[21] 'The war ... in the former Yugoslavia today makes one more step towards atrocity'[22] and '200,000 people could be caught up in the "ethnic cleansing" in the north of Bosnia'.[23]

With this crisis being perceived by the French political leaders as a touchstone of whether Europe could deal with its first security problem after 1989, it was similarly discussed within the public sphere, where it was contended as 'the test of the Yugoslav crisis'[24] or the 'bench test of the new Europe'.[25] Corresponding to such expectations, a quite broad consensus was formed within the political circle on making an immediate response.[26] President Mitterrand suggested that he would 'authorise military action of humanitarian missions',[27] and Prime Minister Pierre Bérégovoy said that 'everything should be done so that peace is restored',[28] while the Socialist Party leader, Laurent Fabius, also called for European intervention 'to stop the massacres'.[29] From the conservative/opposition side, the Union for French Democracy (Union pour la Démocratie Française, UDF) faction's president in the National Assembly, Charles Millon, saw the government's reaction as 'insufficient' and demanded more direct action,[30] while the then leader of the Rally for the Republic (Rassemblement pour la République, RPR), Jacques Chirac, also reproached it as 'much too late and too weak'.[31]

Within the public realm, French commitment was strongly upheld from the start. In August 1992, 61 per cent of the French concurred on France's participation in military combat within the framework of the United Nations (33 per cent objected), while, in December 1992, 76 per cent showed support for the use of force to protect the delivery of humanitarian aid (16 per cent opposed) and 70 per cent to enforce a ceasefire (21 per cent opposed).[32] It is generally pointed out that the mobilisation of French soldiers for the purpose of human rights protection was relatively well accepted (La Balme 2001: 192; Morjé Howard and Morjé Howard 2003: 118; Rathbun 2004: 131–134). Therefore, unlike in Britain, where it was claimed that the use of soldiers should be limited to protection of its tangible interests (especially by conservatives) and Germany, where its constitution prohibited any war engagement, solid support was constructed within French society to get involved in this foreign humanitarian crisis, mixed with an ambition to realise a genuine European security system.[33]

Attention of the French public to the situation was consistently high throughout the war. In January 1994, 85 per cent of those questioned said that they were concerned about the events taking place in the former Yugoslavia (39 per cent: very concerned – 46 per cent: somewhat concerned), clearly overwhelming the 14 per cent who were unconcerned (8 per cent: somewhat unconcerned – 6 per cent: not at all concerned).[34] As Marc and Lise Morjé Howard (2003: 125) confirm that 'public opinion did exert an influence on the French government's policy on Bosnia', support from the society surely boosted its commitment to this war. Hence, France became the largest contributor to UNPROFOR on the ground in Bosnia by eventually sending 6,700 troops during the course of the war.

# France's return to NATO to build a new conflict management system

## *The stalemate in Bosnia and public criticisms: changing France's traditional policy*

Despite Paris's vigorous commitment to the war in Bosnia, the impasse of international negotiations had gradually become evident. The most critical example of this was the failure of the peace plan called the Vance-Owen Peace Plan (VOPP), as discussed in Chapter 3. France's support for this UN and EC-led peace mediation was emphasised by Alain Juppé, new Foreign Minister from March 1993, commenting that 'our only basis … is the Vance-Owen plan';[35] therefore, rejection of the plan by the local groups had a big impact, which is now expressed as 'bitter failure' (Lepick 1996: 81) and a 'turning point' (Gregory 2000: 63).

The aftermath of this long-lasting international negotiation generated severe reprimands against the government, claiming that 'the international community capitulates'[36] and laying blame on 'the failure of Western diplomacy'.[37] Former president Valéry Giscard d'Estaing warned that 'the impotence of the European Community to bring a solution to the crisis of the former Yugoslavia causes more damage to the idea of European Union'.[38] Further continuation of the war would not only make France's ambitions difficult but also bring more recriminations on the government for failing to produce peaceful conditions.

Dissatisfaction with the government's performance was also mirrored in public opinion. On 15 April 1993 (slightly before the collapse of the VOPP), 52 per cent of French considered that the French government [was] not making sufficient effort to try to stop the fighting in ex-Yugoslavia whereas only 31 per cent considered that the government [was] doing everything in its power to stop the fighting. (La Balme 2001: 193)[39]

Additionally, public frustration with the government's performance appeared in the evaluation of the UN peacekeeping in the Balkans. The rate of those respondents who considered the UN engagement inefficient rose from 66 per cent (May 1993) to 76 per cent (May 1994) and finally to 79 per cent (May 1995).[40] Given the French presence in UNPROFOR, it is conceivable that this evaluation was directly connected with the assessment on its handling. Natalie La Balme (2001: 193) explains the negative posture of the French public by contending that 'The French public was indeed frustrated with the performance of the United Nations, and of the French government, in Bosnia'. As a backlash to the high expectation to solve the war swiftly, critical opinions towards the government gradually became widespread in the French public sphere.

At this juncture, the French government also came to grope for an alternative method to solve this crisis in a more effective and decisive manner. 'The lack of progress in international conference and the growing number of reports of

Serb atrocities, including rape camps, made the status quo unacceptable' (Wood 1994: 143). Thus, the government, shifting away from its conventional stance, began reviewing its relationship with NATO. In other words, from a theoretical point of view, in order to fulfil 'general' expectations to halt the violence successfully, the government came to revise its approach in the 'practical' management.

Indeed, changes had, albeit little by little, appeared in French diplomacy from late 1992. The first step was taken by President Mitterrand, who had previously confirmed France's unchanged attitude after the Cold War. In December, he authorised French officers to participate in NATO's Military Committee for the first time since 1966, to discuss preparation for potential implementation of UN activity for a Bosnian peace settlement. Furthermore, to Washington's surprise, Paris in January 1993 gave approval for French troops within the Eurocorps coming under NATO operational command in the event of crises (Gordon 1995: 61; Menon 1995: 26, 2000a: 43).

How was this initial move explained by the government? Foreign Minister Roland Dumas held:

> It is also necessary to consider the means with which the Atlantic Alliance could contribute to this action [here, meaning UN action in Bosnia]. ... it [is] natural that the [North Atlantic] Council gives a mandate to the Military Committee to study the methods of the Alliance's contribution.[41] France will naturally take part in this work.

For this reason, France returned first to the Military Committee rather than any other body. Then, referring to the problems of peacekeeping operations and NATO's role in this mission, he continued:

> We do not wish to call into question the traditional procedure of the integrated defence system; but [when] acting in a new mission, it seems necessary for us to define a new working method. On new problems, new solutions.[42]

This statement reveals that France decided to go back to NATO to look for 'new solutions' to 'new problems', viz. such problems as peacekeeping and conflict management that were demanded in the Balkans. Hence, it was not whether to return to the traditional NATO but how France should participate in the process of creating international governance capabilities to deal with humanitarian contingencies. Here, the purpose of its reconciliation can be clearly indicated.

### *The largest contributor, the largest casualties: how norm dilemmas led France to renew its foreign policy*

As a result of the election in March 1993, French politics entered into the second cohabitation in its history, of the new RPR and UDF coalition under Édouard Balladur's prime ministry. It is said that these politicians, having more Atlanticist/neo-Gaullist traits, were more concerned about weakening France's say

*Rapprochement with NATO* 97

by remaining outside the main NATO bodies, and speeded up its reconciliation with NATO (as did the presidential inauguration of Jacques Chirac in May 1995) (cf. Menon 1995, 2000b).

It is absolutely true that this accelerated France's new cooperation with the Alliance. As discussed, however, the first decision was made in December 1992 by President Mitterrand and the Socialist government. The deadlock of the international mediation efforts steered France to move towards NATO. In this regard, Bozo (1997: 49) argues that 'the turn was in fact taken before the coming to power of Balladur's conservative government and the inauguration of a new phase of cohabitation'. It was a matter of interpretation not simply of Gaullism but of effective policy to suitably meet the social anticipation of stopping the violence in Bosnia. Therefore, he (1997: 60) also states that 'the most explicit objective of the new approach to NATO ... is to restore the credibility and viability of France's policy in the realm of European defence'.

This account demands understanding how the stalemate of international policy affected both the older and newer governments. Given the support for action on foreign humanitarian tragedy, policy to meet this social anticipation was not necessarily promised. If French soldiers were killed over the course of operations, the support would turn to fierce criticism and voices for withdrawal. Moreover, as France had dispatched the largest number of troops to UNPROFOR, it was more likely to suffer casualties among its soldiers and personnel. In the middle of the war in January 1994, 18 French soldiers had been killed and 260 injured, while the number of those killed reached 43 by July 1995 (Gregory 2000: 64 and 84). Therefore, even in France, where military engagement was relatively accepted, possible pull-out was a consideration as Prime Minister Juppé said that 'We should not exclude a process of withdrawal',[43] and Defence Minister Léotard also suggested 'the possibility of a withdrawal' in 1993.[44] Brian Rathbun (2004: 137–139) provides detailed documentation of this point by explicating the discussion within the decision makers' circle at that time.

Of course, such statements should not be literally interpreted; they were rather used as a threat to urge its international partners towards 'a more robust approach to fulfilling the present mission', because France's pull-out could cause a malfunction to the entirety of UNPROFOR activities.[45] On a different occasion, Defence Minister Léotard also confessed that withdrawal would be viewed as 'adding failure on top of failure',[46] and was quite a difficult step for the government to take because it would have had to acknowledge the failure of its conflict management, leaving the tragedy behind. Thus, Foreign Minister Juppé also commented: 'we must avoid two evils: escalation or retreat'.[47]

In opinion polls too, such ambivalence was reflected. Table 5.1 (which was also shown in Table 3.2 of Chapter 3) uncovers how the approach to the war was assessed at that time. On Questionnaire (a), a majority of the French disagreed that the situation in Bosnia should continue – by implication, improvement of the local conditions was strongly demanded. Meanwhile, on concrete measures about what to do, Questionnaire (b) reveals that, although withdrawal was surely rejected, it is also true that a not insignificant portion of the respondents concurred on it,

*Table 5.1* France's public opinion towards intervention in Bosnia in 1994 (in percentage)

|  | 25 Feb | 25 Mar | 29 Jun |
|---|---|---|---|
| *(a) Let things go on as they are now* | | | |
| Favour | 8.0 | 14.5 | 11.0 |
| Oppose | 89.3 | 79.9 | 84.6 |
| Don't Know | 2.7 | 5.6 | 4.4 |
| *(b) Withdraw all troops* | | | |
| Favour | 23.5 | 26.8 | 30.7 |
| Oppose | 71.9 | 67.5 | 62.0 |
| Don't Know | 4.6 | 5.8 | 7.3 |
| *(c) Launch air strikes* | | | |
| Favour | 53.1 | 58.4 | 48.3 |
| Oppose | 40.6 | 33.4 | 45.8 |
| Don't Know | 6.4 | 8.2 | 5.9 |
| Number | 497 | 502 | 502 |

Source: *Flash Eurobarometers* 24: 2/25/94; 25: 3/25/94; 29: 6/29/94 (also see Sobel 1996: 179). Questionnaires are slightly modified for grammatical reasons and order is also changed.

reflecting a gradual increase in support. Obviously, because voices for action do not guarantee the permissiveness of human casualties, the government was struck by the dilemma of stopping the war without incurring damage to its personnel.

Questionnaire (c) shows that air strikes were more controversial because they would put French soldiers in danger. Taking into account the outcome of Questionnaire (a) regarding the demand for improvement of the current situation, public opinion was divided on concrete measures, specifically where military options were concerned. Here a gap becomes apparent between discussions at the general and practical levels.

Despite these difficulties, policy was assessed on whether the goal of stopping the violence was being achieved or not and, consequently, criticisms were hurled against the government. Thus, in the case of France, norm dilemmas became more evident as its commitment deepened. Under these circumstances, France commenced a new relationship with NATO.

## *The construction of a new NATO: French policy under the cohabitation*

The newly formed Balladur government facilitated the reconciliation with NATO. In June, France agreed on the integration of WEU naval task forces into NATO command – the aforementioned monitoring activity in the Adriatic Sea – under the principle of 'NATO first, WEU second' (Grant 1996: 61). As cited in

Chapter 3, RPR deputy, Jacques Baumel, Vice President of the National Assembly's Defence Commission, remarked that 'Western countries must put a halt to the absurd battle pitting NATO against [the] WEU', although he simultaneously added that 'the WEU must not become ... NATO's poor cousin, which takes the leftovers when NATO does not wish to assume certain missions'.[48] In any case, France's policy moved towards the Alliance, placing more stress on effective conflict management. Its cooperation with NATO is summarised in Table 5.2.

The new government's will to take the initiative in the discussion of NATO's activity pushed this trend forwards. For instance, Prime Minister Balladur said that 'Within a reform, France ... must find a defined place' in NATO,[49] while Defence Minister François Léotard similarly stated that 'the Alliance must take on new missions', and that 'France must understand this change and not allow others [to] define it'.[50] Additionally, the RPR leader Jacques Chirac, who had been one of the proponents for the revision of Franco-NATO relations, before being elected as president, declared that

> if France wants to play a determining role in the creation of a European defence entity, it must take into account this state of mind of partners, and reconsider to a large degree the form of its relations with NATO.[51]

Table 5.2 French rapprochement with NATO

| | |
|---|---|
| **1992** | |
| Dec | President Mitterrand allowed French officers to work with the NATO military staff on preparing possible NATO activities in Bosnia |
| **1993** | |
| Jan | French forces within the Eurocorps to come under NATO's Operational Command |
| Apr | Participation in NATO's Military Committee by Gen Jean-Paul Pélisson for discussions related to the Alliance's peacekeeping role |
| Jun | France agreed to integrate NATO and WEU naval task forces operating in the Adriatic Sea with the combined task force to come under NATO |
| **1994** | France became co-chair with the United States of NATO's Senior Defence Group on Proliferation |
| Jan | North Atlantic Summit declared full support for the development of ESDI |
| Sep | Defence Minister, François Léotard, attended an informal gathering of NATO defence ministers in Seville (for the first time since 1966) |
| **1995** | |
| Sep | NATO military exercises were held in France for the first time since 1965 |
| Oct | Defence Minister, Charles Millon (Léotard's successor), attended other informal gatherings (France's Chief Staff General, Jean Phillipe Douin, participated in the Military Committee) |
| Dec | Foreign Minister, Hervé de Charette, announced France's full participation in NATO's Military Committee and participation in IFOR (French ground troops were sent under NATO command for the first time since 1966) |
| **1996** | |
| Jun | Defence Minister Millon attended a formal NATO defence ministers' meeting (for the first time since 1966) |

Source: Summarised from Grant (1996: 60–63), Menon (2000a: 45–55).

Admittedly, President Mitterrand took a more reserved or sometimes uncompromising attitude. He prevented Léotard's attendance at an informal meeting of NATO defence ministers at Travemüde in Germany (October 1993) and Admiral Lanxade was recalled several hours prior to a meeting of the Military Committee in NATO (April 1994) (Menon 2000a: 47). However, on NATO's concrete activity in Bosnia, Mitterrand was principally supportive. He said, referring to the Oslo summit in 1992 (in which NATO members concurred to set an agenda of peacekeeping operations beyond its original territory), that 'what I accepted in 1992 could be applied to the occasion of other missions of peacekeeping ... provided that any French decision ... was made by proper national authorities'.[52] Furthermore, as regards NATO's new role, he endorsed that 'peace-keeping operations required a NATO which was more flexible and able to adapt to the objects of each mission'.[53] On Bosnia, it is hard to find a noticeable difference even under the cohabitation, as Foreign Minister Juppé remarked that 'France [during the cohabitation] has always spoken with one single voice'.[54]

This is because the motive that facilitated the pragmatic turn was a sense of urgency to produce a decisive policy and to build a viable security system. For example, as it was argued at that time that 'the failure of the West in the ex-Yugoslavia weighs very heavily on the credibility of the Alliance on both sides of the Atlantic',[55] and as President Mitterrand also recognised 'the tragedy in Bosnia' as 'becoming unbearable',[56] the still ongoing fighting was viewed as depriving French foreign policy of credibility. Hence, Foreign Minister Juppé stated that 'the Yugoslav crisis ... ha[d] illustrated ... the necessity for adaptation [to the new security environment], particularly in the field of peacekeeping',[57] while Prime Minister Balladur also contended that NATO 'must adapt to its new missions' and 'France takes part in this renovation of the Alliance'.[58] These comments reveal how the Alliance created in 1949 was now required to embark on new tasks and how French decision makers were thinking to take part in it.

Against this background, France agreed to the idea of ESDI being used within the framework of NATO, whereas Paris had once categorically argued for fruition on the outside. When the NATO summit of January 1994 endorsed provision of 'full support for the development of a European Security and Defence Identity',[59] Paris welcomed this decision, with Defence Minister Léotard announcing that it was 'an important step which satisfies French demands'.[60] Chief of the French Defence Staff Admiral Jacques Lanxade (1994: 18) made clear that 'our approach aims at promoting a European security and defence identity, while continuing the process of adjusting the Alliance to its new missions and to the present context'. These instances indicate that the debate was no longer *whether* to go back to the Alliance or not but rather *how* to construct a viable European security system in the post-Cold War period by working from within NATO.

France's new policy orientation was confirmed by its *Defence White Book 1994*, published for the first time since 1972. It reaffirms that participation of France's Defence Minister and the Chief of Staff in NATO meetings would be approved 'on a case-by-case basis by the President of the Republic where the engagement of

French forces or French interests were at stake',[61] while regarding NATO as 'an arena where the European security and defence identity' should 'establish itself'.[62] Accordingly, Léotard and Admiral Lanxade attended a NATO Defence Ministers meeting in Seville in September for the first time after an interval of almost 30 years.

## *The final phase of the war*

On the ground in Bosnia, France and Britain were placed in a similar situation in that the two countries had, respectively, the largest and second largest number of troops in UNPROFOR. Like their London counterparts, the French leaders were opposed to the American proposal of the so-called 'lift and strike' policy as Chapter 3 explicated. In response to the policy proposal to initiate both a flow of weapons to the poorly armed Bosnian Muslims by lifting the embargo and an aerial attack against the Bosnian Serbs, President Mitterrand was reported to have made clear his objection by arguing that 'Serb retaliation would pose too great a danger to the French troops serving in the UN force in the region' (Christopher 1998: 346).[63]

However, Paris gradually broke ranks with London. The crucial difference between these two countries was that the failure of this conflict management would cause fundamental damage to France's ambition to build a European security system – an ambition that its British counterparts did not share. Confronted by the mortar shelling in the Sarajevo market in February 1994, in which 43 civilians were killed by the Bosnian Serb attack, the French leadership stepped up towards a tougher option and called for greater American involvement, as it recognised that a more dissuasive approach was necessarily risking the safety of its troops (Lepick 1996: 81). It was said that President Mitterrand 'appear[ed] to feel the overwhelming need to "do something" even though [France] has 6,700 troops on the ground'.[64]

In particular, the hostage-taking of UNPROFOR soldiers, which occurred directly after NATO's limited air strikes on 22 May 1995, was perceived as 'humiliation' by the French public and speeded up France's move towards forceful measures (La Balme 2001: 194; Rathbun 2004: 142). For example, while putting a picture of the captured soldiers on the front page, an article in a French journal, *Le Point*, expressed it as 'the first test of Chirac',[65] referring to the recent election of president Jacques Chirac in May 1995. He soon proposed the creation of a Rapid Reaction Force (RRF) to protect UNPROFOR, consisting mainly of French and British heavily armed troops. As Chapter 3 discussed, this helped to change the situation significantly, and international conflict management moved on to the final phase: namely, massive air strikes by NATO states and ceasefire negotiations in Dayton.

It is correct that France moved towards NATO because it 'recognized that more intimate relations with NATO, and particularly with the United States, were necessary for influence in out-of-area problems as well as for potential access to the technology that lay behind America's domination of the alliance' (Kaplan 2004: 123, also Bozo 1997: 55; De Wijk 1997: 124–125; Grant 1996: 63). As it was claimed, 'In order to be more European tomorrow, it is necessary to be more Atlanticist'.[66] Even if this was the case, nevertheless, it should be contemplated for what purposes this diplomatic volte-face was initiated. It happened in order to address a foreign crisis in Bosnia, which was unlikely to endanger its own security, but public expectation was that it could not be ignored. This point was plainly articulated within the public realm: Bosnia was viewed as bringing 'no serious impact on the life of our [French] people or that of our neighbours of rich Europe. Apart from the images on television ... the war of Bosnia is not that of the French, no more than it is the war of other Europeans – and even less that of the Americans'.[67] Its policymakers began a new partnership with the Alliance to aptly live up to the social normative expectations emanating from the 'images' of the catastrophe playing out on television.

## Post-Bosnia: discussion on a new NATO

In contrast to the early 1990s, France's attitude towards European security became more reconciliatory with the Alliance. In the post-Bosnian summit in NATO in December 1995, the new Foreign Minister, Hervé de Charette, declared its return to NATO's main bodies, as quoted at the opening of this chapter. As he added that 'it is a question of renovation',[68] and French ambassador to NATO, Gérard Errera, similarly explained France's return as 'to make NATO better suited to its new role in Europe',[69] it was aimed at taking initiative in recreating NATO for the sake of effective crisis response. The same view was also expressed by President Chirac. During his visit to the United States, he stated:

> Our common action in Bosnia underlines the need for the Atlantic Alliance to adapt itself to a universe different from the one in which it was born. This reform must initially specify the modes of action which will enable it to effectively answer the unforeseeable situations of the post-Cold War period.[70]

This concisely depicts the transformation process of a military organisation originally created vis-à-vis Soviet threats to one based around new missions in the post-1989 era, i.e. to deal with such out-of-area missions as Bosnia.

Paris continued this policy by taking an active part in the Berlin North Atlantic Council summit of June 1996. The government approved the participation of French officers in the newly created Policy Coordination Groups (PCG), an advisory committee to North Atlantic Council and the Military Committee for new missions of non-Article 5 (missions other than collective defence) (Menon 2000a: 55, also see Chapter 3). Actually, the setting-up of the PCG is said to reply 'to French criticisms of the weak ties between political and military authorities' (Menon 2000a: 54).

The summit in Berlin officially endorsed the concept of the Combined Joint Task Force (CJTF), the programme to enable European members to utilise NATO's assets in operations under WEU-led missions when the United

States reserves its participation. Through this opportunity of opening the way for Europe's own military operations, France succeeded in gaining concessions from Washington to identify European commanders and headquarters under this CJTF operation. As a consequence, Paris left the summit with great satisfaction (Bozo 1997: 73; Menon 2000a: 53–54).

France's rapprochement, however, stalled in the Madrid summit in 1997 when the United States declined President Chirac's request for more Europeanisation of NATO, including establishment of a new European Deputy to SACEUR and nomination of a European Commander of NATO's Allied Forces Southern Europe (AFSOUTH) in Naples (Bryant 2000: 31; Kaplan 2004: 123; Menon 2000a: 56–57).[71] In light of the American rejection, the government announced that it would remain outside some bodies, such as the IMS and the NPG, despite its suggestion of a possible re-entry, thus making France's full reintegration unlikely. This result is sometimes described as indicating that 'French relations with NATO had cooled noticeably' (Menon 2000a: 59).

Nevertheless, taking account of the discussion thus far, the decision not to go back to these bodies is not so strange. First, apart from the fact that, realistically, it was unlikely that the United States would concede the Commander's position of the AFSOUTH, which has conventionally been occupied by American commanders (Menon 2000a: 57–58), the IMS was considered, at least at that time, more appropriate for dealing with issues of Cold War-style collective defence.[72] Defence Minister Léotard explained the reason by stating that 'the procedures of the integrated military structure were of very little use [in the conflict of ex-Yugoslavia]' ... and 'it is, consequently, for France, merely useless to think of returning', while clearly affirming that NATO came to have '"an excessive weight in the planning of the chain of decisions" for peacekeeping'.[73] Second, concerning the DPC, given that its role was to make decisions relating to the integrated military structure (Grant 1996: 65), it would not choose to return to it for the same reason. Interestingly, although the DPC and the Military Committee (which France instantly rejoined in 1992) 'are both non-integrated bodies that "respect" national sovereignty, ... since they take decisions only by unanimous consent' (Grant 1996: 65), the type which France generally prefers, it decided to remain on the outside of the former but not the latter. Finally, concerning the NPG, its non-re-entry could simply have been because nuclear policy planning was irrelevant when talking about crisis response. The argument of this chapter elucidates why France returned to the main NATO bodies but not others.

In fact, in February 1998, the new Defence Minister, Alain Richard, confirmed that 'while France would remain outside the integrated military structure, it would participate fully in the review of the Strategic Concept and in CJTF staffs and associated operational planning bodies'.[74] This new partnership was sought for the purpose of establishing an effective security management system at the international level. Therefore, it is said that 'the failure to secure Naples for France or for a European has not dramatically altered the position of the French' (Bryant 2000: 34, also see Macleod 2000).

France's change of diplomatic direction should be seen from how its experiences in Bosnia were reflected in creating a new security framework for management of crises. Even though action, including military measures, was largely supported in its domestic society, it did not guarantee that effective policy would be produced immediately; furthermore, growing casualties among its own personnel seriously damaged its political credibility. As a consequence, France's decision makers were placed in a dilemma: to keep deploying their troops could result in more casualties, but withdrawal would trigger more severe denunciation for leaving humanitarian tragedy behind. This brought them to the realisation of the need to construct a viable international security system and accordingly led them to make the historic move of reviewing the traditional diplomacy that had held sway since the days of General de Gaulle. Here can be found a domestic-international linkage in creating the post-Cold War European security order – to appropriately meet social normative expectations emanating from the bottom up, its political leaders were prompted to construct a new security arrangement in the international sphere. Within this linkage, France's return came about. At the same time, through this process, the military alliance created in 1949 was changed into a new organisation by being given a new mission and rationale to address and prevent humanitarian contingencies.

## Conclusion

This chapter has investigated how, over the course of the war in Bosnia, the French decision makers conceived a new appropriate posture of NATO in the post-Cold War period by focussing on France's own rapprochement with the Alliance. At the outset, while immediately reacting to this foreign conflict with support for action from its domestic society, France aimed to realise its ambitions to build Europe's own security capability. Hence, it considered that other states' attempt to attach new missions to NATO would thwart its project. As the war continued without showing any improvement and the number of casualties among French troops rose, criticism was hurled against the government for failing to handle this humanitarian disaster. As a consequence, it resorted to seeking more decisive measures and initiated a review of its relationship with the Alliance, returning to it for the first time since 1966. In other words, the question was not whether to go back to the conventional NATO but how it could solve the war in Bosnia and how it should be reorganised so that recurrence of the same experience could be prevented. In this process, France made a historic turn and voluntarily participated in the discussion of its revitalisation.

It is possible to assume that France's reconciliation can be claimed as a shift of emphasis in the Gaullist traditions: a shift from stressing France's independence from NATO to enhancing its say by participating in the post-Cold War discussions as a significant player. However, this account would have difficulty explaining why it chose to rejoin some NATO bodies, but not others. Because its purpose was to construct a security governance mechanism for crisis response, it went back only to those directly related to this object. To be sure, the governmental and presidential changes from the Socialist Party to the RPR and UDF coalition, and from Mitterrand to Chirac, speeded up this trend, the latter claiming for a more active role of France in NATO. Nevertheless, as the rapprochement had been broached by the Socialist government and President Mitterrand, the fundamental reason to return to NATO for the sake of effective security governance should be taken into account.

The findings of this chapter indicate how normative influence is injected into international organisations. Strong support for action within the French society surely spurred on its government's efforts on Bosnia. Nevertheless, it did not culminate in successful policy because no response to such a foreign crisis was readily available. Moreover, in the actual process of intervention, casualties among French personnel, in turn, caused criticism against the government's handling while generating voices for withdrawal. Thus, the dilemma of action struck its decision makers. Hence, France's leaders sought a more robust approach and were also propelled to set up a series of international frameworks for conflict management so that crises could be addressed in a more effective and swift manner. That is to say, normative influence was not reflected in international organisations spontaneously, but the dilemma that it created led policymakers to design their structures to meet the appropriateness it defined. Therefore, concrete reform of NATO was directed not at military intervention but at crisis response and preventive measures. This perspective clarifies the new roles for NATO that the French leaders envisioned in their reconciliation process.

## Notes

1 Quoted in Grant (1996: 58), originally from Hervé de Charette, speech delivered to the North Atlantic Council, 5 December 1995.
2 Quoted in Gordon (1993: 167), originally from *Propos sur la défense*, no. 16, July–August 1990: 14.
3 France's reintegration, completed in 2009 under President Nicolas Sarkozy, will be touched upon in the concluding chapter.
4 N.B. the DPC was dissolved in 2010 and its responsibilities were absorbed by the North Atlantic Council. See, e.g. www.nato.int/cps/ua/natohq/topics_49201.htm (Accessed on 1 July 2018).
5 Union européenne – conseil affaires générales – Conférence de Presse du Ministre des Affaires Étrangères, M. Hervé de Charrette, *La Politique Étrangère de la France*, January–February, 1996: 113.
6 This definition is also used by Gregory (2000: 19), Howorth (1996: 17).
7 Others were the withdrawal from the Mediterranean fleet from the NATO Allied Forces Mediterranean (AFMED) and pulling out of French troops from the German-Czech border. Additionally, after the Algeria crisis, it had already, in 1963, withdrawn 'French naval forces from NATO Atlantic and Channel Commands (ACLANT and ACCHAN)', ACLANT meaning Allied Command Atlantic and ACCHAN meaning Allied Command Channel, quoted in Menon (2000a: 9).
8 Quoted in Gordon (1993: 167), originally from *Le Monde*, 23 March 1991.
9 David White, 'French Minister rejects idea of multi-national forces', *The Financial Times*, 8 June 1990.
10 Quoted in Menon (1995: 25), originally from 'Allocution à la Cérémonie de Clôture de la Session Plénière du Cours Supérieur Interarmées', *Propos sur la Défense*, no. 24, November–December 1991: 121.
11 Quoted in Menon (1996: 159), originally from Ministere de la Défense, *Un Nouveau débate Strategique*, La Documentation Française, 1993: 8.
12 Interview conducted by Philip Gordon (1993: 168). Regarding French engagement in the Gulf War, see Gordon (1993: 165–167), Howorth (1994: 107–108).

13 Quoted in Menon (2000a: 40), originally from *Le Monde*, 7 July 90.
14 Quoted in Gordon (1993: 167), originally from post summit press conference in Ministére de la Défense, *Propos sur la Défense*, no. 16, July–August 1990: 14.
15 This is based on the interview conducted by Anand Menon (2000a: 42). Also see Gordon (1993: 171). N.B. SACEUR has always been occupied by U.S. commanders; therefore, ARRC would inevitably increase U.S. influence.
16 Also see Boris Johnson, Peter Almond and Stephen Robinson, 'Bush Attacks French Moves on Nato', *The Daily Telegraph*, 8 November 1991. As could be expected, France was opposed to NATO's enlargement eastwards. Although, at the 1991 Rome summit, France reluctantly approved the creation of the North Atlantic Cooperation Council, a council in NATO for the political dialogue between the Atlantic allies and the former Warsaw Treaty Pact, Paris instituted an 'empty chair' policy and absented itself from the meetings on 1 and 10 April 1992 (Menon 2000a: 41).
17 This proposal is originally based on the 4 February 1991 letter 'Security Policy Co-operation within the Framework of the Common Foreign and Security Policy of the Political Union', *Europe Documents*, 21 February 1991: 1, quoted in Gordon (1993: 172) (also see 229, fn. 28).
18 Belgium joined in March 1993, contributing an armoured division. Furthermore, the French 1992 military programme law (loi de programation militaire) endorsed the role of the Eurocorps as 'the key element' for the mission of crisis prevention (Howorth 1994: 122).
19 During the campaign around the referendum for the ratification of the Maastricht Treaty, 'tying Germany down' in the European structure was a strong ground for supporters of this treaty, while certainly opponents of the treaty warned against German domination of it. In both cases, the debate revolved around the issue of controlling Germany (Gordon 1995: 88).
20 Regarding France's view on WEU's Petersberg missions, see Howorth (1994: 122).
21 Florence Hartmann, 'Dans un appel à l'ONU La Bosnie-Herzégovine demande "l'usage de la force" contre la Serbie', *Le Monde*, 25 June 1992.
22 '"Purification ethnique"', *Le Monde*, 7 August 1992.
23 '200,000 personnes pourraient être touchées par le "nettoyage ethnique" dans le nord de la Bosnie', *Le Monde*, 21 August 1992.
24 Alain Gresh, 'L'Europe à l'épreuve de la crise yougoslave', *Le Monde Diplomatique*, January 1992.
25 'La coûteuse myopie de la communauté', *Le Monde Diplomatique*, July 1992. Foreign Minister Duma also said that 'the crisis in Yugoslavia is a bench test for Europe', see Alain Debove and Jean Pierre Langellier, 'Un entretien avec le ministre des affaires étrangères M. Dumas: "La crise yougoslave est un banc d'essai pour l'Europe"', *Le Monde*, 27 August 1992.
26 The National Front, a nationalist party, was the only party that was opposed to French involvement in the war, see Rathbun (2004: Chapter 5).
27 'M. Mitterrand assure qu' "une campagne proprement militaire constituerait une épreuve redoutable"', *Le Monde*, 14 August 1992.
28 'CAMPS SERBES EN BOSNIE: "Il faut que la conscience universelle se révolte" déclare M. Bérégovoy', *Le Monde*, 8 August 1992.
29 'M. Fabius demande que 'l'Europe intervienne pour arrêter les massacres', *Le Monde*, 13 August 1992.
30 'M. Millon (UDF) juge que "insuffisante" la solution proposée', *Le Monde*, 12 August 1992.
31 'Il faut organiser des "opérations aériennes ponctuelles" déclare au "Monde" M. Jacques Chirac', *Le Monde*, 12 August 1992.
32 Quoted in Morjé Howard and Morjé Howard (2003: 310–311) (in the appendix section of their chapter). Additionally, in December 1992, 67 per cent felt that 'France should participate in a military operation in ex-Yugoslavia "because it is intolerable to allow such a civil war to go on in Europe without reacting"', quoted in La Balme (2001: 191).

*Rapprochement with NATO* 107

33 As part of the evidence of the public attention at that time, Marc Morjé Howard and Lise Morjé Howard (2003: 121) provide observable data on how often stories related to this crisis were 'broadcast on the evening news (8 p.m.) on the two major French TV channels, TFI and Antenne 2, from 1990 to 1996'. Their research also confirms, as Figure 3.1 in Chapter 3 has explored, high public attention to the war, while accordingly generating pressure for the government to deal with it properly.
34 Quoted in Morjé Howard and Morjé Howard (2003: 119).
35 'Capitulation de la Communauté Internationale: L'affligeante démolition de la Bosnie multiethnique', *Le Monde Diplomatique*, October 1993.
36 'Le conflit dans l'ex-Yougoslavie Après l'abandon du plan Vance-Owen sous la pression serbe et croate Avis de décès', *Le Monde*, 19 June 1993. Also see 'L'impuissance des Occidentaux à mettre fin au conflit. Les divergences sur la Bosnie s'aggravent entre Américains et Européens', *Le Monde*, 13 May 1993; 'Dix-huit mois de guerre en Bosnie', *Le Monde*, 4 September 1993.
37 'Après l'abandon du plan Vance-Owen sous la pression serbe et croate la partition envisagée de la Bosnie consacre l'échec de la diplomatie occidentale la haine et le feu', *Le Monde*, 19 June 1993.
38 'Capitulation de la Communauté Internationale: L'affligeante démolition de la Bosnie multiethnique', *Le Monde Diplomatique*, October 1993.
39 Some apostrophes removed from the original sentence.
40 Quoted in La Balme (2001: 193).
41 N.B. France had retained its position on the North Atlantic Council even during the Cold War.
42 'Conseil de l'Atlantique Nord – Intervention du ministre d'Etat, ministre des Affaires étrangères, M. Roland Dumas', *Bruxelles*, 17 Décembre 1992, in *La Politique Étrangère de la France*, November–December, 1992: 218–219.
43 Robert Fox, 'Bosnia Crisis: Defence Ministers to Discuss Mobile Reserve Force', *The Daily Telegraph*, 3 June 1995.
44 'La situation dans l'ex-Yougoslavie M. Léotard envisage l'éventualité d'un retrait des casques bleus au printemps', *Le Monde*, 21 December 1993. Also see Claire Trean, 'BOSNIE: La tentation du retrait BOSNIA', *Le Monde*, 11 May 1994.
45 Robert Fox, 'Bosnia Crisis: Defence Ministers to Discuss Mobile Reserve Force', *The Daily Telegraph*, 3 June 1995.
46 'Truppenabzug aus Bosnien wäre ein "weitere Niederlage"', *Frankfurter Allgemeine Zeitung*, 8 January 1994.
47 Quoted in Christopher Lockwood, 'War in Bosnia: Western Allies Forced to Think Again – Foreign Ministers Call for Co-Ordinated Effort on Diplomacy', *The Daily Telegraph*, 19 April 1994.
48 Quoted in Grant (1996: 76, fn. 25).
49 Quoted in Menon (2000a: 45), originally in *Reuters*, 27 May 1993.
50 Quoted in Menon (2000a: 46), originally in *Le Monde*, 13 May 1993.
51 Quoted in Grant (1995: 63), originally in Remarks delivered at a reception in honour of Parisian reserve officers, 8 February 1993.
52 'Sommet de l'OTAN – Interview du Président de la République à l'AFP, Paris, 9 Janvier 1994', in *La Politique Étrangère de la France*, January–February, 1994: 32.
53 Quoted in Menon (2000a: 45), originally from Mitterrand, interview with AFP, Paris, 9 January 1994.
54 Quoted in Lucarelli (2000: 184) (parentheses in the original), originally from *La Politique Étrangère de la France*, September–October, 1994: 34.
55 Claire Trean and Jean De Gueriviere, 'Emergence de l'Europe, ou désengagement des Etats-Unis? Washington paraît mieux disposé envers l'affirmation d'une "identité européenne de défense". Mais l'échec dans l'ex-Yougoslavie porte atteinte aux ambitions des Douze autant qu'à la crédibilité de l'Alliance atlantique', *Le Monde*, 9 January 1994.

56 'Truppenabzug aus Bosnien wäre ein "weitere Niederlage"', *Frankfurter Allgemeine Zeitung*, 8 January 1994.
57 Intervention du Ministre des Affaires Etrangères, M. Alain Juppé, à la 46<sup>e</sup> session de l'IHEDEN, 21 Janvier 1994, *La Politique Étrangère de la France*, January–February, 1994: 94.
58 'Discoures du Premier Ministre, M. Edouard Balladur devant l'IHEDN, Paris, 10 May 1994', *La Politique Étrangère de la France*, May–June, 1994: 73.
59 Ministerial Meeting of the North Atlantic Council/North Atlantic Cooperation Council, NATO Headquarters, Brussels, 10–11 January 1994, Paragraph 4. www.nato.int/docu/comm/49-95/c940111a.htm (Accessed on 1 July 2018).
60 Menon (2000a: 47), originally from *Le Monde*, 8 January 1994.
61 The author relied on the translation by Menon (2000a: 47), also see Bryant (2000: 27), Grant (1996: 62).
62 *Livre Blanc sur la Défense 1994*, Paris: Union générale d'éditions, 1994 : 57 and 56. The author relied on the translation by Gregory (2000: 105). In addition, from the public side, a French newspaper, *Le Monde*, identified NATO as 'the principal defence organisation' (quoted in Bryant 2000: 27).
63 This also illustrates why public opinion was divided in Questionnaire (C) in Table 5.1. On the lift and strike policy seen from the French angle, see Wood (1994: 141–146).
64 Boris Johnson, 'Bosnia: Nato Sleep-Walks into a Dark Future – With Its Credibility at Stake, the Alliance Faces the Toughest Test in Its 45-Year History', *The Daily Telegraph*, 11 February 1994. Adrian Treacher (2003: 75) saw this incident as one of the turning points for French attitudes in this war.
65 Michel Colomès, 'Bosnie: la première épreuve de Chirac', *Le Point*, no. 1185, 3 June 1995: 58–59.
66 Quoted in Bryant (2000: 26), originally from J. C. Casanova, 'Dissuasion concertée', *L'Express*, 28 September 1995: 26.
67 Pierrre Lellouche and François Heisbourg, 'Maastricht or Sarajevo?', *Le Monde*, 17 June 1993.
68 Union européenne – conseil affaires générales – Conférence de Presse du Ministre des Affaires Étrangères, M. Hervé de Charrette, *La Politique Étrangère de la France*, January–February, 1996: 113.
69 Quoted in De Wijk (1997: 124), on 17 January 1996 at a meeting of the ambassadors of the North Atlantic Council.
70 Visite aux États-Unis d'Amérique – Discours du Président de la République, M. Jacques Chirac, devant le Congres des États-Unis d'Amérique, Washington, 1<sup>er</sup> Février 1996, *La Politique Étrangère de la France*, January–February, 1996: 128.
71 AFSOUTH was reorganised as Allied Joint Force Command (JFC) Naples, see jfcnaples.nato.int/page6322744/brief-overview (Accessed on 1 July 2018).
72 For example, see Grant (1996: 65). The author intentionally relied on older expositions to reflect the understandings at that time. Today, as Jo G. Gade and Paal Sigurd Hilde (2014) explain, more various roles have been given to the IMS while addressing complex contemporary security problems (see www.nato.int/cps/en/natohq/topics_64557.htm?) (Accessed on 1 July 2018). Given its increasing roles, it is suggestive of why France made a full return to every NATO body, including the IMS, in April 2009. For example, see Allegra Stratton, 'Sarkozy military plan unveiled', *The Guardian*, 17 June 2008.
73 'Dans les opérations de maintien de la paix M. Léotard estime que les grands commandements de l'OTAN "ont un poids excessif"', *Le Monde*, 26 May 1994.
74 Quoted in Yost (1998: 216). The Strategic Concept was later published in 1999, revising the original 1991 version (see Chapter 3).

# 6 From intervention to prevention

Germany's debate on humanitarianism, pacifism and international responsibility

## Introduction

The end of the Cold War raised a question of whether the newly unified Germany would choose to set out on the path to becoming a military power. Neorealists (whose premise provided the theoretical grounds for the question) predicted that German decision makers would renew their policy stance substantially now that the disappearance of the Communist threat had swept away the constraints that had restricted their freedom of action. These scholars articulated that 'once the new Germany finds its feet, it will no more want to be constrained by the United States acting through NATO than by any other state' (Waltz 1993: 76); 'Security considerations will cause Japan and Germany to emulate the United States and acquire the full spectrum of great power capabilities, including nuclear weapons' (Layne 1993: 37); and 'Without the specific threat [meaning the Soviet threat], ... Germany is likely to reject the continued maintenance of NATO' (Mearsheimer 1990: 6, fn. 1).

However, in contrast to this neorealist prediction, Germany has shown a strikingly unchanged attitude, which has led a number of scholars to turn to cultural/normative perspectives, grounded on constructivism. For example, focussing on a self-restrained attitude towards the use of force (anti-militarism) and a strong attachment to international institutions (multilateralism), John Duffield (1999: 767) argued that 'German state behavior has been marked by a high degree of moderation and continuity with its record in the postwar era'. That is to say, their domestic political context, nurtured in the post-1945 background, has more validity to explain its policy than the power-based neorealist perspective. In fact, Bonn immediately unveiled its conformity to NATO soon after the end of the Cold War and repeatedly indicated little aspiration to be a great power (Berger 1998: 168–170; Katzenstein 1996a: 10). Resonating with this assertion, Hanns Maul (1995/96, 2000; also Harnisch and Maull 2001a) proffered an analytical perspective known as 'civilian power', contending that the unified Germany would continue to cherish the 'culture of reticence' (Kultur der Zurückhaltung) by distancing itself from military engagements.

After the debate between neorealism and constructivism, a new argument has gradually appeared. As Germany was involved in foreign military engagements throughout the 1990s, some scholars lay more emphasis on the 'changes' in its diplomacy and claim that it has become a 'normal state', having dropped its constitutional constraints in foreign policymaking. Starting from the critiques against the so-called 'check book diplomacy' in the Gulf war, namely making a financial contribution but refusing to send troops, Germany has been pressed to increase its military contribution in response to global problems. As this chapter will show, the war in Bosnia became a trigger for Germany's new security policy, in which it officially opened a way for the Federal army's (Bundeswehr) activity in NATO out-of-area. Not only did Germany participate in the monitoring mission of the no-fly zone, but it also supplied 4,000 troops to the international peacekeeping operation under the Implementation Force (IFOR) after the ceasefire. Considering the actual instances of foreign activities in the post-Cold War period, Brian Rathbun (2004: 83) remarks that the explanation treating Germany as having a single dominant political culture of pacifism 'dramatically understates the intensity of the conflict [over German foreign policy] and the extent of Germany's transformation'.

It should be noted that the arguments of this branch, which can be categorised as the 'normalisation' strand,[1] do not necessarily concur on the neorealist understandings, as it is stated that 'Any new assertiveness in Germany should not be seen as inherently threatening but simply ... the adoption by Germany of criteria for foreign policy more similar to those in most other countries' (Gordon 1994: 233). These researchers contend that it is merely becoming a normal state, which can dispatch its troops abroad with no major restriction, as others do.[2]

Thus, two different kinds of views have been provided about German diplomacy in the post-Cold War era. One group stresses the 'continuity' of a cultural hesitation over the use of force from a constructivist angle, while the other revolves around 'changes' to indicate increasing international military engagements from a normalisation branch. For instance, Thomas Berger (2002: 192) maintained how German policy has been strongly coloured by its 'taboos' over military action, whereas others viewed that 'many German leaders now argue that their country should no longer be unnaturally burdened by its history and that it should ... assume a more appropriate range of international responsibilities' (Lefebvre and Lombardi 1996: 564). To be sure, political culture that has been cultivated for nearly a half-century is unlikely to dissipate so swiftly. As will be discussed, Germany's inclination towards anti-militarism can be easily observed in its reaction to the war in Bosnia. On the other hand, it is also true that significant changes in German military activity occurred during the 1990s, *inter alia*, through Bosnia. Here, a question arises as to how to illustrate the situations, in which continuity and changes have been simultaneously discussed.

This chapter considers it through an examination of Germany's involvement in the war in the Balkans, which is said to have been the 'most important theatre for this gradual re-calibration of its security policy' (Hyde-Price 2000: 145, also see Lantis 2002: 79). As with the cases of Britain and France, the outbreak of military clashes attracted huge attention in Germany to urge immediate action to this humanitarian tragedy. When concrete measures were demanded, however, the Helmut Kohl government found itself caught by difficulties. Domestically, its constitution, as well as its anti-military public sentiment, did not allow it to implement foreign military activities. Internationally, nevertheless, Germany was put under pressure to work with its Allies in this military operation – to decline would crucially harm its credibility as a reliable partner. Consequently, the political leaders in Bonn were required to fulfil incompatible social claims at the same time: 'do not ignore humanitarian catastrophe' (humanitarianism), 'do not engage in combat activity' (anti-militarism) and 'do not turn their back on international cooperation' (multilateralism). In other words, a 'trilemma' – not a mere 'dilemma' – of norms struck its decision makers during the war in Bosnia.

This chapter holds that such political conditions led the German government to seek for NATO's reorganisation based upon humanitarian crisis 'prevention'. Because it was demanded that Germany not only change its foreign policy but also adhere to its pacifist principles at the same time, it shifted towards the creation of preventive mechanisms in international politics so that contingencies would be addressed before military intervention became unavoidable. For this reason, its policymakers supported the reorganisation of NATO for security governance in its out-of-area. Thus, beyond the debate of 'change' or 'continuity', there was an argument of how they tried to make compatible conflicting social expectations.

This chapter is structured into five sections. The first section presents an overview of the general characteristics of German foreign policy moulded in the post-war contexts. The second section examines its initial reaction to the war in Bosnia by revealing how normative considerations influenced its decision making. The third section investigates the clash of different normative claims between 'never again Auschwitz' (action to the Bosnian crisis), 'never again war' (non-use of forces) and 'never again alone' (cooperation with its Allies).[3] The fourth section explores how this norm trilemma affected the German policymakers and how they envisioned NATO's new role through the experience in Bosnia. The conclusion summarises the lead up to the reorganisation of NATO and contemplates some theoretical implications on change and continuity of Germany diplomacy after the end of the Cold War.

## The distinctiveness of Germany's foreign policy: reticence and restrictions

### *Foreign policy as a historical product*

One of the most often referred to traits of German foreign policy in the existing literature is the norm of 'anti-militarism' (or pacifism), a strong aversion to the use of armed forces, which had been cultivated during the Cold War. It is argued that the 'lessons from its troubled past', i.e. its conduct during the Second World War, were the critical juncture that gave rise to a strong distaste to engage in issues of a military nature (Berger 1998: 6–7). This notion is accounted for by

## 112  *From intervention to prevention*

Harold Müller (1992: 162) as 'an open refusal to consider military means as a legitimate instrument of foreign policy' and by John Duffield (1999: 780) as the tendency to consider 'peace an absolute value'. Jeffrey Lantis (1996: 19) sees it as the 'Restrictions on a more assertive military posture' to be 'deeply rooted in the public psyche in foreign policy', while Maja Zehfuss (2002: 25) states that 'The non-violence and peacefulness' had 'become a matter of conviction'. Through the practice of these policies over the course of the Cold War period, anti-militarism has acquired strong roots in German society.[4]

Another significant attribute to delineate German foreign policy is the norm of 'multilateralism', a sense of belonging to international organisations. The origin of multilateralism also traces back to the post-war days. The political elites in Bonn at that time intended to anchor Germany within multinational frameworks, such as the European Community (EC) and NATO, in order to live up to its partners' expectations on appropriate behaviour, as well as to thereby establish an equal sovereign status between Germany and its neighbours. Duffield (1999: 781, emphasis original) explains the concept of multilateralism by stating that 'a leading imperative has been to avoid acting alone (*Alleingänge*) or pursuing a special path (*Sonderweg*)' that leads back to the Nazi period. That is to say, to cast away its past image, German decisions should be made through cooperation with its neighbours and through international/multilateral frameworks so that Germany could retain its international reputation as a reliable partner. As with the case of anti-militarism, multilateralism also 'diffused throughout Germany and became embedded in the very definition of German state interests and strategies' (Anderson 1997: 85). Similarly, 'German political elites developed a robust attachment to the institutions of integration, incorporating a strong European identity in their diplomacy' (Bulmer 1997: 49).

These characteristics of German political culture are together called the 'civilian power'. According to Hanns Maull (2000: 56), it is defined as 'a particular foreign-policy identity which promoted multilateralism, institution-building and supranational integration, and tried to constrain the use of force in international relations through national and international norms'. He and his Trier-based collaborators have scrutinised various issues of Germany's involvements in foreign military incidents, particularly in Bosnian and Kosovo, and concluded that more than a decade after the end of the Cold War, 'Most policy changes identified in Germany's foreign policy ... can still be interpreted through the Civilian Power role concept' (Harnisch and Maull 2001c: 146).[5]

An important facet that civilian power proponents stress is Germany's strong attachment to international law and human rights protection. Civilian power researchers contend that not only stipulating its own diplomacy, it has tried to constrain the use of force and to facilitate the promotion of legal obligations, human rights and democratisation through the development of international institutions, which can be expressed as an effort of 'civilising international relations' (Harnisch and Maull 2001b: 3). Hence, humanitarianism, an awareness of human rights protection and observance of international laws relating to it, can also be said as constituting vital components of German foreign policy.

Founded upon these existing accounts, this chapter contemplates how Germany would respond to foreign humanitarian disasters. It is conceivable that voices for action may be raised based upon the humanitarianism when people are exposed to critical human rights conditions. Nevertheless, if military measures are to be required over the course of action, the government will be criticised for running counter to the anti-militarism. Instead, if it chooses inaction due to the aversion to the use of force even though Germany is requested to join international military operations, it will be, in turn, denounced as falling short of multilateralism. In short, it will be put in a 'trilemma' of these three different social norms over appropriateness of German diplomacy. It was the war in Bosnia that actually confronted German decision makers with this problem.

## The Bundeswehr's 'out-of-area' debate before Bosnia

In addition to normative requirements, German military action had been strictly restrained by its constitution. Prior to the end of the Cold War, the widely shared understanding of its constitution (Basic Law, called 'Grundgesetz') was that its military activity was limited to use only for national and collective defence. Article 24 (2) of the constitution provides the juridical ground for Germany's affiliation to NATO, stating that 'the Federation may enter a system of mutual collective security'. Article 87a (1), on the other hand, prescribes that 'the Federation shall build up Armed Forces for defence purposes'.[6] Taking these two clauses into consideration, it had been thought that activity of Bundeswehr operations was confined to its own territorial defence and collective defence of its partners in NATO.

Chancellor Helmut Kohl had confirmed this understanding in February 1984, when NATO's possible operation in the Persian Gulf during the Iran-Iraq War was discussed. He pronounced: 'it is a clear policy of the Federal Republic of Germany, and of my government too, that we send no German soldiers outside of NATO territory' (Inacker 1991: 31, also see Philippi 1997: 61–67). Zehfuss (2002: 32) also states that 'the use of military means outside of NATO territory had not been considered a legitimate component of the FRG's [Federal Republic of Germany] foreign policy before the end of the Cold War'. It had been broadly concurred that the Bundeswehr could be utilised only within the boundary of NATO member states and only for defensive purposes.

The end of the Cold War, however, gradually demanded a more active role of Germany. Two months before its official reunification, the Iraqi invasion of Kuwait in August 1990 beset the Bonn government with this problem. Receiving an enquiry from the United States about the possibility to send its ground troops, the Christian Democratic Union (Christlich Demokratische Union Deutschlands, CDU)/Christian Social Union (Christlich-Soziale Union in Bayern, CSU) and Free Democratic Party (Freie Demokratische Partei, FDP) coalition government declined for constitutional reasons. Instead, the government dispatched five minesweepers to a Western European Union (WEU) naval force located in the Persian Gulf in August 1990 and, immediately before the start of the war, 18 Bundeswehr Alpha jets to Turkey in accordance with Ankara's request under the auspices of NATO's Allied Mobile Force (Longhurst 2004: 57). Furthermore, Bonn provided enormous economic aid to those states affected by Iraqi military action, which amounted to $11.5 billion, about one-sixth of the total cost of the operation (Lantis 1996: 23). Nevertheless, Germany's negative attitude to military engagements wiped out its financial contribution and resulted in reprimands that it amounted to mere 'checkbook diplomacy' (Lantis 1996: 21, also see Leithner 2009: 15), an experience which left no small impact on the government leaders.

With the changes in the international surroundings from the Cold War to the post-Cold War, the expectations on Germany also shifted from staying silent to actively committing to security affairs. Symbolically, it was contended from outside of Germany that 'today it is more relevant to … raise Germany up' than what was once expressed as 'to keep Germany down'.[7] Against this background, Germany's policy on the Balkans was to be discussed.

## Germany's initial response to the Balkans

### *Unilateral recognition of Slovenia and Croatia: public outcry for action*

Germany's reaction to the war in the Balkans started with its unilateral recognition of the newly independent Slovenia and Croatia. This has attracted academic interest in why the reunified Germany suddenly pushed for this policy despite other countries' objections. Analysing this point will make clear how this crisis was perceived in German society.

With the outbreak of the conflicts in Slovenia and Croatia in late June 1991, the EC officially proclaimed that the unity of Yugoslavia should be maintained and any recognition would radicalise the conflict between these new independence-declaring republics and Yugoslavia.[8] Initially, the Bonn government shared this idea as Foreign Minister, Hans-Dietrich Genscher, 'called for the suspension of their independence declaration to create a breathing space for negotiations'.[9] After the continued unsuccessful mediations of the EC, however, a change in Germany's attitude gradually appeared; its political elites moved towards recognition.

From then on, the government vigorously urged its partner states to extend recognition by utilising every opportunity, such as EC meetings. As a result of Germany's advocacy, the EC's legal expertise-body, the Badinter Arbitration Commission (led by a French lawyer, Robert Badinter), was organised to discuss this problem and eventually announced, on 16 December 1991, that the EC would make a final decision about this issue on 15 January 1992, by assessing the fulfilment of conditions such as protection of ethnic minority and human rights. Nevertheless, almost one week later on 23 December, Chancellor Kohl declared that his government would recognise Slovenia and Croatia on 15 January and establish diplomatic relations with them.

The decision was welcomed in German society, as Kohl announced 'a big success for us and German politics'.[10] A German newspaper, *Die Zeit*, described it as 'a Christmas gift' to be presented 'at the right time'.[11] Contrary to this, however, it sparked severe recriminations on the international front for making the dissolution of Yugoslavia a *fait accompli* and igniting secessionism and concomitant friction among the ethnic groups in Bosnia, where military clashes had already sporadically broken out. The French government was particularly furious. In promoting a common European diplomatic initiative laid down in the Maastricht Treaty concluded at the beginning of the same month, President Mitterrand expressed his extreme anger about Bonn breaking step with European policy and condemned the decision as a 'major error'.[12] Furthermore, American Secretary of State Warren Christopher accused Germany of bearing 'particular responsibility' for the escalation of the war.[13]

As a result of receiving such harsh international feedback, this experience became a 'trauma' (Axt 1993: 354) or 'a new lesson' (Müller 1994: 126) of German policy towards the Balkans. Why did Germany unexpectedly opt for this unilateral decision? Today, there is a broad consensus that it was because the government had been severely pressured by its domestic society to do something against the crisis (Axt 1993: 353–54; Calic 1996:59; Gordon 1995: 54–57; Jakobsen 1995: 402–404; Libal 1997; Lucarelli 2000: 134–137; Maull 1995/96: 118–119; van Heuven 1993: 60–61). These researchers unanimously deny alternative explanations, such as the unified Germany's ambition to expand its influence over the Balkans, economic ties with Slovenia and Croatia, religious sympathy to Catholic Croats and the fear of influx of refugees, but instead claim that public outcry to stop the violence played a central role in guiding its unilateral action. Three points are noteworthy here.

First, in Germany, self-determination, which the Germans had enjoyed less than a year before, was regarded as an essential human right. The repeated aggression by Belgrade was considered to give Slovenia and Croatia ample reasons to declare independence (Libal 1997: 8; Smith 1996: 55). Second, as former diplomat Michael Libal's (1997: 40) day-to-day analysis indicates, 'threat of recognition' was employed 'to draw concessions from Yugoslavia'. That is to say, because international recognition would make the breakup of the federation inevitable, it was expected to deter further offensives by Belgrade and encourage it to begin peace talks with these two republics. As a means to stop the violence, recognition was pushed for within the society. Third, even if the second approach failed, Germany anticipated that once the problem became 'internationalised' from an internal conflict within the former Yugoslavia, it would open a way for the United Nations to interpose itself and, under its surveillance, violence would be ended by the international pressure on Belgrade to respect the territorial integrity of these newly independent states (Calic 1996: 66; Gordon 1995: 56; Lucarelli 2000: 141; Philippi 2001: 54–55), contrary to the EC's fear that recognition would instigate ethnic separatism.[14] Therefore, Libal (1997: 161) stated that 'The more Belgrade espoused a solution by force, the more necessary it became to internationalize the conflict'.

116  *From intervention to prevention*

Opinion polls in Germany reveal constantly high support for Slovenia and Croatia's independence (77–78 per cent on average from August–September through December 1991).[15] It is said that Chancellor Kohl was confronted by the thrust from the bottom-up. In a conversation with French President Mitterrand, who warned about the mistake of rapid recognition, he replied: 'without doubt, but the pressure at home is very strong ... my party, my political allies, the Church, the press, not counting 500,000 Croats who live in Germany, everyone is pushing' (Védrine 1996: 615–616).[16] Taking all of these explanations into account, domestic outcry uncovers why the German government abruptly steered towards unilateral recognition.

For the study of this book, this recognition episode proffers an important implication that the violence in the former Yugoslavia did not only catch public attention but also generated pressure for action on the government. Recalling the discussions at that time, Libal (1997: 105) made clear that 'the critical motives for German behaviour ... were rooted in a pervasive pattern of moral and political values', namely 'the ideal of self-determination' and 'the rejection of violence as a means of politics'. This suggests how the war in the Balkans was viewed within Germany.

### *'Big voices, small actions':*[17] *domestic discussion on how to address the war in Bosnia*

As its recognition of Slovenia and Croatia tells, Germany's decision making had been circumscribed by the normative attention to this tragedy. As an indicator of this point, when asked to identify the most urgent tasks facing the government in late 1992, 85 per cent of Germans listed ending the war in the former Yugoslavia, next to a domestic issue of the containment of right-wing extremism (88 per cent) (Asmus 1993: 4). This high figure helps to understand how this 'foreign' news was assessed in German domestic society.

Public debate reveals that immediate action was strongly demanded, especially when the conflict in Bosnia intensified around June 1992. For example, it was argued that '"this meaningless murder" in the collapsing Yugoslavia should never be allowed to happen in Europe today',[18] while it was also stated that the [international] negotiator capitulates',[19] and that 'the entire Bosnia is hellish'.[20]

Within the circle of the decision makers in Bonn, such a sense of emergency was shared beyond the party differences. From the governing parties, the CDU/CSU and the FDP, Prime Minister Kohl said that 'Especially for those in Germany, who still have personal memory of horrors of the war, [images of the horrors and terrors on television] are particularly stirring'.[21] Meanwhile, during the war, Christian Schwarz-Schilling (CDU) stated that 'I have my own experience in the Nazi days. ... something like this should never be allowed to happen again in Europe'.[22] FDP Foreign Minister Klaus Kinkel expressed 'the appalling results in the former Yugoslavia' as 'a challenge to the international community',[23] while Ulrich Irmer (FDP) remarked that '[it] is fought a few hundred kilometres away from us. ... There occurs a bleeding conflict'.[24] From the opposition parties too, government action was urged. For example, the Social Democratic Party (Sozialdemokratische Partei Deutschlands, SPD) submitted a proposition pressing the government to take speedy action against 'the human rights abuse in Serbia and Croatia',[25] while arguing that 'Europe cannot stay inactive',[26] and that it should 'let Bosnian refugees in',[27] instead of showing concern over their influx. From the Green Party too, Gerd Poppe pronounced that 'now the refugees from Bosnia, the victims of politics, must be saved',[28] while Wolfgang Ullmann held that 'This is a war – not an inner-Yugoslav civil war, but this is a war in Europe'.[29] Additionally, Hans Modrow, the last communist premier of East Germany and then a member of the successor of the former East German party, the Party of Democratic Socialism (Partei des Demokratischen Sozialismus, PDS), stated that the war in the former Yugoslavia threatened 'European détente [after the collapse of the Cold War] and peaceful coexistence of states to be a focus of tension'.[30]

As it was said, 'clear words, but action too?';[31] however, when it comes to how this conflict should be approached, there was a divide in the German society, reflected in the citation in this section's title. There was little appetite for concrete measures, which might include military options. The reason for the reluctance towards military involvement can be categorised into three claims. The first of these is the constitutional restriction, as the previous section discussed. In fact, the SPD had already made clear its opposition to Bundeswehr's dispatch because military activity beyond NATO territory was illegal.[32]

The second claim is, as also mentioned, the taboo over military activity, rooted in its anti-militarism. Opinion polls at that time evidently affirm this point. For instance, in August 1992, while 50 per cent of respondents in the former West German areas (40 per cent in the former East German areas) favoured participation as part of a UN peacekeeping operation, only 12 per cent in the former West German areas (8 per cent in the former East German areas) agreed on the Bundeswehr's participations in a combat operation.[33] The comparison with Britain and France, for example, clarifies Germany's hesitation about military involvement – around the same time, 61 per cent of the British supported a dispatch of intervention force, while, in December 1992, 67 per cent of the French felt that France should take part in a military operation in the former Yugoslavia.[34]

This does not mean that the Germans simply wanted to evade their involvement. Instead, they opted for peaceful negotiations through international organisations, Because military action could possibly escalate the war (see the next section). Karin Johnston (2003: 261) says that this view was the product of the merger of anti-militarism and multilateralism; reliance on non-military methods and trust in the authority of international organisations. For instance, two-thirds of the former West Germans (four-fifths of the former East Germans) were in favour of the view that 'nearly all disputes between countries could be solved by negotiations' (Holst 2001: 256; Johnston 2003: 260). Additionally, because mediation efforts were still going on at that time through 'multilateral' organisations such as the United Nations and the EC/EU, peaceful resolution was preferred also against this background.

The third element is a history-contingent issue that no troops can be sent to where the Wehrmacht (the Third Reich's army) tramped. In addition to the legal and normative constraints, Maull (1995/96: 112) argues that 'there was widespread consensus among the political élite that history ruled out any participation of German soldiers in peacekeeping or military operations in former Yugoslavia'. Fearing the rise of historical controversies and antipathy against Germany, Chancellor Kohl had already announced, before the intensification of the war, that no troops would be dispatched in these areas, which was later formulated as the so-called 'Kohl doctrine' (Maull 1995/96: 112; McKenzie 1996: 11; Zehfuss 2002: 31).

The difficulty that the Bonn government faced boils down to this: it was largely contended to halt the catastrophic situations in the Balkans immediately, on which policymakers also concurred. It was, however, another question whether or not the use of military forces should be allowed for this purpose – moreover, strong objection had already been shown within the public space. Furthermore, regardless of its domestic discussion, Germany was internationally anticipated 'to play a larger international and political role than in the past' with its 'size, wealth, and geopolitical position' (Gordon 1994: 230). The next section discusses how international and domestic demands caused a 'trilemma' within its society, which appeared as a result of conflicts between the general-level and practical-level debates.

## Domestic constraints and international responsibility: opening a way for German foreign military activity

### *The opposition's view: fear of escalation by the use of force – the SPD and the Greens*

As the war continued with no sign of abating, 'the call for a military intervention in the Balkan conflict becomes bigger' on the international stage,[35] and accordingly Germany's own participation was gradually debated. The opposition parties took fundamental issue with the ruling parties' movement for German engagement in foreign military operations.[36] The SPD and the Green Party claimed that the dispatch of the Bundeswehr required an amendment under the current constitutional conditions and clarified that, even if they were to concur on it, its activity was allowed only for 'peacekeeping' under the UN credentials and thus any further action was prohibited.[37] SPD members had already articulated this point at the party conference in November 1992, rejecting the idea of Bundeswehr participation in UN peace 'enforcement' (Philippi 1997: 120, also see Rathbun 2004: 97).

The objection of these opposition parties emanated from the concern over escalation of the war by a wrong method. The SPD faction leader, Hans-Ulrich Klose, said that 'military intervention is always problematic ... there lies a danger of escalation',[38] while Heidemarie Wieczorek-Zeul (SPD) remarked that 'The situation in the former Yugoslavia cannot be changed or improved through war, but rather only through diplomacy',[39] and demanded that 'no military intervention' should be put into practice 'to avert further mass murders' in Bosnia.[40] Karsten Voigt (SPD) also claimed that 'for us as Social Democrats, what is prioritised is non-military alternatives to military mobilisation',[41] while Günter Verheugen (SPD) pronounced that 'we [should] always look for a means and a way to solve conflicts and difficulties in a peaceful manner without the use of force'.[42] From the Greens too, Christa Nickels argued that 'history teaches us that the attempt to protect peace with a violent means is controlled by it and that streams of blood are shed'.[43]

What they articulated was that it should be dealt with through the United Nations, which they thought 'must have its own legitimacy'.[44] Peter Glotz (SPD) contended that instead of pushing for NATO's threat of aerial bombardment, 'bring it to the Security Council of the United Nations and also sort it out there. That should be our goal',[45] while Vera Wollenberger (the Greens) stated that 'the Greens support a comprehensive reinforcement of the United Nations'; this is the role of 'UN troops', 'no further political role' in NATO.[46]

The SPD and the Greens' conviction that '"peace enforcement" means "war-engagement"'[47] made them stand firm against the Kohl government. This surely made its political manoeuvring difficult. Because constitutional amendment requires the approval of two-thirds of both the upper and lower houses of parliament, a compromise with the SPD, the largest opposition party, was indispensable.[48] Nevertheless, it would not agree on it and, at best, it would support only Bundeswehr's peacekeeping operations under the United Nations. Therefore, it was hard for the government to meet what was demanded by its European partners at that time, such as monitoring of the non-fly zone in Bosnia, with authority granted to use force if necessary. As a result, it was placed in a quandary between international expectations and domestic restraints.

### *The governing parties' view: international responsibility – the CDU/CSU and the FDP*

Another serious problem that struck the governmental leaders was the concern over Germany's international responsibility, which would be significantly damaged by declining NATO's request for military contribution. As a general tendency grounded in multilateralism, Germany had tried to conform to international expectations as Duffield holds (1999: 782, emphasis original) that 'German leaders have attached [tremendous importance] to *Berechenbarkeit*, or calculability, in foreign policy. They have been anxious for their country to be perceived as a reliable, predictable, dependable partner, a concern they frequently and openly articulate'. In other words, 'never again alone', namely not to leave international cooperation as the Third Reich did, was also daunting as the German involvement deepened, besides the claims of 'never again Auschwitz' (response to humanitarian disasters) and 'never again war' (no military measures) (cf. Harnisch 2001: 52). In this sense, international responsibility was not a mere pressure from the outside but rather a matter of whether Germany could suitably meet its ideal of diplomacy.

Chancellor Kohl warned that 'Germany's isolation in the world would have been catastrophic. It is bad enough as it is. The world does not understand what is being discussed here [in Germany]'.[49] Moreover, its isolation could affect European common action as Chairman of the CDU/CSU faction, Wolfgang Schäuble, stated that German non-participation 'would, above all, ruin a crucial option for a common European Handlungsfähigkeit [capability to act] and thereby circumvent Germany's Bündnisfähigkeit [capability to work with its Allies]'.[50] Germany's credibility was at stake over being questioned whether it could remain as a reliable partner.

It is true that there were some conservative politicians who tried to use this argument as an opportunity to make Germany capable of engaging in various military activities as a 'normal state' (Lucarelli 2000: 209; Rathbun 2004: 90–92). For instance, this sort of preference can be found in the statements, particularly made by Bavarian CSU politicians (the party being more conservative than its sister party, the CDU), such as Theodor Waigel (its party leader and Finance Minister) and Michael Glos.[51] Given such voices, nevertheless, because drastic reform would spark fierce backlash, not only from the opposition parties but also from the public, the Kohl government adopted a strategy called 'salami tactic' to gradually expand 'the functions of the Bundeswehr "slice by slice"' (Philippi 2001: 53).

At first, the cabinet meeting of 16 July 1992 decided that a destroyer and three reconnaissance planes would join the NATO and WEU operation in the Adriatic Sea, a marine patrol delegated by the UN Security Council Resolutions 713 and 757 to monitor economic sanctions against the former Yugoslavia. Continuously, when this mission was expanded and the NATO Airborne Warning and Control System (AWACS) was incorporated into it by UN Security Council Resolutions 815 and 816 in 1993, which authorised the use of force against the breach of the non-fly zone over Bosnia, the Bonn government agreed that those German soldiers already deployed in the earlier operation would remain, although its mission had changed to carry a more military-coloured mandate. In addition, Germany began to participate in UN peacekeeping activity in Africa. The Kohl government, on 21 April 1993, dispatched a battalion of 1,600, including engineers, medical personnel, telecommunication specialists and German forces to the second UN Operation in Somalia (UNOSOM II) (cf. Lantis 1996: 24, 2002: 64–66).[52]

The opposition parties quickly responded to bring three lawsuits against each decision to the Federal Constitutional Court (Verfassungsgericht) in Karlsruhe:

1 The dispatch of troops to the Adriatic Sea by the opposition party, the SPD (on 7 August 1992);
2 The participation of German soldiers in the AWACS operation by the SPD and the FDP (on 2 April 1993); and
3 The deployment of troops in Somalia by the SPD (on 15 June 1993).

Particularly, the second trial was highly controversial. Because NATO was permitted to resort to force in this operation, if it was actually used, German troops participating in it would be inevitably involved in a non-defensive way, which would result in violating Article 87a (1) of the German constitution (the defensive rationale for the Bundeswehr). Therefore, not only the SPD but also the FDP, due to a discord with its senior coalition partner, jointly sued the government.

The FDP members concurred on the participation of the Bundeswehr in the UN peacekeeping operations on the condition of a constitutional amendment; but concerning further military involvement, its members' opinions were divided. Some held a similar view to the CDU/CSU, while others were closer to that of the opposition parties. For instance, Irmer (FDP) stated that German soldiers' participation in NATO AWACS operation had 'clear constitutionally right grounds';[53] soon after this statement, Burkhard Hirsch (FDP, one of the vice Presidents of the Bundestag) denied his colleague's view and articulated that 'I hold the participation of the Bundeswehr in military mobilisations, except for the case of defence, as a violation of the constitution. ... no German government could refer to the constitution when sending our sons to another war'.[54] The seriousness of the dissidence even brought up the possibility of dissolution of the coalition within the FDP.[55]

After all, this debate on the Bundeswehr's foreign activity was put in the hands of the legal body, which President Richard von Weizsäcker criticised as an evasion of political responsibility.[56] First, concerning the German participation in the AWACS operation, the Constitutional Court issued a provisional disposition order on 8 April 1993, which dismissed the lawsuit by judging that Germany's engagements in these operations were limited to non-military support and, more importantly, the withdrawal of its troops would compromise its reliability as a partner in the Atlantic Alliance and the United Nations (Müller 1994: 130; Spohr 2004: 83). Subsequently, on 12 July 1994, the Court delivered a final verdict. It ruled that the use of the Bundeswehr outside the territory of NATO did not violate the constitution as long as it was under international collective defence/security organisations (such as NATO, the WEU and the United Nations), because Article 24 (2) (affiliation to international collective security organisation) had already permitted Germany to act within those frameworks (Lantis 2002: 109; Longhurst 2004: 64). On 15 July, based on this verdict's requirement to gain an approval of an absolute majority from the parliament before dispatching German troops, the Bundestag approved these already-started participations in the Adriatic Sea and Somalia. Germany's military engagements (including after this verdict) in the former Yugoslav War are shown in Table 6.1.

As the Constitutional Court's political consideration of damage to Germany's credibility in case of withdrawal indicates, the fear of a dangerous/pacifist 'Sonderweg' – taking another path that would isolate it from international cooperation – played an important role in directing the government's decision (Longhurst 2004: 67; Müller 1994: 130). Since one-third of AWACS personnel in the Adriatic Sea were from the Bundeswehr, a 'no' would have inevitably caused a major malfunction of this international undertaking (Longhurst 2004: 60). NATO Supreme Allied Commander Europe (SACEUR) General John Shalikashivili stated that in the case of the German crew's withdrawal from NATO

122  *From intervention to prevention*

*Table 6.1* Germany's foreign military engagements from 1992 to 1995

| Case | Contents |
|---|---|
| WEU enforcement of embargo (16 July 1992) | Deployment of navy and aircrafts for monitoring mission in the Adriatic Sea, based on UN Security Council Resolutions 713 (arms embargo) and 757 (economic sanction). |
| NATO AWACS mission in the Adriatic Sea (2 April 1993) | UN Security Council expanded the previous enforcement of embargo and included the reconnaissance mission over the non-fly zone in Bosnia (UN Security Council Resolution 781, 9 October 1992) and the use of force for sanctions (UN Security Council Resolutions 815 and 816, 30 and 31 March 1993). The Bonn government agreed on German soldiers' participation on 2 April 1993, followed by the SPD and the FDP appeal for suspension. |
| The Somali Crisis (21 April 1993) | Send troops and logistical support. |
| The Constitutional Court's Judgement (12 July 1994) | The use of the Bundeswehr outside NATO territories was admitted as legal. |
| The establishment of Rapid Reaction Force, led by Britain and France (30 June 1995) | The dispatch of German Tornado aircraft with pilots and crews (1,500). |
| IFOR: NATO-led peacekeeping operation, after the Dayton Peace Accord (December 1995) | The dispatch of 4,000 German Troops to Croatia and aircraft with pilots and crews (Germany's contribution consisted of logistical, medical and engineering units). |

Source: Summarised from Lantis (2002: 170–171), Yost (1998: 214).

aircraft in the Adriatic Sea, its operation would become 'extremely difficult to handle'.[57] Germany's participation had already become an indispensable part of international activity before the range and engagement of the German army was recalibrated.

Germany's 'international responsibility' had become a major concern among its decision makers. For instance, Defence Minister Volker Rühe claimed:

> Whoever governs in Germany in the next coming years, will be confronted by this situation, in which what matters is, for example, German aircraft will also be sent ... under the roof and in the mission of the United Nations to carry such action out. ... If you principally exclude [these missions], then you will block the possibilities of peace building of NATO and the WEU in the mission of the United Nations. ... This is the question that Social Democrats have to ask themselves and give satisfactory answers.[58]

In addition, Foreign Minister Kinkel also reprimanded the opposition by challenging them: 'to make clear your responsibility so that Germany can stay as a credible ally!'.[59]

Certainly, the ongoing war in Bosnia as such was also an indispensable factor in changing German foreign policy. The stalemate of the international mediation efforts had been repeatedly criticised. It was actually argued that the 'peace plan of the UN-EC mediators Cyrus Vance and David Owen is a scrap paper for the Serbs',[60] and that 'the Alliance demonstrates its incapability to control and the loss of its dignity',[61] while the international efforts were branded as 'the failure of the West'.[62] In the face of the critiques, Foreign Minister Kinkel remarked that 'What matters is ... the success of a European common foreign and security policy and the credibility and reputation of Germany in the world',[63] which suggests that the problem had become not only to end the war in Bosnia.

Through the war in Bosnia, Germany embarked upon a new diplomacy to allow the Bundeswehr's engagement in foreign operations. In this process, there was a clash between the different norms of humanitarianism, anti-militarism and multilateralism. As Chancellor Kohl remarked: 'the task of our Bundeswehr has fundamentally changed after the end of the East-West conflict. The expectations of the international community for the reunited Germany are different from ones given to the old Germany'.[64] There had been a shift from a situation where these three norms were compatible to one where they could collide and cause a trilemma for German decision makers. The next section considers how this experience led them to rebuild Germany's diplomatic orientation.

## Germany's new security policy: the reconstruction of NATO

### The government's view on conflict prevention

Unlike Britain and France, Germany incurred no casualties because it did not send any troops to UNPROFOR for deployment on the ground in Bosnia. Even in the massive air campaign by NATO from late August in 1995, Germany's engagement was principally limited to logistical support. Conversely, if its soldiers had been killed, the government would have been placed in a more serious predicament, given the controversy in the past years.

Germany underwent what was called 'a deep turning point in our post-war history' through the Balkans,[65] as it officially permitted its foreign military activity. However, it is surely too extreme to assume that its normative restraints had been completely removed by this new undertaking. Table 6.2 reveals that an ambivalent attitude still continued even after the Constitutional Court's verdict.

To be sure, 'changes' in the opinion polls can be discovered as the figure in Option 1 rose, while that in Option 3 decreased, from 1992 to 1996. However, it is hard to say that the figure in 1996 for Option 1 is very high as such. Meanwhile, Option 2 had constantly been the most concurred in 1992 and 1996. In other words, 'continuity' of German diplomatic orientation to dislike military involvement can also be observed here.

*Table 6.2* Preference on German foreign activities in 1992 and 1996 (in percentage)

|  | 1992 | 1996 |
|---|---|---|
| 1. I am of the opinion that, as is the case with other countries' military, the Bundeswehr should participate, with no limitation, in any operation under NATO command, which is deployed for missions of the United Nations. | 18 | 29 |
| 2. The Bundeswehr should not participate in any combat operations in missions of the United Nations but only in operations for peacekeeping. | 41 | 44 |
| 3. I am against any participation of the Bundeswehr in any NATO out-of-area action. | 30 | 18 |
| 4. No answer | 11 | 9 |

Source: Noelle-Neumann and Köcher (1997: 1143).

In fact, the government had repeatedly denied the possibility of sending ground troops, and clarified that Bundeswehr troops would in no way be involved in combat operations (Baumann 2001: 170–171; also see Longhurst 2004).[66] Foreign Minister Kinkel stressed the maintenance of the 'culture of reticence' by insisting that the verdict of the Constitutional Court never meant 'a militarisation of Germany foreign policy',[67] whereas Chancellor Kohl even cautioned that 'those who are in favour of the participation of German soldiers in an eventual intervention in the field of the ex-Yugoslavia should know that the German government would never accept it'.[68]

Thus, the conflict of norms over foreign military activity remained in Germany's policymaking. Under these conditions, the necessity of creating international security mechanisms was often claimed to prevent crises from happening. For instance, Defence Minister Rühe made clear, soon after the Court's decision, that 'What is agreed by all Europeans is: *prevention has priority*. Military means is the last possibility'.[69] He also stated that 'the case of Yugoslavia shows how important it is to have the potential will to deter regional crisis *at an early stage*' and 'NATO must have the capability to manage crises and conflicts varying greatly in terms of location, duration and intensity' (Rühe 1993: 136, emphasis added). That is to say, if crises are immediately dealt with before deteriorating, German political leaders could pre-empt military intervention and thereby avoid the repetition of the norm trilemmas that they faced during the war in the Balkans. For this reason, the development of such a 'capability' in NATO was claimed by facilitating its reform.

Specifically, Rühe also expressed what roles NATO should play in the following way. After referring to the situations in Bosnia, he mentioned:

> In the future, we have to be able to defuse potential risks in time, to smother emerging conflicts or to settle them by military means. It makes no sense to be prepared only for a large-scale attack on NATO which has become most unlikely today... 'Collective crisis management' is now as important as 'collective defence' (Rühe 1994: 104).[70]

In a similar context, Foreign Minister Kinkel (1993: 9–10) also remarked that 'if we do not want to suffer from political damage, we have to establish a capability to maintain normality in our domestic and foreign policies'. Arguably, such 'political damage' was experienced by German decision makers as a consequence of the norm trilemma. Hence, he also claimed that 'NATO has to become capable of dealing with the full spectrum of tasks, from collective defence to crisis management and peacekeeping'.[71] Sharing the same view, Chancellor Kohl pronounced that 'stability in the former Yugoslavia is unthinkable with its gigantic and available arsenals. That is why we, the Federal Republic of Germany, have worked hard to establish a *comprehensive system* of confidence building and arms control in this area'.[72]

Given that it was actually contended that 'the dramatic failure of the Western world ... in the former Yugoslavia made evident how little [it was] prepared for it',[73] it is conceivable that this experience facilitated NATO reorganisation. Obviously, it was not a reform for intervention, but German policymakers needed one to achieve security governance to avert different norms clashing with each other, which is why conflict prevention was more contended. Therefore, stressing this point, *The White Paper for Defence 1994*, published for the first time after the German reunification, clarified that 'the European instrument for orders must be effective, so that armed conflicts are efficiently *prevented*'.[74] To make compatible different social claims, NATO's new rationale for security governance was supported by the German government.

In accordance with changed expectations on NATO, Germany also launched a major overhaul of its military for more flexible and rapid reaction, just as it was said that 'the ongoing situation of the transformation of NATO and re-orientation of the Bundeswehr was showing a surprising parallel' (Martin and Schäfer 1993: 1193). The Bundeswehr was divided into two bodies: Main Defence Forces and Crisis Reaction Forces, while priority over training, equipment and personnel was given to the latter (Baumann 2001: 155). In preparation for collective military operations outside NATO areas, high mobile and combat-ready forces were introduced in the three military services, viz. air, marine and ground. Along with these changes, Heeresführungskommando (Army Forces Command) in Koblenz was established in March 1994, and, from 1 January 1995, Germany started to benefit from nationales Führungszentrum (a national command centre) for the first time since the end of the Second World War (Baumann 2001: 155–156; Meimeth 1997: 106).[75]

Surely, it is problematic to see these military reforms as Germany's latent ambition for power maximising, because they were carried out 'only to enable the Bundeswehr to take part in multilateral military operations' (Baumann 2001: 156). Germany still 'lacks the central function of a general staff, i.e. full command' and 'command agency responsible for the Bundeswehr as a whole' (Baumann 2001: 155). These reforms were conducted for conflict management purposes. Put differently, not the disappearance of the Cold War confrontation but normative requirements to take action against humanitarian tragedy prompted its political leaders to establish new military structures. Therefore, Sameera Dalvi's (1998) expression, the Bundeswehr as 'a product of normative influences', precisely depicts the characteristics of its military reforms in the 1990s.

126  *From intervention to prevention*

Does this understanding apply only to the governing parties? Additionally, what undertaking was NATO supposed to carry out by the public? The final sections consider these two questions, respectively.

## *The SPD and the Greens' perspectives: from grand-value conflict to prevention*[76]

Ideas relating to new NATO roles were not a monopoly of the governing parties. '[A]fter bitter inner-conflicts',[77] members of the SPD came to vote for the government's proposals to join Bundeswehr troop deployment. For example, Norbert Gansel (SPD) argued that 'After blockades, threats, shelling, murder and hostage-taking, our duty to help and to militarily protect the peacekeepers now weighs more heavily than any history that forbids us from forcing others to their knees',[78] while Horst Niggemeier (SPD) described 'international isolation' as 'not a desirable objective' for the SPD.[79] Such considerations increasingly generated a new orientation on the role of the Bundeswehr for the purpose of humanitarian crisis response. This political stance was consolidated in the party conference in Hannover of December 1997; the party admitted the Bundeswehr's participation in all kinds of military operations, which eventually modified its policy of 'yes' to peacekeeping but 'no' to peace enforcement (Longhurst 2004: 68).

Certainly, it would be simplistic to consider that the norm of anti-militarism had evaporated in the SPD. Rather, the party, having strong attachment to pacifism,[80] had to undergo a more serious conflict of norms in this process. Its party leader Rudolf Scharping's statement is suggestive in explaining how the SPD redirected its attitude on security policy. He mentioned:

> The conflict in the former Yugoslavia unfortunately shows self-evident truth that good words, good gestures and humanitarian help alone cannot stop this genocide.

Then, he contended that 'The Social Democrats are a party with a long pacifist policy tradition', which had 'never participated in a total war when one was brought to our own country or others'. After stressing this point, he continued:

> For this reason, measures for *conflict prevention* and measures for peaceful mediation of conflicts have absolute priority in the concepts of our foreign policy.[81]

This clarifies how the clash between humanitarian and anti-military norms led this party towards crisis prevention.

As for the Greens, Bosnia brought about what its leader Joschka Fischer called a 'ground value conflict' between 'never again war' and 'never again Auschwitz'.[82] After being confronted by the tragic situations in the Balkans, especially the massacre in Srebrenica in July 1995, its realist group (Realos), in relation to its fundamentalist counterpart (Fundis), moved towards accepting the Bundeswehr's foreign activity for the sake of stopping humanitarian crises. Fischer remarked that 'pacifists cannot also close their eyes from ethnic murders and, when all other methods do not work, they also have to say yes to the last resort'.[83]

This change was boosted primarily by Fisher's initiatives. In an open letter to his party in July 1995, he wrote that 'an attitude of "we are horrified, but we do not want to look" is out of question for our party in the face of the Bosnian catastrophe' (Fischer 1995: 1150). Nina Philippi (1997: 135) points out that this letter marked a 'signal' to steer this party to a new direction. Resonating with this, a realist Green, Waltraud Schoppe (1995: 30), advocated military intervention in case of genocide by saying that 'World society can work only when its members are ready to take responsibility and risk to make human rights respected', and Lukas Beckmann added that inaction would make the West 'co-responsible for the genocide'.[84] In addition, Michael Smith shows that the feminist wing of the party argued for the use of force after witnessing the massacre and rapes in the Balkans. Eventually, those members became 'the vocal supporters of military action' (Smith 1996: 59).

Unsurprisingly, nevertheless, its intra-party conflict lasted. When the bill on German participation in IFOR – NATO-led peacekeeping operations after the ceasefire in the Balkans – was passed by an overwhelming majority of Bundestag members in December 1995 (pro 543: contra 107), the Greens' votes were divided by half and half (22: 22, abstention 7).[85] Additionally, its election programme in 1998 left its traditional aims untouched: the abolition of NATO and the Bundeswehr, although it admitted the latter's use against genocide under the UN flag (Longhurst 2002: 68–69).

It was not until the Greens, along with their senior party the SPD, came to power from 1998 that the party redefined its policy towards NATO. Ironically, these two parties, which severely condemned their predecessor's military involvement in Bosnia, dispatched German troops to NATO's air campaign in Kosovo from March 1999. After having experienced this foreign operation as a governing party, the Greens officially acknowledged the role of NATO as Fischer, as a foreign minister, called NATO 'the foundation of our security partnership'.[86]

Even if admitting NATO's military role, surely the party did not relinquish its anti-militarist credentials. Instead, as its party programme in 2002 writes that 'Our policy is aimed ... to put conflict prevention in front and always to refrain from the use of force' (Bündnis 90/Die Grünen 2002: 15), 'preventive, non-military and violence-free conflict management' had been emphasised since the days of Bosnia.[87] Thoroughly examining the Greens' past records, Christos Katsioulis (2004: 241) argues that 'The central notion, which is found in the Green party programme, is "prevention"'. This suggests that what had been discussed was not simply whether to accept military measures but also how to make humanitarian crisis response compatible with its long-cherished pacifist principles.

Thus, changes can be found in the views of the Social Democrats and the Greens but, at the same time, they also expressed their unchanged adherence to pacifist principles. While changes and continuity were cohabiting in these

128  *From intervention to prevention*

parties' past track, they were steadily moving towards a preventive approach to make compatible these different requirements, which consequently shaped their support towards NATO reorganisation.

## Collective recognition on NATO's new undertakings

These changed expectations on NATO can also be ascertained in the public collective recognition. Figure 6.1 unveils how its importance to German security had been viewed. First of all, an apparent change can be confirmed in the former eastern areas. As Karin Johnston (2003: 262–263) remarks that 'The East Germans have an entirely separate historical and emotional relationship to NATO; consequently, their image of NATO is decidedly different', it is no wonder if they had a negative impression of it. From 1994, however, the rates of those considering it important increased drastically (alternatively, the 'unimportant' rate decreased drastically), getting closer to those of the former western areas. Meanwhile, a slight but significant shift can be found in the west too. The end of the Cold War diminished the significance of NATO; nevertheless, the year 1994 saw the supporting rate reaching the highest point over the past decade including the Cold War era.[88]

A more detailed questionnaire on 'tasks of NATO' clarifies what role it was expected to play (data taken in May 1995, multiple answers) (Noelle-Neumann and Köcher 1997: 1135):[89]

1   To help a NATO partner when attacked (74 per cent);
2   To respond to natural disaster (53 per cent);
3   To secure the possible evacuation of UN peacekeepers from the former Yugoslavia (41 per cent); and
4   To end the war in the Balkans (38 per cent).

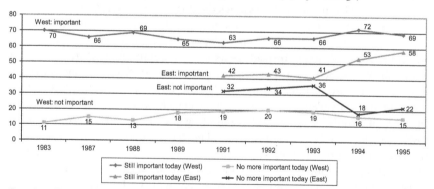

*Figure 6.1* Evaluation on NATO membership in Germany (in percentage)

Question: 'Do you think that it is still important for the security of our country to be a member of NATO, or it is no more important today, or it has never been important?' Figures in per cent. Data of the eastern regions start from 1991.
Source: Noelle-Neumann and Köcher (1997: 1134).

The first and the second options are somewhat natural because the former concerns its original purpose, while the other is a quite general topic. More conspicuous are the third and fourth. Although conflict management had not been originally conceived as one of the original duties of NATO, response to Bosnia, occurring in what was known as its out-of-area, was solidly regarded as its tasks to engage in.

Thus, both changes and continuity can be discovered in the characteristics of German foreign policy. As the same time, conflict prevention was prompted as a third way to avoid repetition of the norm trilemma that Germany faced during the war in Bosnia. Such views were broadly expressed within the different parties and among the public, suggesting how the clash of norms created its new understandings on the role of NATO in the European security system.

## Conclusion

This chapter considered what new rationales of NATO German political leaders came to envision by investigating the conflict of social norms that struck them during the war in Bosnia. First, as with other countries, it was largely articulated in Germany that this tragedy must be stopped. However, when concrete measures were demanded, the government was put in a trilemma over desirable foreign policy, because of the gap between the general discussion and the practical discussion levels. In the domestic realm, military action caused friction with its anti-military norm. In the international realms, the Kohl government was pressed for its participation in the joint military operation to Bosnia and its refusal would crucially impair its credibility as a reliable partner. In short, it was required to fulfil humanitarianism, anti-militarism and multilateralism at the same time although they were inherently compatible.

This chapter argued how this experience led them to the notion of crisis prevention. It is sure that the verdict of the Constitutional Court in 1994 made it possible to send its troops with no legal constraints; nevertheless, aversion to the use of force remained as a strong constitutive element in its future policy. For this reason, its political leaders supported NATO reforms for this sake of conflict prevention with expectations that it would help them to swiftly address crises before military intervention would be unavoidable. Hence, NATO transformation was unanimously upheld within the German political circle, even by those who had opposed its military action.

The introductory section of this chapter reviewed how the existing literature has discussed changes and continuity in German diplomacy. Germany underwent a significant change in its security policy through its engagements in the Balkans. However, it is also true that its anti-military nature still continued to delineate German diplomatic traits. As a consequence, both changes and continuity can be simultaneously discussed in its past trajectory. While contemplating these accounts, this chapter shed light on another aspect of how and why German policymakers came to prefer conflict prevention. This aspect will be missed out if attention is paid to either change or continuity because it emerged out of

130  *From intervention to prevention*

an attempt to meet both requirements, which constituted the expectations for NATO's new roles. Interestingly, Gunilla Fincke and Arzu Hatakoy (2004) also argue 'crisis prevention as a new model of German foreign policy' by extensively analysing Germany's commitment to OSCE, the EU and NATO in the post-Cold War era. By focussing on Bosnia, this chapter explored how the conflict of different norms formed German policymakers' preference on the development of the Alliance to manage contingencies beyond its borders.

## Notes

1 On this usage, e.g. see Hyde-Price (2000: 122–124).
2 In this vein, Adrian Hyde-Price (2000: 168) states, weighing its non-coercive traits and willingness to accept more international responsibility, that Germany is 'now a "normal" civilian power'. Also see Regina Karp (2009), who explores how power, norms and structure interact in German foreign policymaking. Dieter Dettke (2009) examines normalised German foreign policy from a realist perspective, but even his view rests upon defensive realism, not an offensive branch.
3 On these phrases, e.g. see Harnisch (2001: 52).
4 This orientation moulded the political system, which strictly restrained the activity of the Bundeswehr by its constitution (see the next section). Additionally, under the policy of the so-called 'keeping the Germans down' after the end of the Second World War, Germany had agreed to place its armed forces under NATO command even in peacetime and hosted 400,000 NATO troops on its ground since its affiliation to the Alliance, and had no military command agency until 1995 (Katzenstein 1996a: 172, and see Section 4 of this chapter).
5 Anika Leithner (2009: 8) identifies 'responsibility, reliability, multilateralism, predictability, and antimilitarism' as German foreign policy characteristics and contends that 'All of these have become intrinsic components of Germany's self-understanding as a history-conscious nation and have impacted every aspect of German life'. Her monograph explicates how German diplomacy has been shaped by the historical memory of World War II.
6 This translation relies on Lantis (2002: 22–23).
7 This is an expression made by Alyson Bailes (1995: 7), the then Head of Security Policy Department at the British Foreign Common Office.
8 For example, Dutch Foreign Minister Hans van den Broek, holding the EC Presidency at that time, reiterated the reason for refraining from recognition by arguing that 'If we tried to change the borders over there, you would provoke similar claims all over the place and it would never end', quoted in David Usborne, 'EC draws up plan for new Yugoslavia', *The Independent*, 18 October 1991.
9 Quoted in Maull (1995/96: 102).
10 'Ein großer Erfolg für uns', *Der Spiegel*, vol. 52, 23 December 1991: 18.
11 'Zauberformel', *Die Zeit*, No. 51, 12 December 1991.
12 Quoted in Gordon (1995: 60). Also see van Heuven (1993: 61). It should be added that some counter-argue that it was doubtful whether the recognition accelerated Bosnian secession from the former Yugoslavia because its disintegration was inevitable (Jakobsen 1995: 411).
13 Quoted in Gordon (1995: 60).
14 This view is said to come from its relatively strong belief in international law, including the prohibition of the use of force, as well as the fact that, unlike other states, Germany had no strong irredentism in itself, which 'made German opinion less sensitive than others to the inherent problems of the notion of self-determination' (Gordon 1995: 55–56).

*From intervention to prevention* 131

15 Quoted in Johnston (2003: 260).
16 This translation relies on Gregory (2000: 59).
17 Fredy Gsteiger, 'Große Töne, kleine Taten', *Die Zeit*, Nr. 39, 18 September 1992.
18 '"Das sinnlose Morden beenden": Kinkel für Kontrolle der Serbien-Sanktionen', *Süddeutsche Zeitung*, 1 June 1992.
19 'Irrsinn ohne Ende: Die Vermittler kapitulieren, das Gemetzel in Bosnien ist nicht zu stoppen', *Der Spiegel*, vol. 31, 27 July 1992: 116.
20 'Ganz Bosnien ist die Hölle', *Der Spiegel*, vol. 33, 10 August 1992: 128. Also see 'Halb hilft gar nicht', *Die Zeit*, 21 August 1992. Also see Theo Sommer, 'Die Balkan-Falle', *Die Zeit*, 18 September 1992.
21 *Plenarprotokoll*, 12/37, 4 September 1991: 3018.
22 *Plenarprotokoll*, 12/219, 14 April 1994: 18923.
23 *Plenarprotokoll*, 12/101, 22 July 1992: 8608.
24 *Plenarprotokoll*, 12/219, 14 April 1994: 18916.
25 *Drucksache*, 12/2290, 18 March 1992.
26 Peter Glotz (SPD) in *Plenarprotokoll*, 12/33, 19 June 1991: 2561.
27 'SPD: Bosnische Flüchtlinge einreisen lassen', *Süddeutsche Zeitung*, 24 June 1992.
28 *Plenarprotokoll*, 12/113, 15 October 1992: 9641.
29 *Plenarprotokoll*, 12/219, 3 March 1994: 18428.
30 *Plenarprotokoll*, 12/33, 19 June 1991: 2563.
31 'Klare Worte – aber auch Taten?', *Süddeutsche Zeitung*, 29 June 1992.
32 'SPD: Für Blauhelmeinsatz Grundgesetz ändern', *Süddeutsche Zeitung*, 20 May 1992, and 'SPD droht mit Verfassungsklage', *Süddeutsche Zeitung*, 11 July 1992.
33 Quoted in Johnston (2003: 266). As a cross-check, other sources show that, in late summer 1992, some 44 per cent of the former West Germans (24 per cent of the former East Germans) agreed on unarmed peacekeeping, but 14 per cent (11 per cent) favoured a UN peace enforcement, quoted in Müller (1994: 139).
34 The British poll from Wybrow (2003: 40–42) (see Chapter 4) and the French one from La Balme (2001: 191) (see Chapter 5). Additionally, in June 1993, the *Eurobarometer*'s data show that while 60 per cent of the British and 59 per cent of the French were for European military intervention in the framework of the EC's common foreign policy and defence policy, some 44 per cent of Germans were in favour (quoted in Morjé Howard and Morjé Howard 2003: 307, in the appendix section).
35 'Ratlos im Kriegslabyrinth', *Der Spiegel*, vol. 34, 17 August 1992: 130.
36 Another opposition party, the PDS, adopted a comprehensive non-interventionist stance, e.g. see *Plenarprotokoll*, 12/213, 3 March 1994: 18423; Hans Modrow, *Plenarprotokoll*, 12/213, 14 April 1994: 18917.
37 For example, see the SPD's view in *Drucksache*, 12/4710, 6 April 1993 and the Greens in *Drucksache*, 12/4639, 25 March 1993 (The Greens' view on non-military conflict resolution, cf. *Drucksache*, 12/3014, 2 July 1992).
38 *Plenarprotokoll*, 12/219, 14 April 1994: 18910.
39 Her interview in 'Das Nein war deutlich', *Der Spiegel*, vol. 10, 7 March 1994: 24 (I relied on this translation in Rathbun 2004: 96).
40 *Plenarprotokoll*, 12/219, 3 March 1994: 18435.
41 *Plenarprotokoll*, 12/240, 22 July 1994: 21200.
42 *Plenarprotokoll*, 12/98, 24 June 1992: 8166.
43 *Plenarprotokoll*, 13/76, 6 December 1995: 6642. In addition, the Green Party's leader, Joschka Fischer, also made clear the party's opposition to the dispatch of German troops to 'where the Wehrmacht raged in a cruel manner during the Second World War', in *Plenarprotokoll*, 13/48, 30 June 1995: 3974.
44 Vera Wollenberger (Green) in *Plenarprotokoll*, 12/219, 14 April 1994: 18918.
45 *Plenarprotokoll*, 12/219, 3 March 1994: 18432.
46 *Plenarprotokoll*, 12/219, 14 April 1994: 18918. It should be noted that Vera Wollenberger later joined the CDU in 1996, while reverting to her family name Lengsfeld.

132  *From intervention to prevention*

47 Wieczorek-Zeul's words in 'Das Nein war deutlich', *Der Spiegel*, vol. 10, 7 March 1994: 22.
48 In spring 1993, the SPD gained control of a majority of the upper house, Bundesrat, because the CDU lost some state parliamentary elections, which made constitutional changes almost impossible in the upper house, see Lantis (1996: 27).
49 Quoted in Smith (1996: 57–58), originally from *Frankfurter Allgemeine Zeitung*, 1 April 1993.
50 Quoted in Philippi (1997: 84), originally from Wolfgang Schäuble, 'Wir brauchen klare Zielvorstellung', *Nordsee Zeitung*, 18 July 1992.
51 Theodor Waigel's remark on new German foreign orientations in *Plenarprotokoll*, 13/76, 6 December 1995: 6654, and Michael Glos's on 'foreign policy normalisation' in *Plenarprotokoll*, 12/240, 22 July 1994: 21174.
52 Germany also participated in the United Nations Transition Assistance for Cambodia (UNTAC) by sending c.a. 600 Bundeswehr medical corps from May 1992. N.B. UNTAC was a traditional-style peacekeeping operation with no authorisation to use force except for self-defence.
53 *Plenarprotokoll*, 12/219, 14 April 1994: 18915.
54 *Plenarprotokoll*, 12/219, 14 April 1994: 18917.
55 See, for instance, 'Justizministerin schwächt Äußerung zur Koalition ab', *Frankfurter Allgemeine Zeitung*, 7 April 1993. In fact, this decision in the cabinet meeting was made without advance consultation with FDP Foreign Minister Kinkel, which increased the friction between the ruling parties, Lantis (1996: 27).
56 'Karlsruhe berät heute ueber die Awacs-Klage' *Frankfurter Allgemeine Zeitung*, 5 April 1993.
57 Quoted in Smith (1996: 58).
58 *Plenarprotokoll*, 12/213, 3 March 1994: 18433–34.
59 *Plenarprotokoll*, 12/213, 3 March 1994: 18429. Also see Werner Hoyer's (FDP) view in *Plenarprotokoll*, 12/240, 22 July 1994: 21194 and Jürgen Koppelin's (FDP) in *Plenarprotokoll*, 12/240, 3 March 1994: 18428.
60 'Stärker als die ganze Welt', *Der Spiegel*, vol. 19, 10 May 1993: 150. Also see 'Wozu ist die Nato noch', *Die Zeit*, vol. 49, 2 December 1994.
61 Karl Feldmeyer, 'Die Nato ist ratlos', *Frankfurter Allgemeine Zeitung*, 5 December 1994.
62 'Wörner kritisiert Versagen auf dem Balkan, "Der Westen muß Lehren ziehen": Plädoyer für eine weitere Öffnung der NATO nach Osteuropa', *Süddeutsche Zeitung*, 11 September 1993.
63 *Plenarprotokoll*, 13/48, 30 July 1995: 3956. In addition, Karl-Heinz Hornhues (CDU) underscored the necessity for 'credible threat by force' to end the violence in the Balkans (*Plenarprotokoll*, 12/219, 14 April 1994: 18912), while Schäuble argued, at the final stage of the war, that 'if the UN blue-helmets are withdrawn ... then the chances for a political solution of [this] miserable war are dramatically damaged. To avoid this damage, we make a last attempt' (*Plenarprotokoll*, 12/240, 3 March 1994: 18428).
64 *Plenarprotokoll*, 13/76, 6 December 1995: 6632.
65 An SPD politician Walter Kolbow's expression in *Plenarprotokoll*, 12/240, 22 July 1994: 21189.
66 For instance, *Drucksache*, 12/5106, 14 June 1993, which states that Germany's participation was founded upon the ceasefire agreements and consent of local parties.
67 *Plenarprotokoll*, 12/240, 22 July 1994: 21167.
68 Quoted in Lucarelli (2000: 210), originally from *Frankfurter Allgemeine Zeitung*, 20 April 1993.
69 Emphasis added, *Plenarprotokoll*, 12/240, 22 July 1994: 21186.

70 This is Rühe's speech at the Karls University in Prague on 8 October 1993. The author relied on and modified Meimeth's (1997: 95) translation, who used the same material.
71 Quoted in Meimeth (1997: 95), originally from *International Herald Tribune*, 21 October 1993.
72 Emphasis added. *Plenarprotokoll*, 13/76, 6 December 1995: 6634. Additionally, Kohl also stated that 'The former Yugoslavia is just one example, even if [it is] the most frightening one, that war would not be uprooted in Europe in time and perpetually. That is why the evolution of a European security, [as well as] European integration for this purpose, is all the more important'. Helmut Kohl, 'Die NATO ist für neue Mitglieder offen', *Das Parlament*, 21 January 1994.
73 Statement by former defence minister, Rupert Scholz (CDU) (from 1988 to 1989), in 'Die NATO und die Probleme der Erweiterung: Diskussion zwischen zwei Extremen', *Das Parlament*, 11 February 1994.
74 Emphasis added, 'Weißbuch zur Sicherheit der Bundesrepblik Deutschland und zur Lage und Zukunft der Bundeswehr vom 5. April (Auszüge)', *Europa Archiv* 10: 332.
75 Concerning a more detailed explanation, see Young (1996).
76 Another opposition party PDS, consistently objected NATO's military intervention and the sending of the Bundeswehr abroad. This posture remained unchanged, as its party leader, Gregor Gysi, summarised his party's view – he stated: 'I know that terrible crimes happened in the former Yugoslavia. Yet, I would like to warn us about justifying military actions with an identification of what happened in the former Yugoslavia between 1939 and 1945', in *Plenarprotokoll*, 13/76, 6 December 1995: 6648. Regarding this party's opinion, see Müller (1994: 136–137), Longhurst (2002: 69), Philippi (1997: 138–143).
77 'Dabeisein ist alles', *Der Spiegel*, vol. 26, 26 June 1995: 25.
78 *Plenarprotokoll*, 13/48, 30 June 1995: 4012, the author relied on this translation by Rathbun (2004: 99), who used the same material.
79 Quoted in Philippi (1997: 122).
80 On this point about the SPD, see Rathbun (2004: Chapter 4).
81 Emphasis added. *Plenarprotokoll*, 13/76, 6 December 1995: 6635. Also see Scharping (1995).
82 Fischer's interview in 'Das wäre blutiger Zynismus', *Der Spiegel*, vol. 34, 21 August 1995: 29; Joschka Fischer in *Plenarprotokoll*, 13/76, 6 December 1995: 6657.
83 *Der Spiegel*, vol. 34, 21 August 1995: 28.
84 'Die Sorge um die Glaubwürdigkeit der Vereinten Nationen: Bündnis 90/Grüne fordern Kampfeinsatz in Bosnien-Hercegovina', *Frankfurter Allgemeine Zeitung*, 14 May 1993.
85 See *Plenarprotokoll*, 13/76, 6 December 1995: 6673, also See Johnston (2003: 269).
86 Quoted in Katsioulis (2004: 242).
87 Gerd Poppe in *Plenarprotokoll*, 12/240, 22 July 1994: 21184.
88 The same analysis is provided in Horst (2001: 255–256).
89 Top four results are shown out of 14 options.

# 7 The dilemmas of intervention and the reform of NATO

American response to the war in Bosnia

## Introduction

The war in Bosnia was characterised in the United States as 'a problem from hell'. Secretary of State Warren Christopher (1998: 344), who first used this expression,[1] described it as 'the bloodiest since the Second World War'. Indeed, throughout the war (including the war in Croatia), nearly 200 thousand people were killed, and three million were driven from their homes (Gagnon 2006: 1). The news about Bosnia was widely disseminated in the United States and attracted public attention – in the middle of the war, 69 per cent of respondents in one poll said that they had closely followed the situation in Bosnia (very closely 17 per cent and fairly closely 52 per cent).[2]

What do International Relations (IR) theories expect when the United States is confronted by such a foreign war, a superpower country having enormous power and capabilities to engage in military action of its own will? Thinking from the traditional perspective, namely neorealism, American policy should be determined by whether its tangible interests are at stake or not (see Chapter 2). That means, the government will make a hard-headed decision by weighing costs and benefits of action and inaction. In contrast, the constructivist view would contend that American policy is contingent on how inaction towards excessively worsening humanitarian conditions is socially assessed. From this angle, irrespective of whether material interests are involved or not, intervention will be chosen if ignoring humanitarian catastrophe is regarded as normatively inappropriate.

These perspectives help us to understand how the United States actually behaved. Its initial policy seems to be suitably explained by neorealism. When the war broke out, the Washington decision makers tried to stay out of Bosnia by bluntly articulating that no American interests were implicated. However, this attitude did not last long. With the influx of information about the dire humanitarian conditions, the government gradually began its engagements because its inaction was severely condemned as morally wrong within its domestic society. In this change, the constructivist account illustrates why the American government began action despite its perception of the crisis. In analysing its point, it appears necessary to investigate how this foreign crisis was discussed in public and how the pressure for action shaped its policy.

Nevertheless, this constructivist explanation does not fit so neatly with the subsequent developments because humanitarian outcry did not lead to any concrete action straightforwardly. It is true that response to Bosnia was loudly discussed, but this certainly did not mean that people unanimously agreed with their troops being dispatched unconditionally, let alone with their being killed on the battlefield. Along with the criticisms against doing nothing, it was simultaneously warned that intervention would end up becoming 'another Vietnam' through American entanglement. Caught by the contrasting demands for intervention and non-intervention, the government could not set out clear and consistent policy. In fact, Secretary of State Christopher's previously cited phrase had another connotation – in addition to the horrific and brutal conditions of the war, he called the war 'the intractable "problem from hell" that no one can be expected to solve'.[3] This clarifies the intrinsic nature of the handling of the crisis.

Following the theoretical discussions in Chapter 2 to offer separate analyses at the 'general' and 'practical' discussion levels, it can be observed in the American case too that stopping serious humanitarian disasters was generally assumed as desirable, but taking concrete measures to achieve this goal provoked other concerns – especially in the United States, the fear of involvement thwarted the decision makers, as well as the public. Put another way, collective expectations for ideal outcomes were not always realised because of the dilemma caused when action was implemented, which illustrates what caused the American government to vacillate once it commenced its involvement.

Like the previous ones, this chapter also examines how the experiences in Bosnia affected the American view on NATO. Undoubtedly, the United States had been pondering NATO's future role since the end of the Cold War and, in this process, Bosnia gave an impetus for new undertakings beyond its territory, as a well-known statement by Senator Richard Lugar (R-IN) implies: 'NATO would either go out of area or out of business'.[4] However, its initial attitude of trying to keep its distance reveals that the U.S. decision makers did not suppose that NATO would be deployed in this conflict. It was contended that 'The United States had publicly declared its unwillingness to use military power in the case and had insisted as well that NATO should not become involved anywhere "out of area"' (Woodward 1995: 165). Nevertheless, this foreign war, in which its leaders viewed their tangible interests as unthreatened, pushed the Washington government to embark on NATO transformation.

To elucidate the question of how and why the United States came to NATO's new activities through Bosnia, this chapter makes clear that its political leaders needed international mechanisms for security governance to aptly meet various social demands at the same time. In this war, they were demanded to conform to the contrasting claims of doing something about this humanitarian disaster and doing nothing to avoid being involved in it. Furthermore, as the previous chapters explicated, they had head-on disputes with their European Allies due to their disagreement on how to address the war. To avert these problems, they were prompted to set up a series of international frameworks for effective crisis management so that crises would be addressed before deteriorating, which resulted in reinvigorating NATO to launch its new undertakings.

With its power and leadership, this hegemonic country played a significant role not only in conducting the military operation in Bosnia but also in facilitating NATO reorganisation. Nevertheless, even such a country also needed international cooperation to efficiently deal with foreign tragedy without causing friction with its Allies. Investigating the American case will show how its policymakers saw the dilemma of intervention and non-intervention and how they reached a way to redevelop NATO for the sake of international management of foreign contingencies.

This chapter proceeds as follows. The first section examines the George H. W. Bush administration's attitude to Bosnia and its policy change from non-commitment to commitment. The second section discusses the policy taken by the next administration under President Bill Clinton from 1993, with a particular focus on the debates within the domestic society. The third section sheds light on the international aspect, i.e. the diplomatic rows that erupted between Washington and its European partners. The fourth section analyses what the American policymakers envisioned as the role of the post-Cold War NATO. The conclusion section considers theoretical implications drawn from this American case study.

## Policymaking and policy change: decision of the Bush administration

### *Interests, fear and timing: reasons for non-intervention*

The Bush administration chose non-action towards the military clash that broke out in June 1991 in Slovenia and Croatia in 1991, subsequently followed by that of Bosnia in 1992. As touched upon earlier, this decision suitably corresponded to the neorealist account, namely no tangible interests implicated. It can be explicated through three more detailed reasons.

The first reason related to the changes in geostrategic conditions in the post-Cold War world as it is argued that 'Once the superpower rivalry ended, Yugoslavia's international significance diminished considerably, and the successor states are even less significant militarily' (Bert 1997: 64–65). For instance, David Gompert (1996: 125), then special assistant to the Secretary of State, wrote that 'Indeed, the strategic importance of Yugoslavia was waning at the very moment the federation was coming unglued'. Likewise, Secretary of State James Baker made clear that 'Most importantly, unlike in the Persian Gulf, our vital national interests were not at stake' (Baker with DeFrank 1995: 636). Such a view is said to be shared within the decision maker circle as Susan Woodward (1995: 298) states that

> Even President Bush and his chairman of the Joint Chiefs of Staff ... admitted in separate interviews in September and October 1992 that they had yet to be persuaded that there was any political objective or strategic interest for engagement in the Balkans.

As these remarks show, it was difficult to find any compelling incentives for the U.S. to initiate action.[5]

The second reason came from the 'perception' that the conflicts in the Balkans, especially the one in Bosnia, were too complicated to solve from outside because they were rooted in enduring animosities among ethnic groups that dated back several hundred or a thousand years. For instance, Baker's successor, Secretary of State, Lawrence Eagleburger, having served at the American embassy in Belgrade in the 1960s, commented that 'I have said this 38,000 times ... This tragedy is not something that can be settled from outside and it's about damn well time that everybody understood that'.[6] Similar views were also expressed by President Bush, who called the war 'age-old animosities [and] century-old feuds', and Secretary of Defense Dick Cheney, who described the Balkans as 'a hotbed of conflict ... for centuries'.[7] Although this perception is now denied and instead it is argued that it should be understood as 'the product of bad, even criminal, political leaders who encouraged ethnic confrontation for personal, political, and financial gain' (Holbrooke 1999: 23–24; also see Malcolm 1994: 252; Zimmermann 1999: 121), it is often referred to as one of the causes of the Washington government's reluctance and caution over their involvement (Bert 1997; Daalder 2000; Halverson 1996; Holbrooke 1999; Power 2007).

In this light, two military doctrines, which were influential at that time, warned about American involvement – one was the 'Weinberger Doctrine' made public in 1984 by then Secretary of Defense Casper Weinberger, reflecting the Vietnam War, while the other was the 'Powell Doctrine' in 1990 by Chairman of the Joint Chiefs of Staff Colin Powell. Both contended that American military force should be used as a last resort and only when political and military objectives and the clear intention of winning were unequivocally defined to save America's (and its allies') vital national interests.[8] From this point of view, American commitment to the conflict in Bosnia was obviously questioned because of the ambiguity of American interests and the uncertainty of solving this ethnically complex war from the outside. In fact, Powell insisted that 'American GIs were not toy soldiers to be moved around on some sort of global game board' (Powell with Persico 1995: 576).

The third reason was that it was not good timing for the United States to deploy its diplomatic resources in the Balkans. Before the eruption of the first military clash in 1991, it had already been occupied with the Persian Gulf since the invasion of Kuwait by Iraq in 1990. Even after the truce of the war, it had to continuously cope with the Kurdish refugee influx caused by Saddam Hussein's northern Iraq offensive. Seeing such conditions, Warren Zimmermann (1999: 137), the last ambassador to Yugoslavia, wrote that 'Even a great power has difficulty in dealing with more than one crisis at a time'. Furthermore, 1991 was the year of the Soviet Union's collapse and this had occupied much of America's attention. Secretary of State Baker firmly clarified it by stating that 'our central focus for months to come would be on managing the peaceful dissolution of the USSR' (Baker with DeFrank 1995: 637).[9] Hence, the American government did not dare to take any risk in the Balkans and rather considered that it would be a dangerous step to interfere with a conflict in the former Communist territory because it would instigate nationalistic sentiment in the Soviet Union/Russia and simply put President Gorbachev in a more difficult position (Simms 2002: 53).

Accordingly, due to (1) the absence of tangible strategic interests, (2) the perception of this civil war as too complicated to solve from the outside and (3) the preoccupation with other foreign crises, the U.S. government opted for non-intervention. In contrast, European states were more actively addressing the war under the banner of 'the hour of Europe', as examined in the previous chapters. As early as in June 1992, they had already dispatched their troops to Bosnia for humanitarian relief activity under the deployment of UNPROFOR. The Americans welcomed the European initiatives as it was stated 'The Bush administration felt comfortable with the EC's taking responsibility for handling the crisis in the Balkans' (Baker with DeFrank 1995: 636) and that 'the Europeans should take the initiative to bring peace to Bosnia', a crisis occurring in 'Europe's backyard' (Sobel 2001: 183).

*Turnabout*

Despite such a hands-off attitude, the American government gradually started its engagement. This change is now said to have been triggered by the daily-based inflow of information through the media.[10] A critical moment came around August 1992 when the concentration camps run by the local Serb militias were discovered – particularly, a series of reports in *Newsday* by Roy Gutman, who was later awarded a Pulitzer Prize, had huge impact in stirring up public debate. As he recalls, his first article, entitled 'The Death Camps of Bosnia', 'was immediately picked up by news wires, television and radio in the United States and around the world' (Gutman 1993: xiii).[11]

The media incessantly covered the crisis in Bosnia while criticising the government's liability in doing nothing. *The New York Times* reported the details about the ongoing ethnic cleansing in an editorial article entitled 'Shame in Our Time',[12] while other editorials claimed that the international community 'need[ed] to demonstrate that they have learned something from the tragic errors that led to the Second World War'.[13] *The Washington Post* also argued that '[horrific images] and eerily reminiscent accounts are flowing out of the Bosnian war – reminiscent, more and more witnesses are saying, of the Nazi era',[14] while an article by Representative Lee H. Hamilton (D-IN-9) stated that 'After the Cold War, the international community has an opportunity and an obligation to take a fresh look at how to address dire humanitarian crises'.[15] *The Washington Post* also published an article by George D. Kenney, who was deputy chief of Yugoslav affairs at the State Department and submitted a letter of resignation by saying, 'I can no longer in clear conscience support the administration's ineffective, indeed, counterproductive handling of the Yugoslav crisis'.[16] In this article, entitled 'Appeasement in Our Time', Kenney contended that 'What galls me the most about the administration's handling of the crisis is that it doesn't really want to know the facts of the horror in Bosnia, because the more we know, the greater the public pressure to act.'[17] Voices for action were also heard among both Democrat and Republican members. Senator Robert Dole (R-KS) announced that 'What is absolutely clear is that action must be taken now to end Milosevic's murderous rampage',[18] while Senator Larry Pressler (R-SD) held that 'I have risen on numerous occasions to discuss the war being waged in the former Yugoslavia and what I believe this country [meaning America] and the international community should be doing in an attempt to bring an end to the violence, bloodshed and ethnic cleansing in that region of the world'.[19] Likewise, Senator Joseph Biden (D-DE) claimed that 'the plight of Bosnia poses a test of our moral mettle',[20] while Senator Joe Lieberman (D-CT) insisted that 'we are challenged here in these stories [about Bosnia] to be true to our values as Americans',[21] and Senator David Boren (D-OK) stated that 'the hideous policy of "ethnic cleansing" is morally repugnant' and that 'This is truly a decisive test for the post-cold war world'.[22] As far as the author could ascertain, at least 12 resolutions were made in both the Senate and the House of Representatives in 1992, which urged international response by the United Nations to address deteriorating conditions in Bosnia and the former Yugoslavia.[23]

At that time, 'an odd coalition'[24] was formed between the Republican and Democrat camps, just as was seen in the case of Britain (Chapter 4). That is to say, both the so-called hawkish and the so-called dovish figures pushed for action for the sake of stopping the human rights violations. Generally speaking, although the former group seemed to place more value on interstate power politics by weighing the danger of meddling with other country's human rights abuses, Senator Dole, who was one of the most vocal figures in the Senate, former President Ronald Reagan, former Secretary of State Henry Kissinger and former Secretary of State George Shultz all condemned the government's inaction and called for the use of force to end the atrocities.[25] To cite an example, Kissinger contended that 'Putting an end to ethnic cleansing and concentration camps should be the moral objective; preventing an escalation of the crisis beyond the borders of Yugoslavia the political goal'.[26] On the other hand, Democrats such as Senators Biden and Lieberman, and Representatives Frank McCloskey (D-IN-8), Steny Hoyer (D-MD-5) and David Bonior (D-MI-12) advocated military action on humanitarian grounds. For example, Representative McCloskey, whose efforts were explicated by Samantha Power (2007: 298–300), had been calling public attention to Bosnia from the early days, by articulating that 'Genocide is raging unchecked in Europe',[27] although he had opposed the Vietnam War and, during his career as a congressman, voted against the Gulf War.[28]

What was decisive in bringing the topic of Bosnia to the political table was that Democratic presidential candidate Bill Clinton repeatedly attacked President Bush's reluctance by demanding 'urgent and appropriate action to stop the killing'.[29] He pronounced, 'I would begin with air power against the Serbs to try to restore the basic conditions of humanity'.[30] Reacting to his critiques, an ABC news programme ran a profile distinguishing Clinton's and Bush's approaches to Bosnia by extensively quoting Clinton on the need for strong, decisive U.S. leadership (Western 2002: 127). Indeed, opinion poll results had also changed by this time as approval of American air strikes rose from 35 per cent to 53 per cent, while disapproval dropped from 45 per cent (July 1992) to 33 per cent (August).[31] Through such debates, the issue of Bosnia had become a high-profile political agenda.

Eventually, President Bush declared 'measures to penalize Serbia and deliver humanitarian aid, protected by military force if needed, to victims of the inter-ethnic fighting' while denouncing 'the vile policy of ethnic cleansing practiced by the Serbs'.[32] This turnabout was explained as reacting 'to swiftly growing public and political pressure for action against atrocities reported from Bosnia-Hercegovina'.[33] Alternatively, it was also said that 'President Bush, under pressure from Bill Clinton and public opinion, has quickened his response to the carnage in the Balkans'.[34] Given the initially dominant opinions of nonintervention within the Bush administration, the change in its attitude can be contended to be triggered by domestic debates pushing for action in this catastrophic situation.

In all, why the United States commenced its commitment was seen as based upon moral grounds, not upon interest calculations. In questionnaires asking 'the main reason for the United States to consider military intervention', 'moral responsibility to stop ethnic cleansing' (37 per cent) was chosen more than others, such as 'preventing the spread of fighting in Europe' (19 per cent), 'U.S. national security' (15 per cent) and 'no opinion' (13 per cent).[35] Within the decision makers' circle, a similar account was also provided. Richard Holbrooke (1999: 361), who engaged in the lengthy peace negotiation processes as Assistant Secretary of State for European and Canadian Affairs under the Clinton administration, holds in comparison with other various possibilities that 'Strategic considerations were vital to our involvement, but the motives that finally pushed the United States into action were also moral and humanitarian'. Against such a background, American policy towards Bosnia was initiated.

## The debate on concrete measures: policy by the Clinton administration

### *Fear of involvement and fear of inaction*

Bill Clinton's inauguration as President in 1993 brought a change in administration from Republican to Democrat. As discussed earlier, when he was a presidential candidate, Clinton had reprimanded his predecessor's policy on Bosnia, but it was said that he 'ha[d] said nothing on the matter since the election'.[36] After taking office, he finally announced that 'The United States is not, should not become involved as a partisan in a war'.[37] Indeed, while images of atrocities may cause people to call for action, taking measures triggers another problem, specifically, when it entails whether troops should be sent to a foreign war. A 'norm dilemma' caused by the different debates at the general and practical levels struck the Clinton administration. In the American case, it was primarily about the clash between action towards Bosnia and the fear of entanglement.

Concerns over America being bogged down were certainly raised even when calls for action were at their loudest – such voices gained more momentum after concrete measures began to be discussed. Particularly, such caution was expressed in terms of what was called the 'Vietnam syndrome' (Bert 1997: 84). For instance, Senator Ernest Hollings (D-SC) warned that, while being 'revulsed by Serbia's aggression and ethnic cleansing', 'if we learned anything in Vietnam it is that the road to tragedy and quagmire is paved with good intentions'.[38] Likewise, Senator John McCain (R-AZ) also pronounced that 'the overwhelming majority of the American people and the Congress supported United States military involvement [in Vietnam] ... [that has] vanished with time', while adding that 'Let us not be driven by the whims of public opinion'.[39] As America's sensitivities about its soldiers' casualties were explained as deriving from its 'military culture',[40] the risk of soldiers in foreign operations was largely discussed as the question of how to approach any action was considered.

What is more, 18 American soldiers were killed in the military operation in Somalia and their bodies were brutally dragged through the streets in Mogadishu in October 1993, images of which were broadcast worldwide, provoking public outrage in the United States.[41] To be sure, this incident happened outside of the context of Bosnia; nevertheless, it had huge impact, enough to make the Clinton administration not only pull out of Somalia but also review thoroughly American policy of participation in UN peacekeeping in the post-Cold War era, which was embodied in Presidential Decision Directive 25 in May 1994, establishing 'a stringent set of criteria for US military intervention that provided a political argument for refraining from military intervention in almost all circumstances' (Seybolt 2008: 61, fn. 66). Thus, it was argued that 'if we send peacekeepers to enforce a settlement in Bosnia, there will be significant casualties' and that 'It will lead to another Somalia or another Lebanon as surely as night follows day'.[42] This tragic accident in Somalia intensified the fear of involvement and left 'negative reverberations in Washington that seemed to close the door on any possible action in Bosnia' (Woodward 1995: 309).

Within the society, however, this does not mean that voices for action disappeared – they were still strong in the face of the ongoing war. For example, the American Jewish Committee, which in August 1992 issued an open letter in *The New York Times* with a headline 'Stop the Death Camps',[43] had been pushing for American intervention, as the discovery of the concentration camps evoked images of the persecution of the Jews by the Nazi regime. At the dedication ceremony of the Holocaust Museum in April 1993, Elie Wiesel, Jewish novelist and Nobel Peace Prize Laureate, pleaded directly to Clinton, who was present, as follows: 'Mr. President ... As a Jew I am saying that we must do something to stop the bloodshed in that country [the former Yugoslavia]! ... Something, anything must be done'.[44]

Critiques against the government also emerged from the inside of the State Department, accompanying the 'largest wave of resignations in State Department history' (Power 2007: 315). Beginning with George Kenney's aforementioned resignation in August 1992, Marshall Harris (Bosnian desk officer), Jon Western (intelligence analyst) and Steven Walker (Croatian desk officer) followed suit successively in July and August 1993. Harris, for example, explained his resignation by stating, 'I can no longer serve in a Department of State that accepts the forceful dismemberment of a European state and that will not act against genocide and the Serbian officials who perpetrate it'.[45] Ultimately, Zimmermann, who was recalled from the embassy in Belgrade to Washington in protest against the Serbian aggression in Bosnia in 1992 and subsequently took office as Director of the State Department's Bureau of Refugee Affairs, left the Foreign Service due to disagreement with the government's policy.[46] Such a series of resignations surely helped to create a negative image of the government's handling.

As a result, the Clinton Administration was denounced on the grounds that 'After years of vacillation and debate about what America should do about Bosnia, we must also acknowledge that there has not been a clear policy',[47] and that 'American policy in the former Yugoslavia has been morally and politically bankrupt'.[48] The reason for the lack of 'clear policy' can be attributed to the fact that action and inaction were demanded simultaneously. Interestingly, such a dilemma was foreseen in relatively earlier days. For example, Senator John Glenn stated in August 1992 that

> Inserting ourselves into an ongoing war driven by ethnic animosity that is centuries old would require a major U.S. force commitment of indeterminable duration, with the very real probability of casualties. I am not at all sure the American people, outraged as they are about the atrocities occurring in Bosnia, are prepared to make that kind of commitment.
>
> Nevertheless, expressing caution about one end of the spectrum of possible U.S. intervention ... does not mean we should throw up our hands and conclude that we can do nothing about this continuing tragedy but wring our hands. I believe there is a middle ground. I believe the President is pursuing this middle ground in the United Nations.[49]

Presumably, as this 'middle ground' would mean adopting intervention and non-intervention at the same time, frustration was boosted for those who urged more American commitment and for those who feared being dragged into the war.

Ambivalent attitudes can also be observed in opinion poll data. As was referred to at the beginning of this chapter, 69 per cent of Americans said that they were following the situation in Bosnia as of May 1993, which indicates high public awareness of this 'foreign' crisis. On concrete questionnaires, however, contradictory results were shown. When asked to give a good reason to explain why some people 'favoured' America's air strikes, 63 per cent suggested 'a moral obligation' to stop atrocities as a good reason for this claim (very good reason: 17 per cent; good reason: 46 per cent). In contrast, when asked why some people 'opposed' America's air strikes, 73 per cent supposed that this was because 'American soldiers could be killed or wounded' (very good reason: 36

Dilemmas of intervention & reform of NATO 143

per cent; good reason: 37 per cent), whilst 71 per cent believed that this was because 'Air strikes could lead to the involvement of its ground troops' (very good reason: 30 per cent; good reason: 41 per cent).[50] These outcomes make clear that people found reasonable grounds in both pros and cons of intervention – hence, the government was vulnerable to criticism whatever policy it might adopt, just as other opinion polls indicate at the final stage of the war that only 25 per cent of those surveyed thought that the Clinton administration had 'clear and well-thought-out policy on the Bosnian situations', while 65 per cent disagreed.[51]

*The 'lift and strike' policy as a focal point*

Careful investigation of the claims of those calling for American intervention reveals that they did not necessarily push for the dispatch of ground troops. For example, while Congressman McCloskey continuously attacked the government's policy and, despite being a Democrat, even demanded Secretary of State Christopher's resignation for his inadequate handling (Power 2007: 321), 'McCloskey's advocacy stop[ped] at airstrikes' and did not articulate the deployment of American troops on the ground.[52] What he and other proponents contended was to launch strikes from the air to halt the Serb militias' genocide against the Muslim population. Meanwhile, those who opposed American action did not callously say that nothing should be done. They concurred upon limited military operations unless American ground forces should be deployed. More concretely, they supported aerial bombardment because it would create military balance on the ground, deter the Bosnian Serbs from launching further offensives and ultimately open peace negations among the local parties.

Consequently, arguments about Bosnia culminated in a policy called the 'lift and strike'. As Chapter 3 explicated, this policy goes back to 1991 when an arms embargo was imposed against the whole of Yugoslavia after the eruption of military clashes in Slovenia and Croatia. In Bosnia, however, this embargo had worked in favour of the Serb militant groups because armaments and weapons were transferred from the Serbian Republic to them. Therefore, there was increasing pressure for the UN arms embargo to be lifted in order to provide the militarily inferior Muslims with weapons for self-defence and to start air strikes against the Bosnian Serb militias.

The lift and strike policy was broadly upheld in the United States.[53] However, President Clinton never approved it – although he had advocated it during the presidential election campaign. As a candidate, for instance, he commented that 'the United States should take the lead in seeking United Nations authorisation for air strikes ... and should consider whether to push for lifting the United Nations arms embargo that some contend unfairly hurts the Bosnians'.[54] After having been elected, why did he reject this policy? To understand the reason, it is necessary to investigate the troubles that beset him in the international context. He was confronted by vehement objections from the European states.

## Intra-alliance conflict: from the American perspective

As argued in the previous chapters, the Europeans had already deployed their troops to Bosnia since 1992 under UNPROFOR. In the meantime, they had been trying to reach a settlement among the locals. As the war continued, and the Vance-Owen Peace Plan (VOPP) collapsed,[55] however, a more coercive approach was gradually asserted within America. Yet the different political conditions prevailing for the Europeans and the Americans ignited a serious diplomatic row because European soldiers would be put in danger by U.S.-led military operations.

From the American perspective, the arms embargo was merely seen as 'illegal because it violates article 51 of the Charter of the United Nations which gives every country the right to defend itself', said Senator Bill Bradley (D-NJ).[56] Senator Lieberman contended that 'While we wait for the lifting to occur, the people of Bosnia remain under siege – with suffering, death and destruction an intrinsic part of everyday life',[57] whereas Senator Dole also remarked that 'Do we wait another year and see another 100,000 dead?'[58] In both houses of Congress, a number of resolutions were issued to urge President Clinton to terminate the UN embargo.[59]

To break this deadlock, President Clinton proposed that the European states withdraw UNPROFOR and then launch air strikes. This negotiation started in May 1993 with the dispatch of Secretary of State Christopher to Europe. But the Europeans, especially Britain and France, rejected this because it would make the situation even worse by suspending humanitarian relief efforts, and accused 'the United States of "hypocrisy" for not providing ground troops in Bosnia but pushing for a tougher approach against the Serbs'.[60] Their disagreements boiled down to confrontation so intensely that it was dubbed 'the biggest diplomatic rift since Suez 1956', as examined in Chapters 3 and 4.

Confronted by this robust resistance, the United States made some concessions. When a congressional vote on a bill to arm the Bosnian Muslims was split 50–50, Vice President Al Gore exercised his constitutional right as President of the Senate to reject it.[61] Furthermore, on 11 August 1995, President Clinton vetoed the bill 'S21' to unilaterally terminate the UN embargo, sponsored by Senator Dole and cosponsored by 18 Senators, including Biden, Jesse Helms (R-NC), Lieberman, McCain, Mitch McConnell (R-KY) and others.[62] He explained his disapproval by stating that it would 'undermine the chances for peace in Bosnia, lead to a wider war, and undercut the authority of the United Nations'. Besides this, he added that it 'could lead to an escalation of the conflict there, including the almost certain Americanization of the conflict'[63] – i.e. American involvement would become inevitable.

In military operations too, the United States changed its policy to meet the Europeans' request. As discussed in Chapter 3, while harbouring the unresolved friction, NATO states had conducted limited aerial bombardment since February 1994. In the strikes of November 1994, however, 43 British soldiers were captured in retaliation for the NATO attacks. As the British government called for the halting of this air campaign, the United States concurred. National Security Advisor, Anthony Lake, told President Clinton that 'to use NATO air strikes to prevent the fall of Bihac [which was under siege at that time] has only intensified the trans-Atlantic friction'.[64] As it was similarly argued that 'American pressure for airstrikes only exacerbated friction within the alliance' (Sharp 1997: 47), the problem had become not merely about saving Bosnia but also about avoiding further deterioration of America's relationship with its European Allies.

Facing this impasse, Senator Helms remarked that 'With empty threats, hollow ultimatums, and embarrassing flip-flops, the credibility of the United States has been whittled away'.[65] Nevertheless, what would have happened if the lift and strike policy had been actually implemented? Presumably, 'Unilateral lift of the embargo would lead to unilateral American responsibility' (President Clinton),[66] or 'unilateral lifting of the arms embargo would Americanise the war there and give us a very heavy responsibility' (Secretary of State Christopher).[67] Ivo Daalder (2000: 63) explains the pressure from Congress as follows: 'Of course, the congressional actions provided no clear road map for how to resolve the conflict in Bosnia. It was more an expression of frustration with administration policy and a strong belief that the Bosnians possessed a moral right of self-defense than a ready policy course to follow'. As his account implies, the 'expression of frustration', rather than its feasibility as such, seems to have contributed to forming strong support for lift and strike policy.

Frustration was also shown by President Clinton. It was suggested to him by a reporter that Bosnia was 'the most important foreign policy problem of your Presidency, and you are seen as indecisive', and he was then asked, 'Is this frustrating to you in a situation such as Bosnia, where no action might actually be the best action?' He responded candidly: 'Sure it is, because most of the people who criticize don't have a better alternative. And many of them who criticize don't have any alternative'.[68] This signifies that he was placed in a situation where no ready solution was found, but failing to solve this war would trigger criticisms.

Admittedly, Clinton's policy was constrained by what he could not control. As he acknowledged, 'when I took office, the United Nations was already there';[69] the uncoordinated international approach ended up in 'the inherent contradictions in trying to use NATO air power coercively against the Bosnian Serbs when our [American] allies ha[d] troops on the ground attempting to maintain impartiality in performing a humanitarian mission'.[70] Furthermore, it should be added that another problem, called the 'dual key' problem, made the international response more complicated. This means, even if America and the European states could agree on starting bombing, permission from the UN Secretary General was required – thus, NATO decisions could in all cases be overturned by the Secretary General, although the use of force had already been sanctioned by the UN Security Council, which also 'frustrated' the U.S. decision makers.[71] Given their experiences in Bosnia, it is conceivable that they were prompted to overhaul the international security system by reorganising NATO as adjustment to the new environment. The next section explores how these experiences affected the Washington leaders.

## American views on the roles of NATO: from intervention to reorganisation

### Military operation

At the final phase of the war, 350 UNPROFOR personnel were captured by the Bosnian Serb militias in retaliation for NATO's air strikes in May 1995. Upon facing this hostage crisis, Britain, France and the Netherlands organised the Rapid Reaction Force (RRF) to reinforce the lightly armed UNPROFOR. President Clinton authorised the furnishing of up to 17 million dollars to the United Nations for purposes of supporting the RRF.[72] This was surely to assist the new international efforts but was also intended to avoid the withdrawal of UNPROFOR. That is to say, NATO's inner circle had discussed an evacuation plan called 'OPLAN 40104' at that time and, if it were to be carried out, NATO states would provide 82,000 troops, 25,000 of whom would be American soldiers. As Holbrooke (1999: 66) and Daalder (2000: 48) illustrate in more detail, American ground forces would be 'automatically' sent to Bosnia as part of NATO forces – in case of its non-participation, it would significantly jeopardise not only this plan as such but also its credibility as an alliance leader. Therefore, the withdrawal of UNPROFOR became no longer desirable for the United States despite its long-lasting persuasion.

After the build-up of UNPROFOR, NATO launched massive air strikes from late August 1995, which lasted for three weeks. Holbrooke (1999: 92) remarked that 'This was the most important test of American leadership since the end of the Cold War'. Unquestionably, its ability to coordinate the international action and perform the military campaign made evident the indispensable role of the United States in the Alliance, as was indicated by French Foreign Minister Herve de Charette's relieved comment that 'America is back'.[73] The war in Bosnia was terminated with the conclusion of the Dayton Agreement, and it, along with other NATO members, moved towards the discussion of the reconstitution of the European security system.

### What roles of NATO did a hegemonic state find after Bosnia?

Given its leadership and military capability, it was not foreseeable at the outset how the United States would act to bring the war in Bosnia to an end. First of all, political leaders in Washington preferred non-intervention for fear of entanglement and thus did not assume that NATO would play such a role in a conflict occurring beyond its borders. Moreover, it is hard to consider that they had a clear vision on its activity, just as the serious confrontation among its members hampered American policy. In fact, Holbrooke (1999: 361), who was directly involved in the inter-Alliance disputes, describes its graveness as follows:

> Washington's relations with our European allies were worse than at any time since the 1956 Suez crisis. But this comparison was misleading; because Suez came at the height of the Cold War, the strain then was containable.

Bosnia, however, had defined the first phase of the post-Cold War relationship between Europe and the United States, and seriously damaged the Atlantic relationship.

Within the public sphere too, NATO was critically viewed as it was actually argued that 'the hope that [NATO] could be similarly useful in managing local disputes like the Balkans now appears to have been a fantasy',[74] and that 'The visible gap between the alliance's rhetoric about unity and purpose, and its ability to act in a real crisis outside its original purpose of territorial self-defense, is growing'.[75] Likewise, it was also said that NATO was 'still searching for a role in a world with no clear adversary such as that embodied for decades by the Soviet Union'.[76] Such a view was shared on the governmental side, as Secretary of State Christopher (1998: 358) remarked that 'Only a few months before [the conclusion of the Dayton Agreement], many in Europe as well as in the United States had questioned whether NATO had a role to play in the post-Cold War era'.

Despite these negative assessments, why did the American policymakers try to reinvigorate NATO? Specifically, what role of NATO did they envision after their involvement in Bosnia? As considered in Chapter 2, it can be surely supposed that a series of tragic events pushed the United States not only to intervene but also to carry out its reforms so that humanitarian tragedy could be dealt with properly. Surely, this understanding is indispensable because without humanitarian normative pressure for action, American policy would otherwise have remained silent due to the lack of strategic interests and the risk of entanglement.

Nevertheless, if normative pressure had been the sole factor in explaining the Washington leaders' decision, they could have conceived of a NATO that would facilitate military intervention in what is perceived as excessive human rights abuses. In this case, a more aggressive structure of the Alliance should have been preferred to forcefully intervene in other countries' domestic affairs. As investigated thus far, even if action was demanded genuinely to stop humanitarian tragedy, to do so would collide with other social demands; in the American case, it was simultaneously asserted that no troops should be sent to this foreign battlefield. Given the dilemmas that confronted the American political leaders, it is difficult to accept that humanitarian grounds alone led them to embark on NATO's reorganisation.

In fact, even after the war in Bosnia, discussion on foreign deployment of American soldiers was not so different from how it used to be. When President Clinton suggested sending 20,000 American troops to join the Implementation Force (IFOR), namely the NATO-led operation in the post-war Bosnia, he found it rough going to gain approval from Congress, although its mandate was for *peacekeeping* missions limited to only *one year*. As soon as the question of possible deployment was raised, as early as October 1995, Congress warned the President by passing resolutions to require a congressional vote for it.[77] In the end, it was passed in December of that year through the Senate (69: 30) and by the House of Representatives (287: 141),[78] but this reveals that it was not an easy decision to dispatch troops into foreign territories.

Neither was this deployment so widely welcomed within the public sphere. Directly before the aforementioned congressional vote, 54 per cent of the respondents disapproved of the deployment (strongly: 43 per cent; not strongly: 11 per cent), whereas 41 per cent approved of it (strongly: 24 per cent; not strongly: 17 per cent).[79] Interestingly, this result was provided although 'the development of a peaceful solution to the situation in Bosnia' had been hugely appreciated ('very important': 30 per cent; 'somewhat important': 48 per cent), in contrast to 'not too important' (11 per cent) and 'not important at all' (8 per cent).[80] It can be seen that different discussions took place at the general level to assess the value of the peace settlement and at the practical level about the dispatch of troops to a foreign territory.

Thus, the dilemma between normative demands not to ignore humanitarian tragedy and the fear of involvement remained unsolved. This unsolved problem, in turn, pushed the American policymakers to redesign NATO. That is to say, developing an international framework for crisis response would help them to pre-empt the dilemmas of intervention and also avoid the unnecessary confusion that they experienced with their European partners during the war in Bosnia. Indeed, the lack of such international mechanisms had been seen as a source of fundamental problems. For example, concerning Bosnia, President Clinton stated that 'it was the first time we'd ever done anything out of the area of the NATO members themselves. ... It's not been established yet that anyone is capable of solving a civil war in another country'.[81] In other words, it was still not ready and therefore confusion was caused in NATO states' handling. As he added that 'we're working on this',[82] this prompted the U.S. to launch NATO's reorganisation.

President Clinton also claimed that 'we must work to prevent future Bosnias' and that 'we must build the structures that will help newly free nations to complete their transformation successfully to free market democracies and preserve their own freedom'.[83] As this indicates, more emphasis was placed on creating an international system to 'prevent future Bosnias' by building 'the structures' for stability, not creating international mechanisms for intervention.

Similar views were also heard from other officials. Deputy Secretary of State Strobe Talbott (1995: 28) remarked that 'the lesson of the tragedy in the former Yugoslavia is not to retire NATO in disgrace but to develop its ability to counter precisely those forces that have exploded in the Balkans', while Secretary of Defense Les Aspin (1994: 13) stated that 'tragic events in what used to be Yugoslavia underscore the urgency of being prepared to undertake new peacekeeping missions'. Likewise, Holbrooke remarked (1999: 372, emphasis original) that *'There will be other Bosnias in our lives* – areas where early outside involvement can be decisive, and American leadership will be required'.

During the war, the United States had already started an overhaul of NATO. In mid-June 1993, an Inter-agency Working Group (IWG) was set up and soon offered a 'proposal to create more mobile and flexible command structures and forces so that NATO could more easily deploy forces beyond its borders to deal with future Bosnias through so-called Combined Joint Task Forces or CJTFs [*sic*]' (Asmus 2002: 34). In October 1993, the United States formally proposed this 'concept in order to push the alliance further down the road toward out-of-area operations and toward expeditionary doctrine and structures' (Deni 2007: 39). As was explicated in Chapter 3, the CJTF was one of the major reforms of NATO in terms of its out-of-area activities. It is true that the notion of the CJTF itself had already been proposed since the end of the Cold War as a broad idea; nevertheless, it took shape concretely within the U.S. decision-making circle in addressing Bosnia (cf. Asmus 2002; Barry 1996; Yost 1998).

Thus, it is necessary to consider humanitarian normative outcry to understand what led the Washington government to the foreign strife in the Balkans. Without this influence, it would have kept the policy of non-intervention. Once it commenced its engagement, however, it was struck by a question of how to deal with it; while being continuously pressed for action, the Washington leaders simultaneously faced other critiques for the danger of being dragged in it. To avoid the repetition of the same dilemma, the Clinton administration moved towards the reorganisation of NATO to create an international framework of effective security governance.

## Conclusion

Holbrooke (1999: 369) quoted Henry Kissinger (1994), who discussed two traits of American diplomacy. One is found in the tradition of Theodore Roosevelt, representing 'realpolitik' based upon balance of power to secure America's own strategic interests, while the other follows in the lines of Woodrow Wilson by embodying idealism to put forward the truism of American universal values, such as democracy and human rights. Such characteristics can also be seen in its response to Bosnia – some people insisted on non-intervention because they judged none of America's national interests implicated in this foreign strife, while others advocated intervention because turning their eyes away from humanitarian tragedy would run counter to the American values of human rights protection. These different perspectives had reasonable grounds to justify their own claims, which inevitably resulted in constant struggles over desirable foreign policy. What was demanded was to make compatible these contrasting claims at the same time.

This chapter has investigated the dilemmas that the American decision makers faced in Bosnia and, through this experience, what roles they came to envision for NATO in the post-Cold War world. At the outbreak of the war, they, weighing the cost and benefit, cautiously excluded intervention. Despite their initial attitude, the government gradually shifted its policy and began its commitment with the growing call for action. However, this guaranteed that no effective policy would be produced immediately because the government leaders were confronted by a norm dilemma. While being urged by the outcry not to ignore the war, they were also pressured not to deploy American soldiers for fear of involvement. Furthermore, they were struck by a head-on debate with its European Allies due to their uncoordinated international approach. All of these contributed to generating reprimands against the government as indecisive.

## 150  *Dilemmas of intervention & reform of NATO*

Having gone through such dilemmas of intervention, the U.S. political leaders made clear their views of NATO reorganisation for the sake of conflict management. To be sure, it is possible to contend that humanitarian normative pressure propelled an American response to Bosnia and facilitated NATO reforms to cope with similar emergencies. To follow this logic, however, the Washington leaders could have reorganised it to repeat intervention in what are claimed as humanitarian disasters. As explored, it was difficult to find evidence that sending troops into foreign warfare became accepted without hesitation. Instead, its reforms were launched to prevent crises from occurring before international intervention would be needed. Put another way, the presence of a well-developed international organisation would help them to address humanitarian contingencies before they raise the possibility of pre-empting the dilemmas of intervention.

From the traditional IR perspective, it appears that a superpower country has enormous resources to influence the course of alliances by imposing its own will. It is certain that American military capability was indispensable, especially in the final phase of the war in Bosnia, as Sten Rynning (2005: 24) says that 'U.S. leadership is a must'. However, in a world where normative effects transcend territorial borders and define appropriate goals for states to achieve, the United States also needed to arrange common understandings on how to take joint action. In reality, dissidence among NATO members triggered such intense rows that the Washington leaders had to make concessions. This chapter shed light on how and why the United States also sought for international frameworks for conflict prevention in tandem with other states.

## Notes

1 For example, Samantha Power, who later became the U.S. Ambassador to the United Nations under the Barack Obama Administration, used this phrase as the title of her book (Power 2007).
2 On 12 May 1993, in *The Gallup Poll: Public Opinion*, 1993: 95.
3 Quoted in Thomas L. Friedman, 'Bosnia Reconsidered; Where Candidate Clinton Saw a Challenge The President Sees an Insoluble Quagmire', *The New York Times*, 8 April 1993.
4 Quoted Rhodes (2013: 40).
5 Similar statements by American decision makers are also proffered in other expositions, including, to name a few, Halverson (1996: 2), Holbrooke (1999: 24–26), Rynning (2005: 25), Western (2002: 119–120).
6 Quoted in Holbrooke (1999: 23), Power (2007: 282–283).
7 Quoted in Power (2007: 282).
8 For example, Senator William Cohen (R-ME) warned about the danger of intervention by directly citing the Weinberger Doctrine, in S12015, 102nd Congress, 10 August 1992 (ironically, he was later appointed as Secretary of Defense under the Clinton administration and led the American intervention).
9 Also see Woodward (1995: 154–155). Additionally Thomas Halverson argues that 'America has also developed an interest in building a cooperative security, political relationship, first with the Soviet government, and then with Russia'.
10 The effects of the media information are often referred to, e.g. by Halverson (1996: 9), Power (2007: 274–277), Strobel (1997: 147) and Western (2002: 127).

## Dilemmas of intervention & reform of NATO   151

11  His reports have now been converted into a monograph (Gutman 1993). As a crosscheck to confirm the influence of his reports, see Power (2002: 271) and Don Oberdorfer, 'Week of Publicity and Policymaking Started Off With a Chilling Headline', *The Washington Post*, 9 August 1992.
12  'Shame in Our Time, in Bosnia', *The New York Times*, 21 May 1992.
13  'Milosevic Isn't Hitler, But…', *The New York Times*, 4 August 1992.
14  'Atrocity in Bosnia', *The Washington Post*, 3 August 1992.
15  Lee H. Hamilton, 'When It's Our Duty to Intervene; In Cases Like Bosnia, the U.N. Must Alter Its Presumption Against Warfare', *The Washington Post*, 9 August 1992. 'Four More What?', *The Washington Post*, 17 August 1992.
16  Quoted in Don Oberdorfer, 'U.S. Aide Resigns Over Balkan Policy; Administration's Handling of Civil War Decried as "Ineffective"', *The Washington Post*, 26 August, 1992.
17  George D. Kenney, 'Bosnia – Appeasement in Our Time', *The Washington Post*, 30 August 1992.
18  Senator Bob Dole (R-KS) in S8872, 102nd Congress, 25 June 1992.
19  Senator Larry Pressler (R-SD) in S15517, 102nd Congress, 29 September 1992.
20  Senator Joseph Biden (D-DE) in S17706, 102nd Congress, 8 October 1992.
21  Joe Lieberman (D-CT) in S11406, 102nd Congress, 4 August 1992.
22  Senator David L. Boren (D-OK) in S13540, 102nd Congress, 15 September 1992. Also see, Steny Hoyer, (D-MD-5) in E1779, 102nd Congress, 11 June 1992.
23  For example, from the House of Representatives, H.Res.448, 102nd Congress (1991–1992), 12 May 1992; H.Res.470, 102nd Congress (1991–1992), 21 May 1992; H.Res.554, 102nd Congress (1991–1992), 11 August 1992; H.Res.557, 102nd Congress (1991–1992), 12 August 1992; H.Res.546, 102nd Congress (1991–1992), 19 August 1992; H.Res.552, 102nd Congress (1991–1992), 14 September 1992; and H.Res.598, 102nd Congress (1991–1992), 3 October 1992. From the Senate, S.Res.290, 102nd Congress (1991–1992), 29 April 1992; S.Res.300, 102nd Congress (1991–1992), 19 May 1992; S.Res.314, 102nd Congress (1991–1992), 11 June 1992; and S.Res.330, 102nd Congress (1991–1992), 11 August 1992. They are available at www.congress.gov/ (Accessed on 1 July 2018).
24  Jason Vest, 'Battle Cry of the Anti-War Congressman; Frank McCloskey was against U.S. Involvement in Iraq, but He's Seen the People of Bosnia', *The Washington Post*, 19 February 1994.
25  Concerning the views of Reagan, Shultz and Kissinger, see Elaine Sciolino 'Clinton Urges Stronger U.S. Stand On Enforcing Bosnia Flight Ban', *The New York Times*, 11 December 1992.
26  Henry A. Kissinger, 'How to Persuade Serbia the World Means Business: Balkans: What's needed is a coherent program to multiply political and economic pressures on Belgrade. A line must be drawn in the soil', *The Los Angeles Times*, 20 September 1992.
27  David Briscoe, 'Congressman Calls For Possible Air Strikes Against Serbs', *The Associated Press*, 17 November 1992.
28  Jason Vest, 'Battle Cry of the Anti-War Congressman', *The Washington Post*, 19 February 1994.
29  Quoted in Don Oberdorfer, 'Week of Publicity and Policymaking Started Off With a Chilling Headline', *The Washington Post*, 9 August 1992. Halverson (1996: 10) claims that 'Candidate Bill Clinton also used Bosnia as a vehicle to contest President Bush's image as a foreign specialist'.
30  Barton Gellman, 'U.S. Military Fears Balkan Intervention; Dual Combat, Relief Role Seen Unworkable', *The Washington Post*, 12 August 1992.
31  Quoted in Sobel (2001: 183).
32  Quoted in Don Oberdorfer 'Bush Shifts Toward Force to Aid Bosnia', *The Washington Post*, 7 August 1992.

## 152  Dilemmas of intervention & reform of NATO

33  Ibid.
34  'Not Tough Enough With Serbia', *The New York Times*, 7 August 1992.
35  Data taken on 25 February 1993, in *The Gallup Poll: Public Opinion*, 1993: 41.
36  Elaine Sciolino, 'Bush Asks France and Britain to Back Force of Monitors in Kosovo', *The New York Times*, 25 November 1992.
37  Quoted in 'Excerpts From President Clinton's News Conference', *The Washington Post*, 24 April 1993.
38  Senator Ernest Hollings (D-SC) in S12227, 102nd Congress, 11 August 1992.
39  Senator John McCain (R-AR) in S11998, 102nd Congress, 10 August 1992. See similar comments made by Bob Inglis (R-SC-4) in H2433, 103rd Congress, 12 May 1993.
40  William Drozdiak, 'U.S. and Europe In Serious Rift Over Bosnia War; Allies Resent GIs' Absence As Americans Call for Action', *The Washington Post*, 27 November 1994.
41  Concerning how Somalia was discussed in relation to Bosnia at that time, see Paul Lewis, 'Final Reluctant Peacekeepers: Many U.N. Members Reconsider Role in Conflicts', *The New York Times*, 12 December 1993. Also see Wheeler (2000: 198–200), Seybolt (2008: 57–60), Strobel (1997: 141–142).
42  Robert C. Byrd (D-WV) in S5614, 103rd Congress, 12 May 1994.
43  'Stop the Death Camps: An Open Letter to World Leaders', *The New York Times*, 5 August 1992.
44  Quoted in Asmus 2002: 23. Original text is available at 'Elie Wiesel's Remarks at the Dedication Ceremonies for the United States Holocaust Memorial Museum, April 22, 1993', www.ushmm.org/information/about-the-museum/mission-and-history/wiesel (Accessed on 1 July 2018).
45  Quoted in Power (2007: 313).
46  John M. Goshko, 'Diplomat Quits; Bosnia Rift Hinted', *The Washington Post*, 7 January 1994.
47  Senator Kay B. Hutchison (R-TX) in S14843, 104th Congress, 10 October 1995.
48  Senator Robert C. Byrd (D-WV) in S5612, 103rd Congress, 12 May 1994.
49  Senator John H. Glenn, Jr. (D-OH) in S12285, 102nd Congress, 11 August 1992.
50  On 6 May 1993 in *The Gallup Poll: Public Opinion*, 1993: 95–96. In addition, support for American policy changed in accordance with the deepening degree of military commitment. 65 per cent of the respondents favoured the plan of starting American 'airstrikes', whereas 27 per cent opposed. However, the rate dropped to 41 per cent when asked about sending U.S. 'ground troops' if air strikes were to be found not effective, while the rate of those who disagreed increased to 53 per cent (on 16–18 April 1994), *The Gallup Poll: Public Opinion*, 1994: 216. Here a dilemma of involvement can also be observed.
51  On 6–5 June 1995 in *The Gallup Poll: Public Opinion*, 1995: 240.
52  Jason Vest, 'Battle Cry of the Anti-War Congressman', *The Washington Post*, 19 February 1994.
53  Polls reveals that the lift and strike policy was supported by 53 per cent in January and by 61 per cent in May 1993, quoted in Kull and Ramsay (2003: 85).
54  Elaine Sciolino, 'Clinton Urges Stronger U.S. Stand on Enforcing Bosnia Flight Ban', *The New York Times*, 12 December 1992.
55  Concerning the VOPP, the United States was critical because its cabinet members, especially the U.S. ambassador to the United Nations, Madeleine Albright, saw the plan as an appeasement to the Bosnian Serbs' aggression and ethnic cleansing, see Szamuely (2013: 180). Also see David Owen (1996: 170ff), for his criticism of the lack of American support.
56  In S5621, 103rd Congress, 12 May 1994.

## Dilemmas of intervention & reform of NATO    153

57 Senator Joe Lieberman (D-CT) in S11224, 104th Congress, 2 August 1995.
58 Quoted in William Drozdiak, 'Dole Places Bosnia Atop Senate Agenda; GOP Leader Presses End to Arms Ban', *The Washington Post*, 30 November 1994.
59 For example, see S.Res.341, 102nd Congress (1991–1992), 16 September 1992; S.Res.11, 103rd Congress (1993–1994), 21 January 1993; S.Res.104, 103rd Congress (1993–1994), 16 June 1993; S.Res.79, 103rd Congress (1993–1994), 24 June 1993; H.Res.35, 103rd Congress (1993–1994), 19 April 1993; and H.Res.204, 104th Congress (1995–1996), 1 August 1995.
60 Charles Forrest, 'The Coward's Way Out', *The Washington Post*, 12 December 1994.
61 Tom Rhodes and Tim Judah, 'Gore casting vote keeps Bosnian arms ban in place', *The Times*, 2 July 1994.
62 'S.21: Bosnia and Herzegovina Self-Defense Act of 1995', available at www.congress.gov/bill/104th-congress/senate-bill/21 (Accessed on 1 July 2018). Also see Daalder (2000: 64). Concerning Clinton's veto, see 'Statement on Vetoing Legislation To Lift the Arms Embargo Against Bosnia August 11, 1995', in The American Presidency Project, www.presidency.ucsb.edu/documents/statement-vetoing-legislation-lift-the-arms-embargo-against-bosnia (Accessed on July 1 2018), a website run by the University of California Santa Barbara, which holds the leading database of American presidents' speeches and transcripts. Thereafter, this source is referred to as The American Presidency Project.
63 'Message to the Senate Returning Without Approval the Bosnia and Herzegovina Self-Defense Act of 1995 August 11, 1995', in The American Presidency Project, www.presidency.ucsb.edu/documents/message-the-senate-returning-without-approval-the-bosnia-and-herzegovina-self-defense-act (Accessed on 1 July 2018).
64 Quoted in Daalder (2000: 33). Also see Michael R. Gordon, 'U.S., In Shift, Gives Up Its Talk Of Tough Action Against Serbs', *The New York Times*, 29 November 1994.
65 Senator Jesse Helms (R-NC) in S5617, 103rd Congress, 12 May 1994.
66 'Message to the Senate Returning Without Approval', (see fn. 63).
67 Quoted in Royal United Service Institute for Defence Studies 1998: 1214–1215 (the original sources are: the Bill is 104th Congress, 1st Session, S. 21, 4 January 1995 and Christopher's comment is in U.S. Embassy London, *European Wireless File*, 27 January 1995).
68 'Interview with Bob Edwards and Mara Liasson of National Public Radio', 7 August 1995, in The American Presidency Project, www.presidency.ucsb.edu/documents/interview-with-bob-edwards-and-mara-liasson-national-public-radio (Accessed on 1 July 2018).
69 'Interview on MTV's "Enough is Enough" Forum', 19 April 1994, in The American Presidency Project, www.presidency.ucsb.edu/documents/interview-mtvs-enough-enough-forum (Accessed on 1 July 2018).
70 Lake's statement quoted in 'Conflict In The Balkans: The Policy Colliding Missions', *The New York Times*, 4 December 1994.
71 On more detailed accounts on this problem, see Daaldr (2000: 72), Ryning (2005: 27).
72 'Memorandum on Assistance to the United Nations Rapid Reaction Force in Bosnia August 3, 1995', in The American Presidency Project, in The American Presidency Project, www.presidency.ucsb.edu/documents/memorandum-assistance-the-united-nations-rapid-reaction-force-bosnia (Accessed on 1 July 2018).
73 Quoted in Asmus (2002: 125). Concerning America's leadership in this military operation, see Asmus (2002: 124–128), Daalder (2000: Chapters. 3–4), Holbrooke (1999: Chapters 5–7).
74 'Conflict in the Balkans: the Policy Colliding Missions – a special report; U.S. and Bosnia: How a Policy Changed', *The New York Times*, 4 December 1994.

75 John Hoagland, 'NATO: A Sweet, but Misleading, Song', *The Washington Post*, 15 November 1994, quoted in Goldgeier (1997: 98).
76 Ruth Marcus, John F. Harris, 'Behind U.S. Policy Shift on Bosnia: Strains in NATO', *The Washington Post*, 5 December 1994.
77 See S.Res.187 (20 October 1995) and H.Res.247 (30 October 1995). Concerning the pressure from Congress, see Norman Kempster and Elizabeth Shogren, 'Clinton to Consult Congress on Deployment: Balkans: President says he will seek approval before sending troops to Bosnia, but only after peace agreement – based on U.S. participation – is reached', *The Los Angeles Times*, 21 October 1995.
78 S.J.Res.44, 104th Congress (1995–1996), 13 December 1995; H.Res.302, 104th Congress (1995–1996), 13 December 1995.
79 On 23 December 1995 in *The Gallup Poll: Public Opinion*, 1995: 192.
80 On 27 October 1995 in *The Gallup Poll: Public Opinion*, 1995: 156.
81 'Exchange with Reporters in Brussels, Belgium January 9, 1994', in The American Presidency Project, www.presidency.ucsb.edu/documents/exchange-with-reporters-brussels-belgium (Accessed on 1 July 2018).
82 *Ibid.*
83 This statement was made after he said that 'NATO remains the bedrock of security in Europe', 'Remarks to the Conference on Security and Cooperation in Europe in Budapest, Hungary December 5, 1994', in The American Presidency Project.

# 8 Conclusion
## Norm dilemmas and international security governance

### From domestic norms to international institutional redevelopment

#### *Normative pressure and intervention*

This book started with a theoretical puzzle: how to explain the persistence and transformation of NATO in the post-Cold War era. The conventional knowledge of International Relations (IR) tells us that with the demise of military threats, alliances should lose their *raison d'être*. Nevertheless, NATO still exists and has developed new activities after its adversary disappeared – the first case was international conflict management in Bosnia. Investigating the international response to this crisis, the question then became how this former anti-Soviet alliance evolved, through the introduction of reforms, into a security organisation prepared to deal with regional crises outside of its territory.

This book first examined, in comparison with other IR theories, how the war in Bosnia was perceived within the Western states. Neorealists (as well as classical realists) would contend that intervention is conducted based upon cost-benefit calculations. In this context, it can be assumed that certain interests at stake, including strategic and economic ones, prompted the Western states to intervene in the Balkans. Undoubtedly, such considerations should not be omitted to explain this complex social phenomenon, but this book found that they were simply insufficient to understand the international response to this conflict. For instance, some countries, in particular Britain (Chapter 4) and the United States (Chapter 7), were obviously reluctant to get involved due to the lack of relevance to their tangible national interests and, moreover, even feared being bogged down in what they called an ethnic quagmire without exit. If strategic elements had been regarded as crucial, they would have taken swifter measures to protect their interests.

Rather, non-intervention was strategically more stressed in order not to exert adverse influence on the unstable political situation in the Soviet Union and subsequently Russia at that time. Weighing up the importance of retaining a good relationship, the European and American political leaders were concerned that stepping into this former Communist territory would evoke antipathy against the West and ignite nationalistic sentiments in the Soviet Union, which would make Mikhail Gorbachev's political manoeuvring more difficult. Non-intervention was prioritised from the neorealist perspective.

It seems plausible that the influx of refugees might have pushed the Western states to prevent them from coming into their countries. Again, such a possibility should not be dismissed; however, Chapter 2 questioned whether this concern was enough to explicate the entire intervention activities, while, contemplating the argument of Chapter 6, this explanation alone has difficulty in fully accounting for the policymaking by Germany, the country that accommodated the highest number of refugees.

From the neoliberal institutionalist angle, it can be held that NATO's institutional assets enabled its members to address new security problems after the end of the Cold War, as Wallander (2000) states that institutional assets in this highly developed organisation helped its members to adapt themselves to a new political environment. This perspective elucidates why NATO, the most viable military organisation in Europe, was eventually chosen to engage in Bosnia, not other international bodies. Given NATO's assets, however, some examples of counter-evidence were presented. Chapters 2 and 3 made clear that NATO's command structure, geared up for collective defence against aggression by the Communist bloc, was largely viewed as not applicable to such a low-intensity war as Bosnia. More importantly, even allowing for its institutional advantages, it is necessary to investigate the reason why the Western states decided to commit the Alliance to a war occurring in a foreign country and develop it for the sake of what were called 'non-Article 5 missions' in its out-of-area, such as conflict management, peacekeeping and peacebuilding activities. The purposes of NATO's reinvigoration require first to be explored before considering how its assets contributed to initiation of its new undertakings.

After examining these alternatives, this book explored the fundamental reason as to why NATO states took action on the war in Bosnia. As each case study chapter demonstrated, the crisis in Bosnia triggered bottom-up pressure to 'do something' against this humanitarian emergency; this factor played a vital role in moulding state policy towards it. Put another way, regardless of whether it was inside or outside of national borders, and whether it was a direct threat to national interests and security or not, societies expected that grave humanitarian tragedy must be halted and standing still and doing nothing was rendered socially inappropriate. Based on this finding, the book argued that normative explanation had much more validity than other alternative explanations in elucidating the Western states' involvement in the war in the Balkans.

To evince this point, each chapter qualitatively investigated how this foreign crisis was debated within the Western states by comprehensively scrutinising transcripts of parliamentary debates, newspaper archives and public opinion data. At the same time, Chapter 3 provided quantitative data to indicate that this war had been constantly discussed using the strongest expressions, namely genocide and ethnic cleansing. In addition, corresponding to this pressure from the bottom up, it was analysed how political leaders thought about such domestic discussion, and how those states reluctant to take measures changed their behaviour after being confronted by the pressure through the investigation of their statements pronounced in primary materials.

For this ontological reason to treat social ideational elements, the argument of the book rests upon constructivist understandings. Without observing how the war in Bosnia triggered social pressure, international response would not be adequately explicated.

## *Why is social appropriateness not always realised?*

The discussion of the previous chapters, however, revealed that such humanitarian normative anticipation was not necessarily realised automatically – rather conforming to it sparked off what this book calls 'norm dilemmas'. That means that implementing what are considered appropriate clashes with other existing norms as well as interests. Founded around this investigation, this book claimed that norm influence should be examined differently at the *general discussion* and *practical discussion* levels. Humanitarian norms go beyond the boundary of the state and take up various forms of social incorrectness as political agendas; however, their demands do not always fit with other norms and interests, which are valid in the sovereignty-based international system. It was widely contended that the catastrophe in the Balkans must not be ignored, but related action triggered conflicts with the principle of sovereign integrity and the non-use of force. Despite a 'general' consensus on action, the debate over how to put this into 'practice' caused huge controversies.

- Chapter 3 argued that when it comes to how to approach the war in Bosnia, different views among the Western states came to the surface, which resulted in the lack of military backing in the European negotiations at the early stage, the separate monitoring activities by the WEU and NATO authorities in the Adriatic Sea and the simultaneous pursuit of peacekeeping and peace enforcement. In particular, the last instance caused such grave confrontations as to be described as the biggest row since Suez, because the European states vehemently opposed the American plan to launch aerial bombardment, fearing for the safety of their own troops on the ground in Bosnia.
- In the individual member states too, confusion was triggered. Chapter 4 made clear the division in Britain over the use of force. In resonance with the public pressure of 'something must be done', the opposition parties, the Labour Party and the Liberal Democratic Party, urged intervention to protect Bosnian civilians. In contrast, the Conservatives warned that further involvement could lead to British soldiers being killed in a foreign war where no British interests were implicated. On different grounds, however, they unanimously condemned the John Major government's equivocal policy as it vacillated between these opposing claims.

- Chapter 5 showed that action was strongly supported in France as it actually dispatched the largest number of troops in Bosnia, even though it pushed for the EU to boost European security initiatives, not NATO, from whose military bodies it had withdrawn its representatives in 1966. As the war lingered with no improvement, however, the French government gradually faced the call for withdrawal as some of its personnel were killed or wounded in this operation. As a consequence, it was put in a dilemma; if it pulled out, it would be harshly condemned for turning its back on the catastrophe, but if it stayed on, more critiques would be hurled for endangering its troops because of its mishandling.
- Chapter 6 revealed that while it was claimed that Germany should not turn its eyes away from such an Auschwitz-like human rights violation as Bosnia, it was also contended that the use of armed forces should be precluded on its constitutional grounds. At the same time, the Helmut Kohl government was put under international pressure to join NATO military activities irrespective of its own constitutional constraints. Thus, in the case of Germany, a 'trilemma' was caused over its policy: not to ignore the tragedy (humanitarianism), not to use force (anti-militarism) and not to break step with international cooperation (multilateralism).
- Similar scenarios were also being played out on the other side of the Atlantic Ocean. Chapter 7 explained that although the United States initially preferred non-intervention because of the lack of material interests in this 'ethnically complex' conflict, it gradually commenced its engagement with the increase in the calls for action from its domestic society. Nevertheless, this, in turn, gave rise to another criticism that the Bill Clinton administration was dragging the United States into 'another Vietnam'. Additionally, on the international front, it was beset by severe rows with its European partners as it proposed a plan for the start of NATO air strikes. Ultimately, it was reprimanded as failing to show clear leadership in dealing with this first security crisis in the post-Cold War Europe.

Although humanitarian normative concerns propelled international action in each country, all these instances merely contributed to producing incoherent and inefficient policies to address the crisis and to generating more criticism from domestic societies for failing to improve the tragic situations in Bosnia. Thus, what was socially agreed upon as desirable was not always capitalised upon – instead, meeting this social anticipation caused conflicts with other political demands.

### *From norm dilemmas to international security governance*

By shedding light on the discussions at different levels, this book explained the occurrence of a norm dilemma because of the gap between what (cosmopolitan) norms define as appropriate in territorially unconstrained contexts and what other norms and interests, established based upon the sovereign state system, designate as goals that states should achieve. That is to say, responding to humanitarian tragedy in a foreign country inevitably collides with principles and norms of sovereign integrity, non-use of armed forces and aversion of human casualties. As a result of these different claims being expected to be abided by simultaneously, a dilemma was triggered.

In other words, what is questioned is governance of international security in terms of how to live up to social anticipation to address regional emergencies without colliding with other claims. Then, the book proposed an analytical perspective that norm dilemmas led states to reorganise NATO based around the idea of humanitarian crisis 'prevention'. Its member states were prompted to conduct reform of NATO to build an international security governance mechanism. Thus, states came together collectively and found a new rationale in this Alliance. The case study chapters confirmed these traits in the following ways.

- Chapter 3 revealed that even if NATO was expected to deal with a foreign crisis, such a policy would not be produced spontaneously. Rather it could be a source of confusion among its members because of an uncoordinated international response. Reflecting this experience in Bosnia, its overhaul was commenced, in which more stress was laid on early warning, conflict prevention and policy coordination among its members. To be sure, Bosnia became an impetus to embark on its new undertakings; nevertheless, its reform was not intended to provoke eager intervention in other countries' domestic affairs but to pre-empt intervention so as to address conflicts before norm dilemmas confront its members.
- Chapter 4 argued that despite the divided opinions over military operations in Britain, there was broad concurrence on NATO reorganisation. In this regard, it seems that those who opposed intervention agreed on it because they had learned the importance of responding to foreign human rights violation. However, it was hard to find such evidence. Instead, holding the stance that British soldiers should be utilised only to save tangible national interests, they claimed that NATO should develop capabilities for early conflict resolution so that contingencies can be quenched before intervention is inevitable. Thus, normative influence was not necessarily reflected in a direct process but in a way to achieve compatibility with other different demands.
- Chapter 5 discussed how its experiences in intervention activities led France to the idea of developing NATO. Despite the strong support for action on Bosnia, casualties among its own soldiers and personnel damaged the legitimacy of its policy. At this juncture, the French government made a historical turn to the Alliance. The government explained this decision as creating new international capabilities for conflict management so that the dilemmas of intervention would be averted. This point was confirmed by analysing why France rejoined some of NATO's military bodies but not other conventional ones.[1] Against this background, its rapprochement was conducted.
- Chapter 6 showed that through its engagements, Germany reinterpreted its constitution to allow foreign military operations under international organisations. But it would be simplistic to assume that this marked the closure of its pacifist tradition. While adhering to it, German policymakers tried

- to meet both humanitarian normative demands and their foreign military responsibilities, which resulted in their support to develop NATO for conflict prevention. Particularly, such traits can be observed in the Social Democratic Party and the Green Party, the parties that experienced more serious norm dilemmas over the use of force due to their stronger attachment to anti-militarism. While upholding this stance, they pushed for NATO's reform for the purpose of early conflict management.
- Chapter 7 argued that the Washington leaders also concurred on NATO's new undertakings, as they proffered prototype ideas of Combined Joint Task Force (CJTF) amidst the war. Certainly, the United States has enormous resources and capability to wield its power; nevertheless, even such a country had to go through the norm dilemmas in making decisions on Bosnia. As its policymakers made clear the necessity of early conflict management as a series of NATO reforms, they identified its new roles in addressing crises beyond its original purpose and thereby achieving governance of international security.

It is possible to suppose that the rise of normative pressure urged not only intervention in Bosnia but also reforms in NATO to deal with similar contingencies, because ignoring such dire humanitarian situations was simply inexcusable. This book agrees upon the first half account for intervention as discussed thus far. On NATO reorganisation, however, a more detailed explanation is required because the following points would defy explanation. First, it is difficult to illustrate why, despite the relatively solid support for action on Bosnia, dissidence emerged so soon after intervention was actually initiated. If normative influence of humanitarian concerns had been the sole factor to be considered, intervention would have gone ahead with no hesitation. That is to say, norm dilemmas mattered in this context.

Second, the question remains unanswered as to why conflict prevention was the focus of NATO's reorganisation. If implementation of humanitarian norms had been the only concern, NATO could have adopted a more militant and forceful posture towards dealing with human rights abuses everywhere. Instead, what its members needed was an international governance mechanism to address humanitarian catastrophe effectively while avoiding other troubles caused by intervention. The rise of normative pressure explains the intervention, but another account is needed to investigate why a particular form of the Alliance was preferred over others.

The third point is why those who had opposed intervention because of lack of tangible interests or because of anti-militaristic reasons also concurred on NATO's reform to address similar foreign contingencies. Conventional constructivist knowledge tells us that they changed their views through 'learning' (cf. Checkel 2001); in this context, meaning that they learned the significance of intervention for humanitarian purposes over non-intervention. However, as people can have various ideas at the same time, accepting normative influence does not mean that they have discarded all other norms and interests. Rather, in order to make their claims compatible with humanitarian norms, they were propelled to reorganise NATO for conflict prevention, as it can be found, in particular, in the views of the British Conservatives (Chapter 4) and the German left-wing parties (Chapter 6), who disagreed on intervention for interest-based and pacifist reasons but agreed on NATO reform. These anomalies are left unexplained unless the dilemmas caused by humanitarian norms are taken into account.

*Table 8.1* Debates in each case study

|  | Public discussion at the general level | Each government's reaction at the initial stage | At the practical discussion level, intervention caused... | Views on NATO reorganisation |
|---|---|---|---|---|
| Britain |  | Negative due to the lack of interests | Dilemmas between more action and no further involvement |  |
| France | Action should be taken on the humanitarian catastrophe in Bosnia | Agreed to take action, aiming to realise European security system | Dilemmas between more action and no more casualties of French personnel | Creation of international capability for security governance to address out-of-area crises |
| Germany |  | Agreed to take action | Trilemmas between humanitarianism, anti-militarism and multilateralism |  |
| United States |  | Negative due to the lack of interests | Dilemmas between more action and no further involvement |  |

In sum, this book explained a construction of international framework for security governance through NATO's reform. Humanitarian norms are not constrained by territorial boundaries and therefore define response to foreign crises as an appropriate political agenda. Nevertheless, meeting this demand collides with other norms and interests valid in the sovereignty-based world. To rectify, or mitigate at least, this collision, international governance mechanisms are required. This account clarifies why a particular form of NATO, for developing preventive capabilities, was chosen over others.

Table 8.1 summarises the debates through which Britain, France, Germany and the United States moved towards NATO reorganisation.

## Theoretical claims: rationale for adopting and developing a constructivist approach

From a theoretical point of view, the study of this book started with an argument that without considering normative debates within domestic societies, international response to Bosnia cannot be fully explicated. In following the flow of causal logic from the bottom up to state policy, theoretical analogies can be drawn with the form of constructivism developed in particular by Thomas Berger (1998), John Duffield (1999), Ted Hopf (2002), Peter Katzenstein (1996),

Jeffrey Legro (1996, 1997, 2000) and many others. As basic understandings on how normative influence is reflected in international politics are embodied as the 'norm life cycle' by Finnemore and Sikkink (1998), meeting social normative requirements constitutes state legitimate policy. Within this framework, putting an end to the war in Bosnia was set as a goal that states should pursue.

In this line, it appears that NATO's reform was commenced by conforming to the same normative expectations. This book, however, took one more step by questioning such a straightforward way of norm reflection, arguing that meeting normative ideals triggers conflicts with other existing norms and interests. Growing attention has been paid in the constructivist literature to contestations that normative influence causes in this process. As Chapter 2 discussed in more detail, Antje Wiener (2008, 2014), Wayne Sandholtz (2007, 2008), Diana Panke and Ulrich Petersohn (2012, 2016), and Alan Bloomfield (2016), respectively, explained that norms are not incorporated into state policy in a progressive manner but generate contestations – through which they are modified, mixed with other existing ones, and blocked by countermovement against them. Beyond such contestations, however, the book considered how states try to accommodate different claims at the same time. Given that human rights violation is viewed as inexcusable, the rule of sovereign integrity as a convention of international society is unlikely to dissipate overnight, whereas casualties of intervening state soldiers soon generate calls to 'bring our boys back home' (Chapter 2) and crucially damage the legitimacy of state policy. Under these situations, the state is demanded to fulfil these contradictory requirements.

This account explains the cause of norm contestations as emanating from the gap between normative effects beyond territorial limits and conventional practices based upon the Westphalian sovereignty system. Even though reaction to foreign humanitarian tragedy was brought in as a generally desirable goal to be achieved, dilemmas arose when addressing it in other foreign terrains. The book aims to proffer an understanding as to how normative concerns play an agenda setter role in a globalised context and, in turn, how states respond to it by developing international organisations to fill this gap and thereby to meet spreading normative expectations.

## The scope of this book and some implications

### Limits and conditions

The limits of this book's argument should be made clear. It deals with the rise of normative pressure as an independent variable, the pressure for some action to be taken against humanitarian disaster in the Balkans. This would raise a question as to why no action, or lesser action at least, was taken against Somalia and Rwanda in the early 1990s and other numerous civil wars in the world. As touched upon in the earlier chapters, the book acknowledges that the probability of intervention is influenced by other case-by-case conditions such as geographical vicinity of the conflicts, media coverage (particularly aggrandised by the former one) and commitment of regional powers (e.g. the cases of Chechnya and Ukraine in relation to Russia and of Tibet in relation to China). In this study, the international intervention in Bosnia had a great deal to do with the fact that it was regarded as a war that occurred in the backyard of 'Europe' and that 'European' organisations must cope with it (Chapters 3, 4, 5 and 6). While accepting this point, the book examined which element – the strategic or the normative – can explain better the Western states' response to this crisis and, through empirical examination, discussed the necessity to include the latter.

This book is certainly not saying that all the current characteristics of NATO are encompassed within this perspective since it now has various functions resulting from adaptation to the complex security environment in the post-1989 period and especially in the period of war against terror. Its research scope was limited to NATO's first engagement and analysis of how its transformation occurred through the war in Bosnia.

Nor does the book deny the role that a hegemonic leader, i.e. the United States, played in implementing actual military intervention and reforms in NATO.[2] It is unquestionably the most influential member within NATO as its military capability played an important role in carrying out air strikes in the final stage and the ceasefire monitoring after the war.[3] It appears that whatever discussions were deployed within other states, the course that NATO would take was determined by the will of this country. Yet, because its decision was obviously made collectively on a consensus basis, it is necessary to investigate what structure of NATO the hegemon, as well as its partners, delineated in the aftermath of a war happening in what was known as out-of-area. Furthermore, the United States was not only forced to concede its claims for the use of air strikes due to the vehement objections from other European members during the war but also came to seek for internationally shared understandings to perform effective conflict management, just as other members did. Given these points, it should be analysed why the United States also needed an international framework for a more flexible reaction to contingencies. As Chapter 7 provided a more detailed discussion, this question cannot be adequately answered unless the argument put forward by this book is taken into account.

## *NATO's activities after Bosnia*

NATO countries were confronted by the crisis in Kosovo from 1998 to 1999, the conflict between the Kosovo Liberation Army (KLA), pro-independent militia in Kosovo and the Yugoslav National Army (JNA). From 24 March 1999, Western states launched aerial bombardment against Belgrade and other military facilities. In this international response, what was reiterated was the experience in Bosnia. For example, American President Bill Clinton said that 'now we have a chance to take the lessons we learned in Bosnia and put them to work in Kosovo before it's too late'.[4] Additionally, the then NATO Secretary General, Javier Solana, announced that 'One lesson that we have learned from Bosnia, and which we are now applying in Kosovo, is that diplomacy can often only succeed when it is backed up with the credible threat of military force'.[5] These all indicate how crucially the Balkan crisis in the early 1990s directed subsequent international reaction to this regional contingency.

In 2001, when a military clash happened in the northern part of Macedonia (FYRM) between an Albanian ethnic group (NLA: National Liberation Army) and the Macedonian national army, NATO, in tandem with the EU, immediately started mediation efforts and succeeded in reaching a ceasefire agreement without resorting to force.[6] Viewed from the traditional IR perspective, such small-scale violence was unlikely to induce international reaction because it did not directly affect other states' national security. Nevertheless, action was taken immediately so that the crisis would be resolved before deteriorating. The international response to this conflict reveals how the new international crisis preventive system in NATO helped its members to cope with this conflict through peaceful negotiations.

Of course, it was not free from troubles and criticisms. In Kosovo in particular, this military operation was not authorised by the United Nations Security Council due to the Russian and Chinese vetoes, which significantly damaged the legality of its action. Moreover, perverse outcomes caused the Albanians in Kosovo more suffering, while the resulting civilian casualties and bombing errors (notably the Chinese embassy) became a long-lasting bone of contention in the subsequent years.[7] After all, no intervention can escape reprimands as long as it entails the use of military force and infringement of sovereignty.[8] Hence, it can be assumed, states are led towards a preventive approach.

Conflict prevention, which the book examined as one of the key features in NATO's reconstruction, is often mentioned in the contemporary context. The Strategic Concept 2010 also stresses its importance by stating that 'The lessons learned from NATO operations, in particular in Afghanistan and the Western Balkans, make it clear that a comprehensive political, civilian and military approach is necessary for effective crisis management', and that 'The best way to manage conflicts is to prevent them from happening' (North Atlantic Treaty Organization 2010: Paragraphs 21–22).[9] Graeme Herd, John Kriendler and Klaus Wittmann (2013: 28) contend that 'the Strategic Concept declares prevention and management of crises as well as stabilization of post-conflict situations and support of reconstruction as necessary NATO engagements'. Given the stress on conflict prevention in NATO, this book's analysis on its first foreign engagement in Bosnia presents a perspective on how institutional frameworks develop under circumstances where the expectation is that both humanitarian norms and other pressing concerns will be addressed properly.

## *Implications: the responsibility to 'prevent'*

Few would deny that prevention is more desirable if atrocity crimes can be averted. In terms of high costs and risks of responding after they are underway, preventive action would be logically prioritised (cf. United Nations Office on Genocide Prevention and the Responsibility to Protect 2014: 2–3). The problem is, however, that any measures are unlikely to be taken until deadly fighting breaks out, simply because it is not widely known about and does not attract media and public attention.[10] Despite its desirability, conflict prevention is therefore rather more unlikely to be embodied in state policy. In consideration of this difficulty, the findings of this book are suggestive of why NATO states have come to lay emphasis on this aspect.

To be sure, the scenario of institutional development examined in the case of NATO depends on such additional factors at play as the power of member states and differences between regional and global organisations. Nevertheless, the recent debates founded around the United Nations are suggestive. One notable instance is the Responsibility to Protect (R2P), issued by the International Commission on Intervention and State Sovereignty (ICISS), and endorsed by the United Nations in the Outcome Document of the 2005 World Summit (United Nations General Assembly 2005), to reconceptualise the meaning of sovereignty in light of human rights protection, while reflecting the experiences of interventions (and certainly of non-intervention, such as Rwanda).[11]

An intriguing point is that it does not advocate for forceful interventions but teases out acceptable conditions for interventions while making clear that 'sovereignty still matters' and focussing on the operational dimensions of desirable interventions (ICISS: 7).[12] It can be seen how the gap between the conventional sovereign jurisdiction and notions of human rights protection was considered as behind the birth of this concept. Hence, it is not strange to find the ICISS's report beginning with 'the intervention dilemma' (ICISS 2001: 1 and 19) and also discussing as one of its propositions 'the Responsibility to Prevent' (ICISS 2001: Chapter 3). Indeed, Gareth Evans and Mohamed Sahnoun (2002: 102), who co-chaired the ICISS, mentioned that 'the "responsibility to protect" is an umbrella concept, embracing not just the "responsibility to react" but the "responsibility to prevent" and the "responsibility to rebuild" as well'.[13]

Even if there are deep concerns over human rights violations, it does certainly not mean that armed intervention would be encouraged. In more contemporary warfare arenas, such as Ukraine, Syria and the northern areas of Iraq, where the so-called Islamic State reigned, the dire situation may also provoke calls for 'something to be done', but intervention would trigger heated debate over fear of involvement and potential confrontation with regional powers, which would only make the situation more complicated. Although more investigation is needed, the findings of this book provide some implications as to how norm dilemmas depict the nature of contemporary problems in the world and how they pave the path that states aspire to take in international politics, as the notion of the R2P is tightly connected with the Responsibility to Prevent.

## Notes

1 France's return to all of the NATO bodies was completed in 2009 under the Nikolas Sarkozy presidency, with a view to enhance its voice in the new political environment where measures against terrorism are demanded. At that time, the Interior Minister, Michele Alliot-Marie (former Defence Minister), commented that 'France's full participation in NATO will mean a stronger voice for Europe and European defense' and that 'France will have the capacity to truly influence this transformation', in Steven Erlanger, 'Sarkozy Embraces NATO, And Bigger Role for France', *The New York Times*, 8 March 2009.

2 For example, see Fred Chernoff (1995), who refers to the hegemon's role in underpinning the alliance's activities.
3 See, e.g. Rynning (2005: 24).
4 Quoted in Vickers (2000: 56). Originally entitled 'Clinton address to the American Federation of State, County and Municipal Employees, 24 March 1999'.
5 Javier Solana, 'NATO: Ready to Meet the Challenges Ahead', At the Council on Foreign Relations, Washington, 15 March 1999, www.nato.int/docu/speech/1999/s990315a.htm (Accessed on 1 July 2018). Also see Daalder and O'Hanlon (2000: 24–25, 28), Solana (1999).
6 On the Macedonian crisis, e.g. see Judah (2000).
7 On legitimacy problems of this NATO operation and the reviews of its critiques, see Coleman (2007: Chapter 6), Power (2007: 460–473), Szamuely (2013: 500–504), Webber (2012: 66).
8 Robert Pape (2012: 43) proposes a 'pragmatic standard' of humanitarian intervention, considering 'an ongoing campaign of mass homicide', 'a viable plan for intervention with reasonable estimates of casualties' and 'a workable strategy for creating lasting local security'. Although this is an attempt to find a more 'pragmatic' way for intervention, fundamental problems caused by military action will not be solved.
9 Also see Ivanov (2011: 88).
10 Jennifer Welsh (2016: 222–224) presents similar insights on this point. On the Responsibility to Prevent, see Hehir (2012: Chapter 4), Bellamy (2009: Chapter 4).
11 On the evolution of the concept of the R2P, see Hehir (2012: Chapter 2).
12 On how the ICISS intentionally focussed 'not on what interveners are entitled to do ("a right of intervention") but on what is necessary to protect people in dire need', see Bellamy (2008: 620). Also see Acharya (2002), Hehir (2012), Weiss 2016 (in particular Chapter 4); Welsh (2013, 2014).
13 On more detailed discussion and recent development, see United Nations Office on Genocide Prevention and the Responsibility to Protect 2014; Bellamy (2009: Chapters 4–6), Welsh (2016).

# Bibliography

Acharya, Amitav 2002. 'Redefining the Dilemmas of Humanitarian Intervention', *Australian Journal of International Affairs* 56 (3): 373–381.
―――― 2004. 'How Ideas Spread: Whose Norms Matter? Norm Localization and Institutional Change in Asian Regionalism', *International Organization* 58 (2): 239–275.
―――― 2011. 'Norm Subsidiarity and Regional Orders: Sovereignty, Regionalism, and Rule-Making in the Third World', *International Studies Quarterly* 55 (1): 95–123.
Adachi, Kenki 2013. 'Countering Norm Creation: Tug-of-War between Norm Entrepreneurs and Norm Protectors on Access to Essential Medicines', *The Ritsumeikan Journal of International Studies* 26 (1): 1–13.
Adler, Emanuel 1997. 'Seizing the Middle Ground: Constructivism in World Politics', *European Journal of International Relations* 3 (3): 319–363.
―――― 2008. 'The Spread of Security Communities: Communities of Practice, Self-Restraint, and NATO's Post-Cold War Transformation', *European Journal of International Relations* 14 (2): 195–230.
Adler, Emanuel and Barnett, Michael (eds.) 1998. *Security Communities*, Cambridge: Cambridge University Press.
Adler, Emanuel and Pouliot, Vincent (eds.) 2011. *International Practices*, Cambridge: Cambridge University Press.
Adler-Nissen, Rebecca 2014. 'Stigma Management in International Relations: Transgressive Identities, Norms and Order in International Society', *International Organization* 68 (1): 143–176.
Almond, Mark 1994. *Europe's Backyard War: The War in the Balkans*, London: Mandarin.
Anderson, Jeffrey J. 1997. 'Hard Interests, Soft Power, and Germany's Changing Role in Europe', in P. J. Katzenstein (ed.), *Tamed Power: Germany in Europe*, Ithaca, NY: Cornell University Press: 80–107.
Art, Robert J. 1996. 'Why Western Europe Needs the United States and NATO', *Political Science Quarterly* 111 (1): 1–39.
Asmus, Ronald D. 1993. 'Germany's Geopolitical Maturation: Strategy and Public Opinion after the Wall', *Rand Issue Paper*, February.
―――― 2002. *Opening NATO's Door: How the Alliance Remade Itself for a New Era*. New York: Columbia University Press.
Asmus, Ronald D., Kugler, Richard L. and Larrabee, F. Stephen 1993. 'Building A New NATO', *Foreign Affairs* 72 (4): 28–40.
Aspin, Les 1994. 'New Europe, New NATO', *NATO Review* 42 (1): 12–14.
Axt, Heinz-Jürgen 1993. 'Hat Genscher Jugoslawien Entzweit?: Mythen und Fakten zur Außenpolitik des Vereinten Deutschlands', *Europa-Archiv* 48 (12): 351–360.
Aybet, Gülnur 2000. *A European Security Architecture after the Cold War: Questions of Legitimacy*, Basingstoke: Macmillan.

# Bibliography

Bailes, Alyson J. 1995. 'European Defence and Security: The British Approach', *RUSI Journal* 140 (6): 6–10.

Baker, James A. III with DeFrank, Thomas M. 1995. *The Politics of Diplomacy: Revolution, War, and Peace, 1989–1992*, New York: G.P. Putnam.

Barnett, Michael 2013. *Empire of Humanity: A History of Humanitarianism*, Ithaca, NY: Cornell University Press.

Barry, Charles 1996. 'NATO's Combined Joint Task Forces in Theory and Practice', *Survival* 38 (1): 81–97.

Baumann, Rainer 2001. 'German Security Policy within NATO', in V. Rittberger (ed.), *German Foreign Policy since Unification: Theories and Case Studies*, Manchester: Manchester University Press: 141–184.

Bellamy, Alex J. 2008. 'The Responsibility to Protect and the Problem of Military Intervention', *International Affairs* 84 (4): 615–639.

—— 2009. *Responsibility to Protect: The Global Effort to End Mass Atrocities*, Cambridge: Polity.

Bennett, Andrew and Checkel, Jeffrey T. 2015. *Process Tracing: From Metaphor to Analytic Tool*, Cambridge: Cambridge University Press.

Berger, Thomas U. 1998. *Cultures of Antimilitarism: National Security in Germany and Japan*, Baltimore, MD: The Johns Hopkins University Press.

—— 2002. 'A Perfectly Normal Abnormality: German Foreign Policy after Kosovo and Afghanistan', *Japanese Journal of Political Science* 3 (2): 173–193.

Bert, Wayne 1997. *The Reluctant Superpower: United States' Policy in Bosnia, 1991–95*, New York: St. Marti's Press.

Betts, Alexander and Orchard, Phil (eds.) 2014. *Implementation and World Politics: How International Norms Change Practice*, Oxford: Oxford University Press.

Bially Mattern, Janice 2001. 'The Power Politics of Identity', *European Journal of International Relations* 7 (3): 349–397.

—— 2005. *Ordering International Politics: Identity, Crisis, and Representational Force*, New York: Routledge.

Bloed, Arie, and Wessel, Ramses A. 1994. *The Changing Functions of the Western European Union*, Dordrecht: M. Nijihoff.

Bloomfield, Alan 2016. 'Norm Antipreneurs and Theorising Resistance to Normative Change', *Review of International Studies* 42 (2): 310–333.

Bloomfield, Alan and Scott, Shirley V. 2017. *Norm Antipreneurs and the Politics of Resistance to Global Normative Change*, London: Routledge.

Bozo, Frédéric 1997. 'France', in M. Brenner (ed.), *NATO and Collective Security*, Basingstoke: Macmillan: 52–75.

Bryant, Janet 1996. 'Changing Circumstances, Changing Policies? The 1994 Defence White Paper and Beyond', in T. Chafer and B. Jenkins (eds.), *France: From the Cold War to the New World Order*, London: Macmillan Press: 79–92.

—— 2000. 'France and NATO from 1966 to Kosovo: Coming Full Circle?', *European Security* 9 (3): 21–37.

Bukovansky, Mlada 2002. *Legitimacy and Power Politics: The American and French Revolutions in International Political Culture*, Princeton, NJ: Princeton University Press.

Bulmer, Simon J. 1997. 'Shaping the Rules? The Constitutive Politics of the European Union and German Power', in P. J. Katzenstein (ed.), *Tamed Power: Germany in Europe*, Ithaca, NY: Cornell University Press: 49–79.

Bündnis 90/Die Grünen 2002. *Die Zukunft ist grün: Grundsatzprogramm von Bündnis 90/Die Grünen*, Berlin: Bündnis 90/Die Grünen.

Calic, Marie-Janine 1996. 'German Perspectives', in A. Danchev and T. Halverson (eds.), *International Perspectives on the Yugoslav Conflict*, London: Macmillan: 52–75.

Chandler, David 2006. *From Kosovo to Kabul: Human Rights and International Intervention*, London: Pluto.

Chayes, Antonia Handler and Weitz, Richard 1996. 'The Military Perspective on Conflict Prevention: NATO', in A. Chayes and A. H. Chayes (eds.), *Preventing Conflict in the Post-Communist World: Mobilizing International and Regional Organizations*, Washington, DC: Brookings Institution: 381–427.

Checkel, Jeffery T. 2001. 'Why Comply? Social Learning and European Identity Change', *International Organization* 55 (3): 553–588.

Chernoff, Fred 1995. *After Bipolarity: The Vanishing Threat, Theories of Cooperation, and the Future of the Atlantic Alliance*, Ann Arbor, MI: University of Michigan Press.

Christopher, Warren 1998. *In The Stream of History: Shaping Foreign Policy for a New Era*, Stanford, CA: Stanford University Press.

Claude, Inis L. Jr. 1966. 'Collective Legitimization as a Political Function of the United Nations', *International Organization* 20 (3): 367–379.

Cloward, Karisa 2014. 'False Commitments: Local Misrepresentation and the International Norms against Female Genital Mutilation and Early Marriage', *International Organization* 68 (3): 495–526.

Coleman, Katharina P. 2007. *International Organisations and Peace Enforcement: The Politics of International Legitimacy*, Cambridge: Cambridge University Press.

——— 2013. 'Locating Norm Diplomacy: Venue Change in International Norm Negotiations', *European Journal of International Relations* 19 (1): 163–186.

Cottey, Andrew 1996. 'Developing the Conflict Prevention Agenda', in J. M. O. Sharp (ed.), *About Turn, Forward March with Europe: New Directions for Defence and Security Policy*, London: IPPR/Rivers Oran Press: 183–196.

Crawford, Neta C. 2002. *Argument and Change in World Politics: Ethics, Decolonization, and Humanitarian Intervention*, Cambridge: Cambridge University Press.

Daalder, Ivo H. 2000. *Getting to Dayton: The Making of America's Bosnia Policy*, Washington, DC: Brookings Institution Press.

Daalder, Ivo H. and O'Hanlon, Michael E. 2000. *Winning Ugly: NATO's War to Save Kosovo*, Washington, DC: Brookings Institution.

Dalvi, Sameera 1998. 'The Post-Cold War Role of the Bundeswehr: A Product of Normative Influences', *European Security* 7 (1): 97–116.

De Wijk, Rob 1997. *NATO on the Brink of the New Millennium: The Battle for Consensus*, London: Brassay.

Deni, John R. 2007. *Alliance Management and Maintenance: Restructuring NATO for the 21st Century*, Aldershot: Ashgate.

Dettke, Dieter 2009. *Germany Says "No": The Iraq War and the Future of German Foreign and Security Policy*, Baltimore, MD: Johns Hopkins University Press.

Deutsch, Karl W., with Burrell, Sidney A., Kann, Robert A., Lee, Maurice Jr., Lichterman, Martin, Lindgren, Raymond E., Loewenheim, Francis L., and Van Wagenen, Richard W. 1957. *Political Community and the North Atlantic Area: International Organization in the Light of Historical Experience*, Princeton, NJ: Princeton University Press.

Donia, Robert J. and Fine, John V. A. 1994. *Bosnia and Hercegovina: A Tradition Betrayed*, New York: Columbia University Press.

Duffield, John S. 1994/1995. 'NATO's Functions after the Cold War', *Political Science Quarterly* 109 (5): 763–787.

―――― 1999. 'Political Culture and State Behaviour: Why Germany Confounds Neorealism', *International Organization* 53 (4): 765–803.

―――― 2001. 'Transatlantic Relations after the Cold War: Theory, Evidence, and the Future', *International Studies Perspectives* 2 (1): 93–115.

Evans, Gareth and Sahnoun, Mohamed 2002. 'The Responsibility to Protect', *Foreign Affairs* 86 (6): 99–110.

Eznack, Lucile 2012. *Crises in the Atlantic Alliance: Affect and Relations among NATO Members*, New York: Palgrave Macmillan.

Farrell, Theo 2001. 'Transnational Norms and Military Development: Constructing Ireland's Professional Army', *European Journal of International Relations* 7 (1): 63–102.

Fierke, Karin M. 1996. 'Multiple Identities, Interfacing Games: The Social Construction of Western Action in Bosnia', *European Journal of International Relations* 2 (4): 467–498.

Fincke, Gunilla and Hatakoy, Arzu 2004. 'Kriesenprävention als Neues Leitbild der Deutschen Außenpolitik: Friedenspolitik mit Zivilen und Militärischen Mitteln?', in S. Harnisch, C. Katsioulis and M. Overhaus (eds.), *Deutsche Sicherheitspolitik: Eine Bilanz der Regierung Schröder*, Baden-Baden: Nomos-Verlagsgesellschaft: 59–87.

Finnemore, Martha 1996a. *National Interests in International Society*, Ithaca, NY: Cornell University Press.

―――― 1996b. 'Constructing Norms of Humanitarian Intervention', in P. J. Katzenstein (ed.), *The Culture of National Security: Norms and Identity in World Politics*, New York: Columbia University Press: 151–185.

―――― 2003. *The Purpose of Intervention: Changing Beliefs about the Use of Force*, Ithaca, NY: Cornell University Press.

―――― 2008. 'Paradoxes in Humanitarian Intervention', in R. M. Price (ed.), *Moral Limit and Possibility in World Politics*, Cambridge: Cambridge University Press: 197–224.

Finnemore, Martha and Sikkink, Kathryn 1998. 'International Norm Dynamics and Political Change', *International Organization* 52 (4): 887–917.

―――― 2001. 'Taking Stock: The Constructivist Research Program in International Relations and Comparative Politics', *Annual Review of Political Science* 4: 391–416.

Fischer, Joschka 1995. 'Die Katastrophe in Bosnien und die Konsequenz für unsere Partei', *Blätter für Deutsche und Internationale Politik* 40 (9): 1141–1152.

Flockhart, Trine 2014. 'Post-Bipolar Challenges: New Visions and New Activities', in S. Mayer (ed.), *NATO's Post-Cold War Politics: The Changing Provision of Security*, Basingstoke: Palgrave Macmillan: 71–88.

Gade, Jo G. and Hilde, Paal Sigurd 2014. 'Enduring Rules, Changing Practices: NATO's Post-Cold War Military Committee and International Military Staff', in S. Mayer (ed.), *NATO's Post-Cold War Politics: The Changing Provision of Security*, Basingstoke: Palgrave Macmillan: 159–175.

Gagnon, V. P. Jr. 2006. *The Myth of Ethnic War: Serbia and Croatia in the 1990s*, Ithaca, NY: Cornell University Press.

Gentry, John A. 2006. 'Norms and Military Power: NATO's War against Yugoslavia', *Security Studies* 15 (2): 187–224.

Gheciu, Alexandra 2005. *NATO in the "New Europe": The Politics of International Socialization After the Cold War*, Stanford, CA: Stanford University Press.

Giddens, Anthony 1990. *The Consequences of Modernity*, Cambridge: Polity Press.

Glaser, Charles L. 1993. 'Why NATO is Still Best: Future Security Arrangements for Europe', *International Security* 18 (1): 5–50.

Glaurdić, Josip 2011. *The Hour of Europe: Western Powers and the Breakup of Yugoslavia*, New Haven, CT: Yale University Press.

Glenny, Misha 1996. *The Fall of Yugoslavia: The Third Balkan War*, London: Penguin Books.
Goldgeier, James M. 1999. *Not Whether but When: The U.S. Decision to Enlarge NATO*, Washington, DC: Brookings Institution Press.
Gompert, David C. 1996. 'The United States and Yugoslavia's Wars', in R. H. Ullman (ed.), *The World and Yugoslavia's Wars*, New York: Council on Foreign Relations: 122–144.
Gordon, Philip H. 1993. *A Certain Idea of France: French Security Policy and the Gaullist Legacy*, Princeton, NJ: Princeton University Press.
—— 1994. 'The Normalization of German Foreign Policy', *Orbis* 38 (2): 225–243.
—— 1995. *France, Germany and the Western Alliance*, Oxford: Westview Press.
Gordon, Phillip H. and Shapiro, Jeremy 2004. *Allies at War: America, Europe, and the Crisis over Iraq*, New York: McGraw-Hill.
Goulden, John 1996. 'NATO Approaching Two Summits: The UK Perspective', *RUSI Journal* 141 (6): 29–32.
Gow, James 1996. 'British Perspectives', in A. Danchev and T. Halverson (eds.), *International Perspectives on the Yugoslav Conflict*, London: Macmillan: 87–99.
—— 1997. *Triumph of the Lack of Will: International Diplomacy and the Yugoslav War*, London: Hurst & Co.
Gow, James, Paterson, Richard and Preston, Alison 1996. *Bosnia by Television*, London: British Film Institute.
Grant, Robert P. 1996. 'France's New Relationship with NATO', *Survival* 38 (1): 58–80.
Gregory, Shaun 2000. *French Defence Policy into the Twenty-First Century*, London: Macmillan Press.
Guicherd, Catherine 1993. 'The Hour of Europe: Lessons from the Yugoslav Conflict', *Fletcher Forum of World Affairs* 17 (2): 159–181.
Hall, Rodney Bruce 1999. *National Collective Identity: Social Constructs and International Systems*, New York: Columbia University Press.
Halverson, Thomas 1996. 'American Perspectives', in A. Danchev and T. Halverson (eds.), *International Perspectives on the Yugoslav Conflict*, London: Macmillan: 1–28.
Hansen, Lene 2006. *Security as Practice: Discourse Analysis and the Bosnian War*, London: Routledge.
Harnisch, Sebastian 2001. 'Change and Continuity in Post-Unification German Foreign Policy', *German Politics* 10 (1): 35–60.
Harnisch, Sebastian and Maull, Hanns W. (eds.) 2001a. *Germany as a Civilian Power?: The Foreign Policy of the Berlin Republic*, Manchester: Manchester University Press.
—— 2001. 'Introduction', in S. Harnisch and H. Maull (eds.), *Germany as a Civilian Power?: The Foreign Policy of the Berlin Republic*, Manchester: Manchester University Press: 1–9.
—— 2001. 'Conclusion: "Learned Its Lesson Well?": Germany as a Civilian Power Ten Years after Unification', in S. Harnisch and H. Maull (eds.), *Germany as a Civilian Power?: The Foreign Policy of the Berlin Republic*, Manchester: Manchester University Press: 128–153.
Harries, Owen 1993. 'The Collapse of the West', *Foreign Affairs* 72 (4): 41–53.
Heathcoat-Amory, David 1994. 'Britain's Security Policy: Current Issues and Practical Realities', *RUSI Journal* 139 (5): 2–5.
Hehir, Aidan 2012. *The Responsibility to Protect: Rhetoric, Reality and the Future of Humanitarian Intervention*, Basingstoke: Palgrave Macmillan.
—— 2013. 'The Permanence of Inconsistency: Libya, the Security Council, and the Responsibility to Protect', *International Security* 38 (1): 137–159.

Hellmann, Gunther and Wolf, Reinhard. 1993. 'Neorealism, Neoliberal Institutionalism, and the Future of NATO', *Security Studies* 3 (1): 3–43.

Herd, Graeme P., Kriendler, John and Wittmann, Klaus 2013. 'NATO's Genesis and Adaptation: From Washington to Chicago', in G. P. Herd and J. Kriendler (eds.), *Understanding NATO in the 21st Century: Alliance Strategies, Security and Global Governance*, New York: Routledge: 16–32.

Hobson, John M. 1997. *The Wealth of States: A Comparative Sociology of International Economics and Political Change*, Cambridge: Cambridge University Press.

—— 2000. *The State and International Relations*, Cambridge: Cambridge University Press.

Holbrooke, Richard C. 1999. *To End a War*, New York: Modern Library.

Holst, Christian 2001. 'Public Attitudes and Elite Attitudes: Towards a New Foreign-Policy Consensus?', in W. Eberwein and K. Kaiser (eds.), *Germany's New Foreign Policy: Decision-Making in an Interdependent World*, Basingstoke: Palgrave: 251–263.

Holzgrefe, J. L. and Keohane, Robert O. (eds.) 2003. *Humanitarian Intervention: Ethical, Legal, and Political Dilemmas*, Cambridge: Cambridge University Press.

Hopf, Ted 1998. 'The Promise of Constructivism in International Relations Theory', *International Security* 23 (1): 171–200.

—— 2002. *Social Construction of International Politics: Identities and Foreign Policies, Moscow, 1955 and 1999*, Ithaca, NY: Cornell University Press.

Howorth, Jolyon 1994. 'The Debate in France over Military Intervention in Europe', in L. Freedman (ed.), *Military Intervention in European Conflicts*, Oxford: Blackwell Publishers: 106–124.

—— 1996. 'France and European Security 1944–1994: Re-reading the Gaullist "Consensus"', in T. Chafer and B. Jenkins (eds.), *France: From the Cold War to the New World Order*, London: Macmillan Press: 17–38.

—— 2001. 'European Defence and the Changing Politics of the European Union: Hanging Together or Hanging Separately?', *Journal of Common Market Studies* 39 (4): 765–789.

Hurd, Douglas 2003. *Memoirs*. London: Little, Brown.

Hurd, Ian 1999. 'Legitimacy and Authority in International Politics', *International Organization* 53 (2): 379–408.

—— 2005. 'The Strategic Use of Liberal Internationalism: Libya and the UN Sanctions, 1992–2003', *International Organization* 59 (3): 495–526.

—— 2007. *After Anarchy: Legitimacy and Power in the United Nations Security Council*, Princeton, NJ: Princeton University Press.

—— 2010. 'Constructivism', in C. Reus-Smit and D. Snidal (eds.), *The Oxford Handbook of International Relations*, Oxford: Oxford University Press: 298–316.

Hurrell, Andrew 1998. 'Society and Anarchy in the 1990s', in B. A. Roberson (ed.), *International Society and the Development of International Relations Theory*, London: Pinter: 17–42.

Hyde-Price, Adrian G. V. 2000. *Germany and European Order: Enlarging NATO and the EU*, Manchester: Manchester University Press.

Inacker, Michael J. 1991. *Unter Ausschluss der Öffentlichkeit?: Die Deutschen in der Golfallianz*, Bonn: Bouvier Verlag.

International Commission on Intervention and State Sovereignty (ICISS) 2001. *The Responsibility to Protect*, Ottawa: the International Development Research Centre.

Ivanov, Ivan Dinev 2011. *Transforming NATO: New Allies, Missions, and Capabilities*, Lanham, MD: Lexington Books.

Jakobsen, Peter Viggo 1995. 'Myth-making and Germany's Unilateral Recognition of Croatia and Slovenia', *European Security* 4 (3): 400–416.
Johnston, Alastair Iain 2001. 'Treating International Institutions as Social Environments', *International Studies Quarterly* 45 (4): 487–515.
Johnston, Karin 2003. 'German Public Opinion and the Crisis in Bosnia', in R. Sobel and E. Shiraev (eds.), *International Public Opinion and the Bosnia Crisis*, Lanham, MD: Lexington Books: 249–282.
Johnston, Seth A. 2017. *How NATO Adapts, Strategy and Organization in the Atlantic Alliance since 1950*, Baltimore, MD: Johns Hopkins University Press.
Judah, Tim 2000. 'Greater Albania', *Survival* 43 (2): 7–18.
Kahl, Colin H. 2007. 'In the Crossfire or the Crosshairs? Norms, Civilian Casualties, and U.S. Conduct in Iraq', *International Security* 32 (1): 7–46.
Kaplan, Lawrence S. 2004. *NATO Divided, NATO United: The Evolution of an Alliance*, Westport, CT: Praeger.
Karp, Regina 2009 'Germany: A "Normal" Global Actor?', *German Politics* 18 (1): 12–35.
Katsioulis, Christos 2004. 'Deutsche Sicherheitspolitik im Parteiendiskurs: Alter Wein in Neuen Schläuchen', in S. Harnisch, C. Katsioulis and M. Overhaus (eds.), *Deutsche Sicherheitspolitik: Eine Bilanz der Regierung Schröder*, Baden-Baden: Nomos-Verlagsgesellschaft: 227–252.
Katzenstein, Peter J. 1996a. *Cultural Norms and National Security: Police and Military in Postwar Japan*, Ithaca, NY: Cornell University Press.
——— 1996b. 'Introduction: Alternative perspectives on National Security', in P. Katzenstein (ed.), *The Culture of National Security: Norms and Identity in World Politics*, New York: Columbia University Press: 1–32.
Kaufman, Joyce P. 2002. *NATO and the Former Yugoslavia: Crisis, Conflict, and the Atlantic Alliance*, Oxford: Rowman & Littlefield Publishers.
Kay, Sean 1998. *NATO and the Future of European Security*, Lanham, MD: Rowman & Littlefield Publishers.
Kelleher, Catherine McArdle 1995. *The Future of European Security: an Interim Assessment*, Washington, DC: Brookings Institution.
Kent, Gregory 2006. *Framing War and Genocide: British Policy and News Media Reaction to the War in Bosnia*, Cresskill, NJ: Hampton Press.
Keohane, Robert O. 1984. *After Hegemony: Cooperation and Discord in the World Political Economy*, Princeton, NJ: Princeton University Press.
Keohane, Robert O. and Martin, Lisa 1995. 'The Promise of Institutionalist Theory', *International Security* 20 (1): 39–51.
Kerton-Johnson, Nicholas 2009. 'Coercing Solidarism: the Secular and Religious in US Exceptionalism', in R. Durward and L. Marsden (eds.), *Religion, Conflict and Military Intervention*, New York: Routledge: 111–128.
King, Gary, Keohane, Robert O. and Verva, Sidney 1994. *Designing Social Inquiry: Scientific Inference in Qualitative Research*, Princeton, NJ: Princeton University Press.
Kinkel, Klaus 1993. *Verantwortung, Realismus, Zukunftssicherung: Deutsche Außenpolitik in einer sich Neu Ordnenden Welt*, Bonn: Auswärtiges Amt, Refarat Öffentlichkeitsarbeit.
Kissinger, Henry A. 1964. *A World Restored: Metternich, Castlereagh and the Problems of Peace 1812–22*, New York: Grossert and Dunlap.
——— 1965. *The Troubled Partnership: A Re-Appraisal of the Atlantic Alliance*, New York: Harper and Row.
——— 1994. *Diplomacy*, New York: Simon & Schuster.

Kitchen, Veronica M. 2009. 'Argument and Identity Change in the Atlantic Security Community', *Security Dialogue* 40 (1): 95–114.

—— 2010. *The Globalization of NATO: Intervention, Security and Identity*, Abingdon: Routledge.

Kramer, Steven Philip 1994. *Does France Still Count? The French Role in the New Europe*, Washington, DC: Praeger.

Krasner, Stephen D. 1999. *Sovereignty: Organized Hypocrisy*, Princeton, NJ: Princeton University Press.

Kratochwil, Friedrich V. 1989. *Rules, Norms, and Decisions: On the Conditions of Practical and Legal Reasoning in International Relations and Domestic Affairs*, Cambridge: Cambridge University Press.

Krebs, Ronald R. and Jackson, Patrick Thaddeus 2007. 'Twisting Tongues and Twisting Arms: The Power of Political Rhetoric', *European Journal of International Relations* 13 (1): 35–66.

Kull, Steven and Ramsay, Clay 2003. 'U.S. Public Opinion on Intervention in Bosnia', in R. Sobel and E. Shiraev (eds.), *International Public Opinion and the Bosnia Crisis*, Lanham, MD: Lexington Books: 69–106.

La Balme, Natalie 2001. 'Public Opinion and the International Use of Force', in P. Everts and P. Isernia (eds.), *Public Opinion and the International Use of Force*, London: Routledge: 186–204.

Lantis, Jeffrey S. 1996. 'Rising to the Challenge: German Security Policy in the Post-Cold War Era', *German Politics and Society* 14 (2): 19–35.

—— 2002. *Strategic Dilemmas and the Evolution of German Foreign policy Since Unification*, Westport, CT: Praeger.

Lanxade, Jacques 1994. 'French Defence Policy after the White Paper', *RUSI Journal* 139 (2): 17–21.

Layne, Christopher 1993. 'The Unipolar Illusion: Why New Great Powers will Rise', *International Security* 17 (4): 5–51.

Lefebvre, Stephane and Lombardi, Ben 1996. 'Germany and Peace Enforcement: Participating in IFOR', *European Security* 5 (4): 564–587.

Legro, Jeffrey W. 1996. 'Culture and Preferences in the International Cooperation Two-Step', *American Political Science Review* 90 (1): 118–137.

—— 1997. 'Which Norms Matter? Revisiting the "Failure" of Internationalism', *International Organization* 51 (1): 31–63.

—— 2000. 'Whence American Internationalism', *International Organization* 54 (2): 253–289.

Leithner, Anika 2009. *Shaping German Foreign Policy: History, Memory, and National Interest*, Boulder, CO: FirstForumPress.

Lepick, Oliver 1996. 'French Perspectives', in A. Danchev and T. Halverson (eds.), *International Perspectives on the Yugoslav Conflict*, London: Macmillan: 76–86.

Libal, Michael 1997. *Limits of Persuasion: Germany and the Yugoslav Crisis, 1991–1992*, London: Praeger.

Lindley-French, Julian 2006. *The North Atlantic Treaty Organization: The Enduring Alliance*, London: Routledge.

Liska, George 1962. *Nations in Alliance: The Limits of Interdependence*, Baltimore, MD: Johns Hopkins Press.

Longhurst, Kerry 2004. *Germany and the Use of Force: The Evolution of German Security Policy, 1990–2003*. Manchester: Manchester University Press.

Lucarelli, Sonia 2000. *Europe and the Breakup of Yugoslavia: A Political Failure in Search of a Scholarly Explanation*, The Hague: Kluwer Law International.

Macleod, Alex 2000. 'France: Kosovo and the Emergence of a New European Security', in P. Martin and M. R. Brawley (eds.), *Alliance Politics, Kosovo and NATO's War: Allied Force or Forced Allies?* New York: Palgrave: 113–130.

Major, John R. 1999. *The Autobiography*, London: HarperCollins.

Malcolm, Noel 1994. *Bosnia: A Short History*, New York: New York University Press.

March, James G. and Olsen, Johan P. 1998. 'The Institutional Dynamics of International Political Orders', *International Organization* 52 (4): 943–969.

Martin, Mathias and Schäfer, Paul 1993. 'Militärische Dimensionen der Neuen Deutschen Außenpolitik', *Blätter für Deutsche und Internationale Politik* 10: 1185–1199.

Maull, Hanns W. 1995/1996. 'Germany in the Yugoslav Crisis', *Survival* 37 (4): 99–130.

——— 2000. 'Germany and the Use of Force: Still a "Civilian Power"?', *Survival* 42 (2): 56–80.

Mayer, Sebastian (ed.) 2014. *NATO's Post-Cold War Politics: The Changing Provision of Security*, Basingstoke: Palgrave Macmillan.

McCalla, Robert B. 1996. 'NATO's Persistence after the Cold War', *International Organization* 50 (3): 445–475.

McKenzie, Mary M. 1996. 'Competing Conceptions of Normality in the Post-Cold War Era: Germany, Europe, and Foreign Policy Change', *German Politics and Society* 14 (2): 1–18.

Mearsheimer, John J. 1990. 'Back to the Future: Instability in Europe After the Cold War', *International Security* 15 (1): 5–57.

——— 1994/1995. 'The False Promise of International Institutions', *International Security*, 19 (3): 5–49.

Meimeth, Michael 1997. 'Germany', in M. Brenner (ed.), *NATO and Collective Security*, Basingstoke: Macmillan: 52–75.

Menon, Anand 1995. 'From Independence to Cooperation: France, NATO and European Security', *International Affairs* 71 (1): 19–34.

——— 1996. 'The "Consensus" on Defence Policy and the End of the Cold War: Political Parties and the Limits of Adaptation', in T. Chafer and B. Jenkins (eds.), *France: From the Cold War to the New World Order*, London: Macmillan Press: 155–168.

——— 2000a. *France, NATO and the Limits of Independence 1981–97: The Politics of Ambivalence*, London: Macmillan Press.

——— 2000b. 'Domestic Constraints on French NATO Policy', *French Politics, Culture and Society* 18 (2): 49–68.

Moore, Rebecca R. 2007. *NATO's New Mission: Projecting Stability in a Post-Cold War World*, London: Praeger Security International.

Morgenthau, Hans J. 1967. 'To Intervene or Not to Intervene', *Foreign Affairs* 45 (3): 425–436.

Morjé Howard, Marc, and Morjé Howard, Lise 2003. 'Raison d'état or Raison populaire? The Influence of Public Opinion on France's Bosnia Policy', in R. Sobel and E. Shiraev (eds.), *International Public Opinion and the Bosnia Crisis*, Lanham, MD: Lexington Books: 107–134.

Müller, Harald 1992. 'German Foreign Policy after Unification', in P. B. Stares (ed.), *The Germany and the New Europe*, Washington, DC: Brookings Institution: 126–173.

——— 1994. 'Military Intervention for European Security: The German Debate', in L. Freedman (ed.), *Military Intervention in European Conflicts*, Oxford: Blackwell Publishers: 125–141.

Noelle-Neumann, Elisabeth and Köcher, Renate (eds.) 1997. *Allensbacher Jahrbuch der Demoskopie 1993–1997*, 10, München: K. G. Saur.

North Atlantic Treaty Organization 2010. *Strategic Concept for the Defence and Security of the Members of the North Atlantic Treaty Organization*, Brussels: NATO Public Diplomacy Division, available at www.nato.int/nato_static_fl2014/assets/pdf/pdf_publications/20120214_strategic-concept-2010-eng.pdf (Accessed on 1 July 2018).

Owen, David 1996. *Balkan Odyssey*, London: Indigo.

Panke, Diana and Petersohn, Ulrich 2012. 'Why Some International Norms Disappear', *European Journal of International Relations* 18 (4): 719–742.

――― 2016. 'Norm Challenges and Norm Death: The Inexplicable?', *Cooperation and Conflict* 51 (1): 1–17.

Pape, Robert A. 2012. 'When Duty Calls: A Pragmatic Standard of Humanitarian Intervention', *International Security* 37 (1): 41–80.

Paris, Roland 2014. 'The "Responsibility to Protect" and the Structural Problems of Preventive Humanitarian Intervention', *International Peacekeeping* 21 (5): 569–603.

Philippi, Nina 1997. *Bundeswehr-Auslandseinsätze als Außen- und Sicherheitspolitisches Problem des Geeinten Deutschland*, Frankfurter Am Main: Peter Lang.

――― 2001. 'Civilian Power and War: The German Debate about Out-of-Area Operations 1990–99', in S. Harnisch and H. Maull (eds.), *Germany as a Civilian Power?: The Foreign Policy of the Berlin Republic*, Manchester: Manchester University Press: 49–67.

Powell, Colin L. with Persico, Joseph E. 1995. *My American Journey*, New York: Random House.

Power, Samantha 2007. *"A Problem from Hell": America and the Age of Genocide*, New York: Harper Perennial.

Price, Richard M. 1998. 'Reversing the Gun Sights: Translational Civil Society Targets Land Mines', *International Organization* 52 (3): 613–644.

Ramet, Sabrina Petra 1996. *Balkan Babel: The Disintegration of Yugoslavia from the Death of Tito to Ethnic War*, Boulder, CO: Westview Press.

Ramsbotham, Oliver, and Woodhouse, Tom 1996. *Humanitarian Intervention in Contemporary Conflict: A Reconceptualization*, Cambridge: Polity Press.

Rathbun, Brian C. 2004. *Partisan Interventions: European Party Politics and Peace Enforcement in the Balkans*, Ithaca, NY: Cornell University Press.

Rees, Wyn G. 1998. *The Western European Union at the Crossroads: Between Trans-Atlantic Solidarity and European Integration*, Oxford: Westview Press.

Reus-Smit, Christian 1997. 'The Constitutional Structure of International Society and the Nature of Fundamental Institutions', *International Organization* 51 (4): 555–589.

Rhodes, Matthew 2013. 'U.S. Perspectives on NATO', in G. P. Herd and J. Kriendler (eds.), *Understanding NATO in the 21st Century: Alliance Strategies, Security and Global Governance*, New York: Routledge: 33–49.

Rifkind, Malcolm 1995. *UN Peacekeeping: Past Lessons and Future Prospects*, Edinburgh: David Hume Institute.

Risse, Thomas 2000. '"Let's Argue!": Communicative Action in World Politics', *International Organization* 51 (1): 1–41.

Risse, Thomas, Ropp, Stephen C. and Sikkink, Kathryn (eds.) 1999. *The Power of Human Rights: International Norms and Domestic Change*, Cambridge: Cambridge University Press.

Risse-Kappen, Thomas 1994. 'Ideas Do Not Float Freely: Transnational Coalitions, Domestic Structures, and the End of the Cold War', *International Organization* 48 (2): 185–214.

―― 1995. *Cooperation among Democracies: The European Influence on U.S. Foreign Policy*, Princeton, NJ: Princeton University Press.
―― 1996. 'Collective Identity in a Democratic Community: The Case of NATO', in P. J. Katzenstein (ed.), *The Culture of National Security: Norms and Identity in World Politics*, New York: Columbia University Press: 357–399.
Roberts, Adam 1996. *Humanitarian Action in War: Aid, Protection and Impartiality in a Policy Vacuum*, Adelphi Paper 305, Oxford: Oxford University Press.
Robinson, Piers 1999. 'The CNN Effect: Can the News Media Drive Foreign Policy?', *Review of International Studies* 25 (2): 301–309.
Royal United Service Institute for Defence Studies 1998. *Documents on British Foreign and Security Policy, Volume 1: 1995–1997. Vol. 1*, London: Stationary Office.
Rühe, Volker 1993. 'Shaping Euro-Atlantic Policies: A Grand Strategy for a New Era', *Survival* 35 (2): 129–137.
―― 1994. 'Rede des Deutschen Verteidigungsministers, Volker Rühe, am 8. Oktober 1993 an der Karls-Universität in Prag (Auszug)', *Europa-Archiv* 3: 101–104.
Rynning, Sten 2005. *NATO Renewed: The Power and Purpose of Transatlantic Cooperation*, Basingstoke: Palgrave Macmillan.
Sandholtz, Wayne 2007. *Prohibiting Plunder: How Norms Change*, New York: Oxford University Press.
―― 2008. 'Dynamics of International Norm Change: Rules against Wartime Plunder', *European Journal of International Relations* 14 (1): 101–131.
Scharping, Rudolf 1995. 'Deutsche Außenpolitik muß Berechenbar Sein', *Internationale Politik* 50 (8): 38–44.
Schimmelfennig, Frank 2001. 'The Community Trap: Liberal Norms, Rhetorical Action, and the Eastern Enlargement of the European Union', *International Organization* 55 (1): 47–80.
―― 2003. *The EU, NATO and the Integration of Europe: Rules and Rhetoric*, Cambridge: Cambridge University Press.
Schoppe, Waltraud 1995. 'Menschenrechte und Außenpolitik: Soll die Moral die Außenpolitik Dominieren?', *Internationale Politik* 50 (8): 27–30.
Seybolt, Taylor B. 2008. *Humanitarian Military Intervention: The Conditions for Success and Failure*, Oxford: Oxford University Press.
Sharp, Jane M. O. (ed.) 1997. *Honest Broker or Perfidious Albion?: British Policy in Former Yugoslavia*, London: Institute for Public Policy Research.
Silber, Laura and Little, Allan 1995. *The Death of Yugoslavia*, London: Penguin Books.
Simms, Brendan 2002. *Unfinest Hour: Britain and the Destruction of Bosnia*, London: Penguin Press.
Sjursen, Helene 2004. 'On NATO's identity', *International Affairs* 40 (4): 687–703.
Sloan, Elinor C. 1998. *Bosnia and the New Collective Security*, Westport, CT: Praeger.
Smith, Martin A (ed.) 2006. *Where is NATO Going?*, London: Routledge.
Smith Michael E. 1996. 'Sending the Bundeswehr to the Balkans: The Domestic Politics of Reflexive Multilateralism', *German Politics and Society* 14 (4): 49–67.
Snyder, Glenn Herald 1997. *Alliance Politics*, Ithaca, NY: Cornell University Press.
Sobel, Richard 1996. 'U.S. and European Attitudes toward Intervention in the Former Yugoslavia', in R. H. Ullman (ed.), *The World and Yugoslavia's Wars*, New York: Council on Foreign Relations: 145–181.
―― 2001. *The Impact of Public Opinion on U.S. Foreign Policy since Vietnam: Constraining the Colossus*, New York: Oxford University Press.

Solana, Javier 1996a. 'NATO in Transition', *Perceptions: Journal of International Affairs* 1 (March-May), available at sam.gov.tr/wp-content/uploads/2012/01/9.-NATO-IN-TRANSITION.pdf (Accessed on 1 July 2018).
—— 1996b. 'Nato's Role in Bosnia: Charting a New Course for the Alliance', *NATO Review* 44 (2): 3–6.
—— 1999. 'NATO's Success in Kosovo', *Foreign Affairs* 78 (6): 114–120.
Sperling, James and Papacosma, S. Victor (eds.) 2012. *NATO after Sixty Years: A Stable Crisis*, Kent, OH: Kent State University Press.
Spohr, Kristina Readman 2004. *Germany and the Baltic Problem after the Cold War: The Development of a New Ostpolitik, 1989–2000*, London: Routledge.
Strobel, Warren P. 1997. *Late-Breaking Foreign Policy: The News Media's Influence on Peace Operations*, Washington, DC: U.S. Institute of Peace Press.
Szamuely, George 2013. *Bombs for Peace: NATO's Humanitarian War on Yugoslavia*, Amsterdam: Amsterdam University Press.
Talbott, Strobe 1995. 'Why NATO Should Grow', *New York Review of Books* 42, 10 August: 27–30.
Thies, Wallace J. 2009. *Why NATO Endures*, New York: Cambridge University Press.
Thompson, Mark 1999. *Forging War: the Media in Serbia, Croatia, Bosnia and Hercegovina*, Luton: University of Luton Press.
Towle, Philip 1994. 'The British Debate about Intervention in European Conflicts', in L. Freedman (ed.), *Military Intervention in European Conflicts*, Oxford: Blackwell Publishers: 94–105.
Towns, Ann E. 2012. 'Norms and Social Hierarchies: Understanding International Policy Diffusion "From Below"', *International Organization* 66 (2): 179–209.
Treacher, Adrian 2003. *French Interventionism: Europe's Last Global Power?* Aldershot: Ashgate.
United Nations General Assembly 1999. 'Report of the Secretary-General pursuant to General Assembly resolution 53/35. 15 November', available at www.un.org/en/ga/search/view_doc.asp?symbol=A/54/549 (Accessed on 1 July 2018).
—— 2005. *2005 World Summit Outcome*, available at responsibilitytoprotect.org/world%20summit%20outcome%20doc%202005(1).pdf (Accessed on 1 July 2018).
United Nations High Commissioner for Refugees 2000. *The State of the World's Refugees: Fifty Years of Humanitarian Action*, Oxford: Oxford University Press.
United Nations Office on Genocide Prevention and the Responsibility to Protect 2014. *Framework Analysis for Atrocity Crimes: A Tool for Prevention*, available at www.un.org/en/genocideprevention/documents/publications-and-resources/Framework%20of%20Analysis%20for%20Atrocity%20Crimes_EN.pdf (Accessed on 1 July 2018).
van Heuven, Marten H. A. 1993. 'Testing the New Germany: The Case of Yugoslavia', *German Politics and Society* (29): 52–63.
Védrine, Hubert 1996. *Les Mondes de François Mitterrand: à l'Élysée 1981–1995*, Paris: Fayard.
Vernet, Daniel 1992. 'The Dilemma of French Foreign Policy', *International Affairs* 68 (4): 655–664.
Vickers, Rhiannon 2000. 'Blair's Kosovo Campaign: Political Communications, the Battle for Public Opinion and Foreign Policy', *Civil Wars* 3 (1): 54–70.
Wallander, Celeste A. 2000. 'Institutional Assets and Adaptability: NATO After the Cold War', *International Organization* 54 (2): 705–735.
Wallander, Celeste A. and Keohane, Robert O. 1999. 'Risk, Threats, and Security Institutions', in H. Haftendorn, R. O. Keohane and C. A. Wallander (eds.), *Imperfect Unions: Security Institutions over Time and Space*, Oxford: Oxford University Press: 21–47.

Walt, Stephen M. 1987. *The Origins of Alliances*, Ithaca, NY: Cornell University Press
—— 1997. 'Why Alliances Endure or Collapse?' *Survival* 39 (1): 156–179.
—— 2000. 'NATO's Future (In Theory)', in P. Martin and M. R. Brawley (eds.), *Alliance Politics, Kosovo and NATO's War: Allied Force or Forced Allies?* New York: Palgrave: 12–25.
Waltz, Kenneth N. 1979. *Theory of International Politics*, New York: McGraw-Hill.
—— 1993. 'The Emerging Structure of International Politics', *International Security* 18 (2): 44–79.
Walzer, Michael 1977. *Just and Unjust Wars: a Moral Argument with Historical Illustrations*, New York: Basic Books.
Webber, Mark 2007. *Inclusion, Exclusion and the Governance of European Security*, Manchester: Manchester University Press.
—— 2012. 'NATO's Post-Cold War Operations in Europe', in J. Sperling and S. V. Papacosma (eds.), *NATO after Sixty Years: A Stable Crisis*, Kent, OH: Kent State University Press: 56–80.
Webber, Mark, Croft, Stuart, Howorth, Jolyon, Terriff, Terry and Krahmann, Eleke 2004. 'The Governance of European Security', *Review of International Studies* 30 (1): 3–26.
Webber, Mark, Sperling, James and Smith, Martin A. 2012. *NATO's Post-Cold War Trajectory: Decline or Regeneration?* Basingstoke: Palgrave Macmillan.
Weiss, Thomas G. 2016. *Humanitarian Intervention: Ideas in Action*, 3rd edition, Cambridge: Polity Press.
Welsh, Jennifer M. 2013. 'Norm Contestation and the Responsibility to Protect', *Global Responsibility to Protect* 5 (4): 365–396.
—— 2014. 'Implementing the "Responsibility to Protect": Catalyzing Debate and Building Capacity', in A. Betts and P. Orchard (eds.), *Implementation and World Politics: How International Norms Change Practice*, Oxford: Oxford University Press: 124–143.
—— 2016. 'The Responsibility to Prevent: Assessing the Gap between Rhetoric and Reality', *Cooperation and Conflict* 51 (2): 216–232.
Wendt, Alexander 1992. 'Anarchy is What States Make of It: The Social Construction of Power Politics', *International Organization* 46 (2): 391–425.
—— 1994. 'Collective Identity Formation and the International State', *American Political Science Review* 88 (2): 384–396.
—— 1999. *Social Theory of International Politics*, Cambridge: Cambridge University Press.
Western, Jon 2002. 'Source of Humanitarian Intervention: Beliefs, Information and Advocacy in the U.S. Decisions on Somalia and Bosnia', *International Security* 26 (4): 112–142.
—— 2005. *Selling Intervention and War: The Presidency, the Media, and the American Public*, Baltimore, MD: Johns Hopkins University Press.
Wheeler, Nicholas J. 2000. *Saving Strangers: Humanitarian Intervention in International Society*, Oxford: Oxford University Press.
Wiener, Antje 2008. *The Invisible Constitution of Politics: Contested Norms and International Encounters*, Cambridge: Cambridge University Press.
—— 2014. *A Theory of Contestation*, Heidelberg: Springer.
Williams, Michael C. 2007. *Culture and Security: Symbolic Power and the Politics of International Security*, London: Routledge.
Wood, Pia Christina 1994. 'France and the Post Cold War Order: The Case of Yugoslavia', *European Security* 3 (1): 129–152.
Woodward, Susan L. 1995. *Balkan Tragedy: Chaos and Destruction after the Cold War*, Washington, DC: Brookings Institution.

Wybrow, Robert J. 2003. 'British Attitudes toward the Bosnian Situation', in R. Sobel and E. Shiraev (eds.), *International Public Opinion and the Bosnia Crisis*, Lanham, MD: Lexington Books: 33–68.

Yost, David S. 1998. *NATO Transformed: The Alliance's New Roles in International Security*, Washington, DC: United States Institute of Peace Press.

Young, Thomas-Durell 1996. 'German National Command Structures after Unification: A New German General Staff?', *Armed Forces and Society* 22 (3): 379–417.

Zarakol, Ayşe 2008. *After Defeat: How the East Learned to Live with the West*, Cambridge: Cambridge University Press.

Zehfuss, Maja 2002. *Constructivism in International Relations: The Politics of Reality*, Cambridge: Cambridge University Press.

Zimmermann, Warren 1999. *Origins of a Catastrophe: Yugoslavia and Its Destroyers*, New York: Times Books.

# Index

Note: Boldface page numbers refer to tables; italic page numbers refer to figures and page numbers followed by "n" denote endnotes.

Acharya, Amitav 28
Adler, Emanuel 14n8, 19
Adriatic Sea: divisions among European states on deployment of monitoring forces in 39–41; NATO and WEU monitoring activities in 45, 120; Operation Maritime Monitor in 41
African Union Mission in Sudan (AMIS) 2
Albright, Madeleine 47, 152n55
Allied Rapid Reaction Corps (ARRC) 65, 91–2, 106n15
Allied Forces Southern Europe (AFSOUTH) 103, 108n71
American Presidency Project 10, 153n62
'Appeasement in Our Time' 138
Ashdown, Paddy 66, 67, 70, 75, 77, 85n111
Aspin, Les 148
Atlantic Alliance 49, 75, 102, 121
Aybet, Gülner 52

Badinter, Robert 114
Badinter Arbitration Commission 114
Baker, James 136–8
Balladur, Édouard 96–100
Barnett, Michael 19, 33n10
Baumel, Jacques 99
Bérégovoy, Pierre 94
Berger, Thomas 110, 161
Biden, Joseph 139, 144
Blair, Tony 77
Bloomfield, Alan 28, 30, 162
Boban, Mate 44
Bonior, David 139
Bonsor, Sir Nicholas 71, 75

Boren, David 139
Bosnia: from anti-Soviet alliance to security governance framework for humanitarian contingencies 56; Britain's incremental engagement 66–9; Britain's view on reform of NATO through 62–80; British government's view 63–5, **73**; Bundeswehr's 'out-of-area' debate before 113–14; constructivism and 3–4; credibility of NATO and military intervention 47–52, **48**; Dayton Accords 50–2; domestic pressure and stalemate of European mediation activity in 41–4; European states' mediation efforts towards Balkans 36–41; final phase of the war 101–2; France and war in 92–4; French engagement at the initial stage 92–3; greatest transatlantic rift since Suez 45–7; humanitarian intervention and 3–4; Labour and Liberal Democrats' view 65–6; NATO's activities after 163–4; outbreak of the war in 36–7; reforming NATO through 35–56; reorganising NATO for effective crisis management 52–6; setback of international mediation and discussion over military intervention 41–7
Bosnia Herzegovina 1, 38–9, 43, 52–3, 67, 94
Bosnian Muslims 44, 46, 60n56, 75, 101, 144
Bozo, Frédéric 87, 97
Bradley, Bill 144
Brioni Agreement 37
Budgen, Nicholas 71

## Index

Bukovansky, Mlada 3
Bundeswehr 130n4, 132n52, 133n76; FDP and 121; 'out-of-area' debate before Bosnia 113–14; SPD opposition to 117
Bush, George H. W. 37, 136–40; interests, fear and timing and reasons for non-intervention 136–8; turnabout 138–40

Campbell, Sir Menzies 71
Carrington, Lord Peter 37, 38, 64
Carter, Jimmy 50
de Charette, Hervé 87, 89, 102, 146
Cheney, Dick 137
Chevénement, Jean-Pierre 90
Chirac, Jacques 51, 94, 97, 99, 101–4
Christian Democratic Union (Christlich Demokratische Union Deutschlands, CDU) 113, 119–23
Christians 23
Christian Social Union (Christlich-Soziale Union in Bayern, CSU) 113, 119–23
Christopher, Warren 47, 75, 115, 134–5, 143–5, 147
Clark, David 65, 70, 75
classical realism 1, 16–17, 33n5, 155
Clinton, Bill 13, 46, 47, 75, 136, 140–3; fear of involvement and fear of inaction 140–3; 'lift and strike' policy as a focal point 143
Cold War 6, 7, 8, 17, 35, 37, 66, 87; Franco-NATO relations during and after 89–90
Combined Joint Task Force (CJTF) 53–4, 78, 102–3, 148–9
Common Foreign and Security Policy (CFSP) 37, 40, 91–2
*The Congressional Record* 10
constructivism 3, 6, 9, 11, 14–16, 19–20, 109, 161; and Bosnia 3–4
Cook, Robin 77
'cooperative security community' 19
Cormack, Patrick 64
Council of the WEU 45
Crawford, Neta 23, 33n10
crisis management: humanitarian 88; international 77, 88; NATO's new roles in 20; reorganising NATO for effective 52–6
Croatia 37–8; Germany's unilateral recognition of 114–16; outbreak of the war in 36–7
Cunningham, Jack 65

Daalder, Ivo 145
*The Daily Telegraph* 9, 62, 66–70, 72, 76, 82n41
Dalvi, Sameera 125
Davies, Quentin 64
Dayton Accords 50–2
Dayton Agreement 146
'The Death Camps of Bosnia' 138
Defence Planning Committee (DPC) 88–9, 91, 103, 105n4
*Defence White Book 1994* 100
Deni, John 7, 18
*Der Spiegel* 9, 51
d'Estaing, Valéry Giscard 95
Deutsch, Karl 19
Dicks, Terry 72
*Die Zeit* 9, 115
Dole, Robert 47, 49, 139
*Drucksache* 10
Duffield, John 109, 112, 119, 161
Dumas, Roland 90, 96

Eagleburger, Lawrence 21, 137
Errera, Gérard 102
"ethnic cleansing" 4, 10, 22, 41, *42*, 43, 50, 66–7, 94, 138–41, 152n55, 156
Eurocorps 91–2
European Community (EC) 21, 36; NATO and 91
European Community Conference on Yugoslavia (The Hague) 37
European Handlungsfähigkeit 120
European Security Defence Identity (ESDI) 40, 91–2
European Union (EU) 11, 18; NATO and 91
Evans, Gareth 165
Eznack, Lucile 7

Fabius, Laurent 94
Farrell, Theo 28
Federal Constitutional Court (Verfassungsgericht) 120
Fierke, Karin 24
*The Financial Times* 9, 51
Fincke, Gunilla 130
Finnemore, Martha 4, 23, 26, 28, 33n10, 162
Fischer, Joschka 126–7
France: attitude towards European security 91; changing traditional policy 95–6; ESDI, CFSP and Eurocorps 91–2; final phase of the war and 101–2; French

engagement at initial stage 92–3; Gaullist legacies and French security policy 89–92; largest contributor, the largest casualties 96–8; norm dilemmas led to renew its foreign policy 96–8; policy under the cohabitation 98–101; public reaction to the government's policy 93–4; return to NATO to build a new conflict management system 95–102; stalemate in Bosnia and public criticisms 95–6; and war in Bosnia 92–4

*Frankfurter Allgemeine Zeitung* 9, 42

Free Democratic Party (Freie Demokratische Partei, FDP) 113, 119–23

French security policy: ESDI, CFSP and Eurocorps 91–2; Franco-NATO relations during and after Cold War 89–90; French attitude towards European security 91; Gaullist legacies and 89–92; NATO and EC/EU 91

de Gaulle, Charles 2, 40, 87, 89
Gaullism 88–9, 97
Gaullist legacies and French security policy 89–92
'genocide' 4, 10, 22–4, 41, 42, 43, 50, 66, 126–7, 139, 142–3, 156, 164
Genscher, Hans-Dietrich 114
Germany: CDU/CSU and the FDP 119–23; collective recognition on NATO's new undertakings 128–9; distinctiveness of foreign policy of 111–14; domestic constraints and international responsibility 118–23; domestic discussion and war in Bosnia 116–18; fear of escalation by use of force 118–19; governing parties' view 119–23; government's view on conflict prevention 123–6; humanitarianism and 109–30; initial response to the Balkans 114–18; international responsibility and 109–30; new security policy of 123–9; opening way for German foreign military activity 118–23, **122**, **124**; opposition's view 118–19; pacifism and 109–30; reconstruction of NATO and 123–9; reticence and restrictions 111–14; SPD and the Green Party 118–19, 126–8; unilateral recognition of Slovenia and Croatia 114–16
German foreign policy: Bundeswehr's 'out-of-area' debate before Bosnia 113–14; distinctiveness of 111–14; as historical product 111–13; reticence and restrictions 111–14

Ghali, Boutros Boutros 69
Giddens, Anthony 23
Glenn, John 142
Glos, Michael 120
Glotz, Peter 119
Gompert, David C. 136
Gorbachev, Mikhail 21, 138, 156
Gordon, Philip 7, 89
Gore, Al 144
Grant, Sir Anthony 75
Great Britain: attacks from the left and pressure to 'do something' more 70–1; attacks from the outside 74–6; attacks from the right and pressure to pull out of Bosnia 71–2; and Bosnia 63–6; difficulties in humanitarian intervention 68–9; diplomatic row with the United States 74–6; discussion inside 72–4; domestic debates in 1993–1995 69–72; final phase of the war 101–2; government's policy change and public debate 66–8; incremental engagement 66–9; from intervention to prevention 76–9; John Major government's steering under attacks from inside and outside 69–76; media discussion after stalemate of international mediation efforts 69–70; and reorganisation of NATO 76–9; view on reform of NATO through Bosnia 62–80
Green Party 117, 118–19, 126–8
*The Guardian* 9, 66, 68–70
Gulf War 37, 65, 90, 139
Gutman, Roy 138

Hamilton, Lee H. 138
Hamilton, Sir Archibald 71
Hannay, Sir David 46
*Hansard* 10
Hansen, Lene 24
Harding, Sir Peter 46
Harris, Marshall 141–2
Hatakoy, Arzu 130
Heath, Sir Edward 75
Heathcoat-Amory, David 78
Heeresführungskommando (Army Forces Command) 125
Helms, Jesse 144–5
Herd, Graeme 164
Hirsch, Burkhard 121

## 184  Index

Hogg, Douglas 64
Holbrooke, Richard 52, 59n37, 140, 146, 148–9
Hollings, Ernest 141
Holocaust 66
Holocaust Museum 141
Hopf, Ted 161
Howard, Lise Morjé 94
Hoyer, Steny 139
humanitarian intervention 4; difficulties in 68–9
humanitarianism: Chandler on 34n23; Germany and 109–30
human rights consciousness 23
Hurd, Douglas 62–4
Hussein, Saddam 137

Implementation Force (IFOR) 52, 110, 127, 147
*The Independent* 1, 9, 66–9
institutionalism, neoliberal 3, 11, 15–18, 40, 156
International Commission on Intervention and State Sovereignty (ICISS) 8, 165, 166n12
'International Conference on Former Yugoslavia' (ICFY) 43–4, 50
International Military Staff (IMS) 54, 88–9, 103
International Security Assistance Force (ISAF) 2
international security governance 1–13, 155–65; from norm dilemmas to 31–2; social norms and 2–6
international security management 29–32
intra-alliance conflict 144–5
Iran-Iraq War 113
Ivanov, Ivan Dinev 8, 18
Izetbegovic, Alija 44, 52

Jews 141
Johnston, Karin 117, 128
Johnston, Seth 7, 18
Joxe, Pierre 90
Juppé, Alain 95, 97

Kadijevic, General Veljko 37
Kaplan, Lawrence 7
Karadzic, Radovan 44
Katsioulis, Christos 127
Katzenstein, Peter 161
Kaufman, Gerald 65
Kay, Sean 55

Kelleher, Catherine McArdle 8
Kenney, George D. 138, 141
Kinkel, Klaus 116, 122–5
Kissinger, Henry 139, 149
Kitchen, Veronica 8, 24
Kohl, Helmut 91, 111, 113–29, 133n72, 158
'Kohl doctrine' 118
Kosovo Liberation Army (KLA) 163
Kriendler, John 164

Lake, Anthony 145
Lantis, Jeffrey 112
Lanxade, Jacques 100
*La Politique Étrangère de la France* 10
Legro, Jeffrey 162
*Le Monde* 9, 51
*Le Monde Diplomatique* 9
Léotard, François 97, 99–103
*Le Point* 101
Libal, Michael 115–6
Lieberman, Joe 139, 144
Lindley-French, Julian 8
Livingstone, Ken 70
London Conference 43, 69
'London Declaration' 39
Lubbers, Ruud 40
Lucarelli, Sonia 93
Lugar, Richard 135

Maastricht Treaty 37, 91–2, 115
McCain, John 47, 141
McCalla, Robert 17
McCloskey, Frank 139, 143
Major, John 12, 43–4, 62–79, 157
Malcolm, Noel 39
Mattern, Janice Bially 7
Maull, Hanns 112, 118
Mearsheimer, John 1
de Michelis, Gianni 37, 57n3
Middle East 37
military intervention: in Bosnia (1994) 48; credibility of NATO and 47–52; dilemmas of 47–50; setback of international mediation and discussion over 41–7
Millon, Charles 94
Milosevic, Slobodan 37, 45, 52, 139
Mitterrand, François 39, 47, 49, 87–8, 91–101, 104–5, 115–16
Modrow, Hans 117
Moore, Rebecca 8
Morjé Howard, Marc 94, 107n33

# Index

Müller, Harold 112
Muslims 38, 44, 48, 50, 143

NATO Airborne Warning and Control System (AWACS) 120–1
NATO reforms **54**, 55–6; Britain's view on 62–80; dilemmas of intervention and 134–50
NATO Training Mission-Iraq (NTM-I) 2
neoliberal institutionalism 11, 15, 17–18
neorealism 2, 16–17, 109, 134
Neville-Jones, Baroness Pauline 45, 55
*Newsday* 138
*The New York Times* 9, 49, 51, 138, 141
Nickels, Christa 119
Niggemeier, Horst 126
'non-Article 5 missions' 17, 32, 53, 89, 102, 156
norm dilemmas 155–65; from domestic norms to international institutional redevelopment 155–61; international security governance and 31–2; rationale for constructivist approach 161–2; theoretical claims 161–2
North Atlantic Council 45, 52, 87, 90, 102
North Atlantic Treaty Organization (NATO): activities after Bosnia 163–4; agreeing in principle, disagreeing in practice 27–9; American views on roles of 146–9; brief theoretical comparison 2–3; Britain's view on the reorganisation of 76–9; changes at the international level 52–5; classical realism and neorealism 16–17; construction of new 98–101; constructivism 3–4, 19–20; credibility of, and military intervention 47–52; Dayton Accords 50–2; defining new role of 52–5; dilemmas caused by normative influence 25–6; dilemmas of military intervention 47–50; and EC/EU 91; gradual engagements 44–5; humanitarian intervention and Bosnia 3–4; and its persistence 16–20; neoliberal institutionalism 17–18; no agreement on role of 39–41; no international frameworks for security management 26–7; from normative expectations to international security management 29–32; normative pressure and intervention 155–7; from norm dilemmas to international security governance 31–2; norms and dilemmas 4–6; post-Bosnia 102–4; post-Cold War 1–13; reconstruction of 123–9; reforming through Bosnia 35–56; reorganisation of 2–6, 24–9, *30*, 52–6; research question 20; responding to one norm while conforming to others 29–31; review of existing literature 16–20; security governance to manage norm dilemmas 55–6; social appropriateness not realised 157–8; social norms and international security governance 2–6; 'Standardization Organization' 54; state-society relations 20–4; Supreme Allied Commander Europe (SACEUR) 18, 91, 103, 121; transformation of, and research question 1–2; on the use of force 44–5
Nuclear Planning Group (NPG) 88–9, 103

*The Observer* 67
Operation Active Endeavour 2
Operation Allied Provider 2
'Operation Deliberate Force' 51
Operation Eagle Assist 2
Operation Maritime Monitor 41
'Operation Sharp Guard' 45
Operation Unified Protector 2
Organisation for Security and Co-operation in Europe (OSCE) 18, 130
Ottoman Turks 23
Outcome Document of the 2005 World Summit 165
Owen, Lord David 43–4, 69, 123
Owen-Stoltenberg Plan 50

pacifism, and Germany 109–30
Pakistan Earthquake Relief Operation 2
Panke, Diana 28, 162
Papacosma, Victor 8
Paris, Roland 25, 34n12
Party of Democratic Socialism (Partei des Demokratischen Sozialismus, PDS) 117, 131n36, 133n76
Petersberg Declaration 40, 93
Petersohn, Ulrich 28, 162
Philippi, Nina 127
*Plenarprotokoll* 10
'political bargaining' 7
Poos, Jacques 37
Poppe, Gerd 117
Portillo, Michael 65, 78
post-Bosnia NATO 102–4

post-Cold War NATO 1–13
Powell, Colin 46, 137
'Powell Doctrine' 137
Presidential Decision Directive 25 141
Pressler, Larry 139

Rapid Reaction Force (RRF) 51, 76, 101, 146
rapprochement with NATO 99: France and war in Bosnia 92–4; France's return to NATO to build new conflict management system 95–102; Gaullist legacies and French security policy 89–92; overview 87–9; post-Bosnia NATO 102–4
Rathbun, Brian 64, 97
Reagan, Ronald 139
Resolute Support Mission 2
Richard, Alain 103
Rifkind, Malcolm 26, 47, 51, 64, 69, 72, 75–9
Risse, Thomas 31
Risse-Kappen, Thomas 19, 26
Robertson, George 65
Rühe, Volker 49, 122, 124
Rynning, Sten 8

Sahnoun, Mohamed 165
Sandholtz, Wayne 28, 30, 162
Schoppe, Waltraud 127
Second World War 66, 111, 125, 138
Shalikashivili, John 18, 121
'Shame in Our Time' 138
'Shame of Camp Omarska' 66
Shea, Jamie 40
Shultz, George 139
Simms, Brendan 40, 46
Sjursen, Helene 19
Slocombe, Walter B. 53
Slovenia 37–8; Germany's unilateral recognition of 114–16; outbreak of the wars in 36–7
Smith, Martin 8
Smith, Michael 127
Soames, Nicholas 78
Social Democratic Party (Sozialdemokratische Partei Deutschlands, SPD) 117, 118–19, 126–8
social norms, and international security governance 2–6
Solana, Javier 2, 53, 55, 163
Soviet Union 1, 15, 18–21, 37, 39, 92, 138, 147, 155–6

Sperling, James 8
Standing Naval Force Mediterranean (STANAVFORMED) 41
state-society relations 20–4; constructivist explanations for intervention 22–4; normative pressure 22; strategic reasons 20–2
Stoltenberg, Thorvald 44
Strategic Concept 2010 164
*Süddeutsche Zeitung* 9
Suez crisis 27, 46, 146
*Sunday Telegraph* 67
Supreme Allied Commander Europe (SACEUR) 18, 91, 103, 106n15, 121

Talbott, Strobe 148
Tapsell, Sir Peter 71
Thatcher, Margaret 64
Thies, Wallace 7, 46
Third Reich 118, 119
*The Times* 9, 66
Tudjman, Franjo 37, 52

UN Charter 4, 29–30, 93, 144
Union for French Democracy (Union pour la Démocratie Française, UDF) 94
United Nations 1, 4, 18, 38, 41, 43, 46, 48, 71, 79, 94–5, 115, 117, 119–24, 145
United Nations High Commissioner for Refugees 21
United States: American views on the roles of NATO 146–9; debate on concrete measures 140–3; decision of the Bush administration 136–40; hegemonic state and Bosnia 146–9; intra-alliance conflict 144–5; military operation 146; policy by the Clinton administration 140–3; policymaking and policy change 136–40
UN Operation in Somalia (UNOSOM II) 120
UN Protection Force (UNPROFOR) 38–9, 41, 45, 50–2, 66, 71, 76, 93–7, 101, 123, 138, 144, 146
UN Security Council 38–9, 40, 93, 164
UN Security Council Resolution 836 45
U.S. Air Force 52

Vance, Cyrus 38, 43–4, 70, 123
Vance-Owen Peace Plan (VOPP) 43–5, 70, 95, 144
Verheugen, Günter 119
'Vietnam syndrome' 141

Vietnam War 137, 139
Viggers, Peter 71
Vincent, Sir Richard 49
Voigt, Karsten 119
von Weizsäcker, Richard 121

Waigel, Theodor 120
Walker, Steven 142
Wallander, Celeste A. 17
Waltz, Kenneth 1, 17, 33n5
Warsaw Treaty Organisation 39
*The Washington Post* 9, 47, 49
Webber, Mark 8
Wehrmacht (the Third Reich's army) 118
Weinberger, Casper 137, 150n8
'Weinberger Doctrine' 137
Western, Jon 141
Western European Union (WEU) 18, 40–1, 45, 54, 91–3, 98–9, 102, 113, 120–2, 157

White Christians 4
*The White Paper for Defence 1994* 125
Wieczorek-Zeul, Heidemarie 118
Wiener, Antje 7, 28–9, 30, 34n20, 162
Wiesel, Elie 141
De Wijk, Rob 8
Williams, Michael 7
Wilson, Woodrow 149
Wittmann, Klaus 164
Wollenberger, Vera 119
Woodward, Susan 37, 42, 136
Wörner, Manfred 40

Yost, David 8, 39
Yugoslav National Army (JNA) 163
Yugoslav People's Army (JNA) 38
Yugoslav War 2, 121; 1991–1993 **44**

Zehfuss, Maja 112–13
Zimmermann, Warren 137, 142